THE RUSSIAN RESEARCH CENTER

The Russian Research Center was established February 1, 1948. It is supported by the Carnegie Corporation on a grant covering the period until July 1, 1958. The major objective of the Research Center is the study of Russian institutions and behavior in an effort to make for better understanding of international actions and policy of the Soviet Union. The participating scholars represent all of the social sciences. In accord with the expressed wish of the Carnegie Corporation, the fields of anthropology, psychology, and sociology, which have hitherto played little part in Russian studies in this country, are strongly represented. The staff of the Center are grateful to the Carnegie Corporation not only for the opportunity to carry out their studies under favorable circumstances, but also for the moral encouragement and intellectual stimulation which have been provided by contact with individual officers and trustees of the Corporation.

RUSSIAN RESEARCH CENTER STUDIES

1. *Public Opinion in Soviet Russia: A Study in Mass Persuasion*, by Alex Inkeles
2. *Soviet Politics—The Dilemma of Power: The Role of Ideas in Social Change*, by Barrington Moore, Jr.
3. *Justice in Russia: An Interpretation of Soviet Law*, by Harold J. Berman
4. *Chinese Communism and the Rise of Mao*, by Benjamin I. Schwartz
5. *Titoism and the Cominform*, by Adam Ulam
6. *Documentary History of Chinese Communism*, by Conrad Brandt, Benjamin Schwartz, and John K. Fairbank
7. *The New Man in Soviet Psychology*, by Raymond A. Bauer
8. *Soviet Opposition to Stalin: A Case Study in World War II*, by George Fischer
9. *Minerals: A Key to Soviet Power*, by Demitri B. Shimkin
10. *Soviet Law in Action: The Recollected Cases of a Soviet Lawyer*, by Harold J. Berman and Boris A. Konstantinovsky
11. *How Russia Is Ruled*, by Merle Fainsod
12. *Terror and Progress USSR: Some Sources of Change and Stability in the Soviet Dictatorship*, by Barrington Moore, Jr.

TERROR AND PROGRESS USSR

TERROR

AND

PROGRESS USSR

SOME SOURCES OF CHANGE AND
STABILITY IN THE SOVIET DICTATORSHIP

Barrington Moore, Jr.

1954

HARVARD UNIVERSITY PRESS · CAMBRIDGE

Distributed in Great Britain by
GEOFFREY CUMBERLEGE
Oxford University Press
London

This volume was prepared under a grant from the Carnegie Corporation of New York. That Corporation is not, however, the author, owner, publisher, or proprietor of this publication and is not to be understood as approving by virtue of its grant any of the statements made or views expressed therein.

To E. C. M.

PREFACE

At the outset it must be confessed that the aim of this study is a rash one. It is an attempt to weigh, with an eye to the future, the sources of stability and the potentialities for change in the Bolshevik regime. Unquestionably my performance has fallen short of this goal, which many thoughtful scholars would regard as essentially a foolish one. To be sure, the results of a search for future developments in the Soviet Union cannot be set down with the assurance, precision, and colorful language of *The Farmer's Almanac*. Yet I hope that the following pages may be distinguished from this venerable document on certain additional grounds. There are enough clear signs of strength and identifiable spores of weakness in crucial parts of Soviet society so that one can discern rough outlines of possible future developments. To locate these points and assess them is a challenging and exciting task. This book is therefore mainly an exploratory foray, marked by some of the dangers and risks of such adventures. There is no shining definite pot of gold at the end of our search, but the reader himself can best judge from the conclusions whether or not the effort was worth while.

The organizing principle with which this study began was one of showing the kinds of situation that confront different people in Soviet society, the ways in which they see their situation and respond to it, and how their behavior sometimes modifies and sometimes perpetuates it. Instead of writing a treatment of the Soviet system with the conventional categories of politics, economics, the family, and the rest, I wanted to see what could be accomplished by viewing it in terms of a series of situations and a series of people, from the factory worker on the assembly line to the leaders in the Kremlin. By noting how the situations are related to one another, one can locate at least some of the major sources of internal strain and stability in Soviet society, as in any other. In the same fashion, external factors which affect the situations facing various people in the society can be taken into account.

Though this principle of organization was necessarily modified considerably as the work progressed, much of it remains. The first chapter introduces the reader to those who manipulate the control levers in Soviet society and the problems that confront them. The second carries this theme somewhat further by showing how some of the levers work in industry, and the significance of the counterpressures that are generated as the machinery of leadership grinds against the demands and desires of the population. A third chapter focuses on the peasants' reactions to this machinery and some of the problems that their response creates for the Communist leadership. Since intellectuals are often a source of change and innovation in modern industrial society, the next two chapters are devoted to the position of the scientist and the creative artist in Soviet society. There follows, in Chapter 6, an appraisal of organized terror, a major factor that plays an important part in the life of nearly every Soviet citizen. Here I have also discussed the much debated question of whether or not socialism inevitably requires terror as one of its major instruments.

While each of the above chapters sheds some light, I hope, on specific aspects of the problem of change and stability in the Soviet dictatorship, the final chapter tries to assess the clues we have found and to explore what meaning they might have for the future. Inevitably the position one takes in attacking such a problem depends partly on one's underlying philosophical assumptions. Without defending them here, I shall merely try to make them explicit.

At any given moment in time, it seems to me, some future developments are such remote possibilities that practical men are justified in calling them impossible. On the other hand, other future events are so probable as to be nearly inevitable. In between lies the range of effective human action. It has been well argued of late that social scientists have put too much emphasis on prediction and have not paid enough attention to inquiring about what events are desirable and how they might be brought about. From the latter standpoint the task of social science becomes less one of straightforward prediction and more one of discovering the range of possibilities in a given situation and the variety of consequences that follow any particular course of action.

The application of this viewpoint to the Soviet case leads therefore to a search for the range of alternative possibilities before the USSR. Simultaneously it requires a search for the consequences of whatever choices are made by the Communist leaders and by ordinary citizens. For example, with appropriate knowledge about Soviet society, it should be possible to make sensible estimates of the consequences of either a "soft" or "tough" domestic or foreign policy, without knowing which one the rulers will adopt. In the last chapter, I have tried to combine factual data with this general viewpoint by outlining a tentative and simple theoretical framework. To the extent that it stands the test of critical analysis, it may help in assessing future events as indices of stability or of change in specified directions. Anyone who studies the Soviet Union finds provisional meanings for specific incidents, such as major changes in personnel or the adoption of new policies, by measuring them against a background composed of both general theory and the immediate facts of the case. These two lenses through which we look at social reality are perhaps always slightly out of focus with one another. But some clarity can be gained if we have a general idea of the direction in which we ought to look.

Throughout the study the test that I have tried to apply in including or omitting any particular piece of information was the clue that it might give to the future, rather than its desirability in rounding out our image of the present. To a considerable extent the two objectives of course overlap and require the same kind of information. But in fairness to the reader it should be made clear that the chief aim of this study is to grapple with a problem and not to mine new facts. In certain areas, particularly in connection with Soviet science and the arts, it has been necessary to break new ground, mainly to supply some answers to our problem. Moreover, in areas that have been studied quite intensively by other scholars, inclusion of many additional details from the original sources seemed essential.

Speaking of Russian source materials, one of my less charitable colleagues once remarked to me that the chief instrument in research on the Soviet Union must be a crystal ball. A word or two about the sources may aid those who are not specialists on Soviet affairs to make up their minds about the validity of the interpretations in this study. There are two major types of factual material, each subject to its own form of unreliability. One type is Soviet printed sources, ranging from laws, Party pronouncements, and newspaper items to fictional treatments of daily life. Out of this material it is possible to construct a moderately complete account of what the Kremlin is trying to do to the population and to deduce many of the difficulties facing the regime. Perhaps the most serious omission from any account limited to such sources would be the operations of the secret police, which turn up very rarely in these materials.

The second type of information is obtained from interviews with refugees from the Soviet regime. Most of the interviews used in this work were carried out in 1950–51 by the Russian Research Center's Project on the Soviet Social System. This project, supported in part by the United States Air Force, monitored by the Air Research and Development Command, Human Resources Research Institute, Maxwell Air Force Base, Alabama, Contract AF 33(038)–12909, has produced a large body of data now under intensive analysis by members of the Center's staff. I have been very fortunate in being able to draw upon this body of material and in having been able to take part in the interviewing for a period of about three weeks. This experience, together with close acquaintance with a few former Soviet citizens in the United States, has, I think, given me valuable insight into the reliability and inevitable distortion of this body of information.

Other interviews were selected from the Russian Research Center series, conducted in 1949 by Professor Merle Fainsod and Mr. Paul Friedrich. In addition, a large number of interviews from a variety of other sources, gathered in the files of the Russian Research Center, were carefully examined. Although not cited directly, they contributed some important clues that influenced the final interpretation.

Most of the former Soviet citizens interviewed by the Harvard group were still in displaced persons' camps in Europe, a factor to be considered in weighing their reliability as sources. While the nature of the bias and dependability varies of course from individual to individual, it seems clear that fears about eligibility for emigration made many refugees reluctant to discuss fully the "delicate" questions of Party and secret police controls. In a few other cases, one would run into the opposite type of situation, in which imagination, together with the refugee's desire to compete for the attention of Western interviewers, led to sensational accounts whose connection with Soviet realities can be most generously described as dubious. Unfortunately, therefore, some of the most important questions remain those for which the information is least trustworthy. As one gets down to the substance of daily life and direct personal experience, the distortion appears to be considerably less, although even here one must be extremely cautious in the use of such data.

It is definitely not true, as is occasionally claimed, that all of the refugees, or even a substantial number of them, are "soreheads" or misfits, who could not get along in the USSR and who therefore represent the rejects of this social system. Many of them are not refugees in the sense of having made a deliberate decision to flee, which they then carried out through careful planning. Instead, they were forced to go to Germany as workers or were swept back with the retreating German armies. During their lives in the USSR, most of the refugees interviewed apparently tried to be good Soviet citizens, and many had achieved positions of considerable responsibility.

In using both types of sources, I have pushed the inferences that could be drawn from them as far as possible, stopping short of the point of uncontrolled speculation where one guess is as good as another. At the same time, through both formal documentation and in the choice of phrasing, I have tried to give the reader a clear idea of the reliance that can be placed upon any specific assertion. In some instances my interpretation rests, without citing specific items, upon a residue of impressions derived from a large number of similar incidents in either the interview sources or in Soviet printed materials. Wherever this is true, I have merely indicated the general nature of the evidence in the course of the discussion.

Though a book may bear the name of a single author on its title page, like any other cultural product it is the work of many hands. I should like to begin my acknowledgment to the work of others with a brief word about two recently published books by authors with whom I have discussed common problems, and who were kind enough to let me read their drafts at various stages before publication, as well as to offer comments upon my views. Since all three of us were engaged in pursuing our intellectual quarry wherever it led us and crystallizing our views on paper at roughly the same time, our association during this period was a very loose one. Nevertheless, the later date of publication of my study has given me the advantage of being able to take account of their views.

One of these works is Merle Fainsod's *How Russia Is Ruled* (Harvard University Press, 1953), a superb analytical description of the growth and contemporary functioning of Soviet political institutions. Where we treat the same subject matter our differences are confined largely to shadings of emphasis. Where Professor Fainsód in a concluding chapter comments upon future possibilities, however, the differing intellectual standpoints from which we start make themselves felt. His analysis is couched primarily in terms of internal tensions and the ability of the present regime to control them. Along, of course, with other considerations, this analytical framework leads him to foresee two main possibilities: a continuation of the existing system in roughly its present form, or the diffusion of the dictator's power among rival elites and the "transformation of Soviet totalitarianism into some type of constitutional order" (p. 500). As he expresses rather strong doubts about the latter outcome, his estimate boils down essentially to the proposition that no fundamental changes are to be expected in the near future.

In *The Dynamics of Soviet Society* (New York, 1953) W. W. Rostow argues quite a different thesis. Though his analysis of the Soviet system covers a great deal of ground, topically and historically, his major interest appears to be focused on the struggle for supreme power released by Stalin's death. His central argument, as I read it, is that this struggle is likely to compel the various contestants to reach back into the society for popular support and to "bring politically into play the dissatisfactions and positive aspirations of various groups" (p. 256). In other words, he anticipates that the Soviet dictatorship could disintegrate from the top downward. Naturally he is too wise a scholar to say that such an outcome is inevitable. He also considers very carefully both the possibilities of a continuation of the Stalinist system under new management, and a potential diffusion of authority which could lead to a constitutional order, in roughly the manner envisaged by Professor Fainsod. Nevertheless, the weight of his argument leans toward the conclusion that a catastrophic fate may await the Soviet dictatorship in the fairly near future.

My chief differences with these two works does not lie in the facts, or in the interpretation of considerable bodies of fact, that we must necessarily use in common. Rather our major differences lie in the broad implications to be drawn from these facts. It seems to me that the range of alternatives posed by Professors Fainsod and Rostow does not encompass adequately all the possibilities, or even all those that can be considered rather probable. Instead they represent, I think, the two extremes between which the course of Russian history is likely to flow. Likewise, although both take into account the possible diffusion of the dictator's power, the present situation contains forces that could push such a development in directions that would have very different consequences. Either a rationalist technocracy or a limited and traditionalist despotism appear to be very distinct possibilities. The nature of these possibilities and their sources in the present situation I have tried to explore in some detail.

One can reply that my own intellectual framework for posing the alternatives before the USSR is also too narrow. Professor Michael Karpovich has made this suggestion, among many other valuable comments, for which I should like to express my very warm thanks. Unquestionably future events and the critical observations of other scholars will call for the modification of my present viewpoint and possibly even its complete rejection. At the moment all I can say is that it covers the facts of the situation as I now see them and that it was used to bind together these facts only after the raw materials had been studied intensively and other schemes tried and discarded. In other words, I would argue that the narrowness is inherent in the Soviet system and in the nature of its contacts with the outside world. This limitation seems to me to render improbable certain political developments most of us would like to see.

Professors Alexander Gerschenkron and Philipp Frank generously gave me the benefit of their specialized knowledge. The Director of the Russian Research Center, Professor Clyde Kluckhohn, has played a major part in giving this book whatever virtues it may possess. Through an anthropological alchemy that I do not fully understand, he has transmuted both highly individualistic scholars and the believers in collective intellectual enterprise into a harmonious yet stimulating group, in which many of the advantages of both procedures are realized. I am in his debt for numerous penetrating comments.

The staff of the Russian Research Center has provided valuable help at many points. Mr. Robert Feldmesser, a Graduate Student Fellow, unearthed much useful material in the early stages of the undertaking. At later stages Mrs. Helen Parsons and Mrs. Elizabeth Fainsod cheerfully found excellent typing assistance in response to my importunate demands.

The help of all these people has been very great. That of my wife, Elizabeth Carol Moore, has been equally indispensable and much more varied. Where clarity and logical consistency are still lacking, it is due largely to my inability to meet her exacting yet affectionately expressed demands. Nearly every paragraph bears their imprint. In addition to her services as editor and severe critic she has helped me in gathering material and in verifying the sources in Russian and other languages. She has also taken from my shoulders the technical problems and the minor crises that always plague the writing of a book and has borne with innate gaiety many personal deprivations that were the result of my having to concentrate on this task for a much longer time than I had anticipated. Finally, she has carried out the trying task of compiling an index. The warmest public thanks that I can express are therefore quite inadequate in relation to my feelings.

The fertile mind of my good friend, Professor Herbert Marcuse of Columbia University, supplied the original suggestion for the main title of this book. He is sincerely thanked for his contribution.

My thanks are also due to *The Review of Economics and Statistics* for permission to quote from an article by Stuart A. Rice in the February 1952 issue.

October 26, 1953   Barrington Moore, Jr.

CONTENTS

1. The Instruments of Control   1

2. The Politics of Industrialization   32

3. The Peasants' Role in the Workers' State   72

4. Communist Beliefs on Science and Art   98

5. Scientist and Artist in the Police State   114

6. The Impact and Function of Terror   154

7. Images of the Future   179

   Notes   233

   Index   251

TERROR AND PROGRESS USSR

chapter 1

THE INSTRUMENTS
OF CONTROL

"Never before has the unity of Soviet society been so monolithic . . . as at the present time," said Georgii Maksimilionovich
Malenkov, Chairman of the Council of Ministers, on August 8,
1953. Ordinarily this ritual formula might have no more impact
on a Soviet audience than the minor interruption of a radio commercial on an American audience, forced to hear that "this year's
Buick is even better than last year's." But to the Soviet delegates,
assembled from all parts of the USSR for a special session of
the Supreme Soviet, Malenkov's words must have had a certain
piquancy lent by the immediately preceding events. Only a few
weeks earlier the newspapers had briefly informed the Soviet
public that Malenkov had brought about the arrest of Lavrentii P.
Beriya, chief of the dreaded secret police and perhaps the most
powerful of Malenkov's rivals in the "monolithic" society.

The frequency with which the claim of unity is repeated
would be enough to evoke skepticism about its truth, even if
there were no other evidence to the contrary. At the same time
the Soviet dictatorship has survived many phases of growth and
change, through invasion and bloody intrigues among its leaders,
for the better part of two generations. Unity of a sort there seems
to be. How is it brought about? How are the activities of millions of Soviet citizens related to one another, their billions of
daily choices coördinated to produce a living society? It is in-
conceivable that the highest leadership with all its turmoil is
merely an excrescence upon the larger society or that the latter
can pursue its daily life undisturbed by the storms and lightning
flashes at the top.

In any society order of some kind must exist in the way people get their living, reproduce themselves, guard against danger, or carry on other activities necessary for group existence. Methods of achieving this ordering of the separate choices of individuals show great variation. The American sociologist, William Graham Sumner, writing in the early years of this century, put a heavy stress on the importance of deeply rooted popular custom, rules that nobody makes, that are not enforced by any courts, but that nevertheless guide a substantial segment of human behavior. His work was an important part of a larger stream of thought that influenced people to look away from kings and battles as the moving springs of history and to search among mass phenomena for the explanation of the past and the present. Perhaps we have looked too hard and too long in this direction alone. In a small society with a simple technology such customary rules may be all that is necessary to solve the problem of order. Cases are known where a tribal chieftain or a set of institutions we would recognize as political are evidently unnecessary for the society to exist.

The situation in the USSR could scarcely be more different. Perhaps no government can maintain itself without some support in popular sentiment and custom. But these factors are definitely not the crucial ones in bringing about an ordered relationship in the behavior of the some 200 million human beings who make up the population of the Soviet Union. Especially in the form that it has taken in the USSR totalitarian dictatorship may be regarded as a substitute for other forms of coördination with a stronger groundwork in popular consensus.* For about the past twenty years Soviet society has been one enormous bureaucracy. The state has swallowed society. The behavior of nearly every adult male during his waking hours is heavily determined by his place within this bureaucracy, which confronts him with a set of alternatives in such a way as to make many of the choices

---

* The reasons for the erosion of this consensus in Russia and the rise of a substitute form constitute fascinating historical and sociological problems about which specialists are far from agreed. But we cannot look into these questions here.

among them obligatory. The same is true of course for the many Soviet women who are gainfully employed. As for children and housewives, the alternatives they face and the choices they make in daily life reflect rather closely the position of the breadwinner in this bureaucratized society. It is bureaucratized in the sense that the decisions of any adult are made within the framework of other decisions, reached at a higher level in an all-embracing administrative system. The peasant, the soldier, the worker, the artist, and the scientist play their roles in accordance with a web of decisions that ultimately originate in, or are approved by, the Presidium (formerly the Politburo), the highest organ of the Communist Party of the Soviet Union.* The Party Presidium now constitutes the most important single device through which the actions of Soviet citizens are connected with one another. Though by no means the only such device, it can be regarded as an indispensable one, for if it suddenly ceased to perform its functions, the entire fabric of Soviet society could be expected to disintegrate with astonishing rapidity.

If it is agreed that under the Bolshevik system the Party Presidium is the most important institution that gears together the various parts of Soviet society, we seem to be up against a blank wall of ignorance about this body that bars any hope of further analysis. It is quite true that we know extremely little about the process through which decisions are reached in the Kremlin. Nor will ingenuity carry us very reliably or very far in any attempt at long-distance mind-reading. But we do know quite well what the major decisions taken by the Kremlin have been. The record of Soviet policy at home and abroad is plain for all to see, even if valuable details that might alter our interpretation are sometimes missing. Furthermore we can see at least the major outlines of the chief problems that in an objective sense

---

* The name of the Politburo was changed to Presidium at the Nineteenth Congress of the Communist Party in the fall of 1952. The name of the Party was also changed from All-Union Communist Party (Bolshevik) to Communist Party of the Soviet Union. The term "Party Presidium" will be used to avoid confusion with the Presidium of the Supreme Soviet.

now confront the Kremlin leadership. The situation that they face does not have a completely random and unlimited number of possible outcomes. Even if we cannot predict what their exact response to the situation will be, it may be possible, through analysis of the situation and its component parts, to specify the range of alternatives and at the same time to indicate some of the consequences of different choices. This is a very different procedure, it may be noted, from merely projecting past trends into the future.

In regard to the situation facing the Party Presidium in the second half of the twentieth century, it is important to point out that the major decisions concerning the fundamental nature of the Soviet system are already a matter of history. Through rapid industrialization, the collectivization of agriculture, dictatorship within the Party, and the use of organized terror, Stalin succeeded in organizing and focusing the energies of Russian society in a manner that withstood the deep wounds of armed invasion and revealed itself capable of considerable expansion beyond the boundaries of the old Russian empire. These crucial decisions were made during the late twenties and early thirties. Though important internal problems remain, some of which are in a sense the consequence of Stalin's success, it does not seem likely that his followers, even if they quarrel further among themselves, will again try to remake Russian society on so grand a scale.

For the past twenty years the major problems confronting the top leadership of the Communist Party of the Soviet Union have concerned not the internal structure of their own system, but the relationship of that system to the outside world. In turn their appraisal of the situation abroad enters in as a major component of decisions that affect the life of every Soviet citizen. How many hours a Ukrainian miner or Central Asiatic peasant will work next year, and how much he will receive for this work, depends heavily on the leaders' appraisal of political trends in Washington, London, Paris, and other key centers. Particularly during the decade between the victory at Stalingrad and Stalin's death Soviet policy reflected a chain of commitments that derived from its increasingly expansionist foreign policy. This policy required the maintenance of a large body of men under arms, an emphasis on heavy industry at the expense of the general population's standard of living, ever greater pressure to extract the last ounce of produce from the peasantry through the machinery of the collective farms, and strict enforcement of conformity of all groups by means of terror and propaganda. No one link in this chain of commitments can be readily singled out as the causal one. Nor does the Kremlin enjoy a completely free hand in adapting to this set of dynamic relationships or in trying to control them. Both Moscow and Washington form parts of a larger system of world politics that has certain dynamic tendencies and properties of its own. Since the closing years of World War II these properties have manifested themselves in the form of intense rivalry between the two strongest powers, the United States and the USSR.

Despite the limitations on their freedom of action, stemming both from the larger arena of world politics and from internal causes, the new Soviet leaders have shown several signs of an attempt to break free of the chain of commitments that characterized the last years of the Stalinist era. A policy that is new in certain important respects has been launched and to some extent carried out, in spite of dramatic internal struggles. Its goal seems to be to reduce commitments and to seek popularity, both at home and abroad, without making the amount or kind of concessions that would threaten vital and hard-won political gains. In other words, it may be interpreted as a minor retreat, executed to consolidate positions already held.

Among the first domestic measures taken by the new regime were a liberal amnesty (March 28, 1953) and a cut in retail prices (April 1) that affected a wide variety of consumers' goods, among them bread, vodka, clothing, and matches. Perhaps recalling an earlier painful experience in 1947 when on December

14 the government had simultaneously abolished bread rationing and sharply devaluated the ruble, the Soviet population again anticipated a currency devaluation when the government announced the new retail price cuts. On June 28, 1953, the Minister of Finance found it necessary to quash rumors about devaluation, at the same time stating that the state loan for 1953 had been set at half the amount for the previous year. These soothing messages dovetailed into the announcements made by Malenkov on August 8, 1953, in which important concessions were made to the peasantry, some reduction was to be given in the emphasis on heavy industry, and an increase planned in the production of consumers' goods.

The policy of limited retreat also appeared in the Soviets' relations with the outside world. An announcement by the Chinese Communists on March 29, 1953, of far-reaching concessions on the prisoner of war issue, which had long blocked truce negotiations in Korea, was immediately supported by Molotov, Soviet Minister of Foreign Affairs. Although there is as yet no clear evidence about where the initiative for the Chinese move really lay, Soviet approval was timed suggestively. In Germany, the other major diplomatic front, the same policy of concessions marked the statement by East German leaders on June 10, 1953, promising the correction of previous "mistakes." Here, however, the policy suddenly backfired in a series of riots and strikes, openly directed against the Soviets and requiring strong military force for their suppression. On June 26, 1953, less than ten days after some degree of order had been restored in the German satellite area, the Presidium of the Supreme Soviet of the USSR adopted a decree branding as a spy and traitor Lavrentii P. Beriya, the man primarily responsible for internal security matters in the Soviet sphere of the world.[1] Presumably Malenkov had won the Party leaders' assent to this act, and possibly that of the military, some time before.

As the Berlin incidents and the rumors about ruble devaluation indicate, the new policy has not been a completely unqualified success. Under Stalin, from 1929 onward, the response of the Party leadership to foreign and domestic problems showed at least one constant aspect: a demand for faster and faster industrialization, accompanied by heavy sacrifices from the mass of the population and modified only by occasional sops thrown to the working man and the peasant. Moreover, after World War II the totalitarian features of the Stalinist regime were gradually intensified, and Party control was tightened in those areas, particularly in agriculture and intellectual life, where some signs of weakness had been shown. Events appeared to be heading toward a major purge shortly before Stalin's death, at the time of the arrest of the Kremlin doctors and in the wave of accusations that spread outward after this incident. The dramatic release of the doctors, together with the public announcement of their innocence, announced on April 3, 1953, can now be seen as part of the larger pattern of recasting Stalinist policy. But so far the new regime has by no means reversed former major policies, nor has there yet been any basic change in the major institutional features of the Soviet system since Stalin's death.

On the whole, it seems most improbable that under the present leadership severe changes will be made in the general functions and structure of the Soviet control system, which has proved itself effective despite actual and potential weaknesses. Before probing for these soft spots and examining the sources of stability within this apparatus, it is necessary to sketch briefly, mainly for the nonspecialist in Russian affairs, the form and functions of this complicated system.

In general, the Soviet leadership has at its command three main instruments of control which it can use to enforce its decisions and to focus the energies of the Soviet population in the desired directions. One of these is the Party. The second is composed of the secret police and the military forces, which together constitute the instruments of violence. The third channel of control is, in a sense, a residual category, which many citizens of the USSR and the official press often lump together under the term "Soviet apparatus." It includes three major elements: (1) ministries administering economic activities (such as transport, coal, oil, chemicals, metallurgy, etc.), together with ministries directing noneconomic activities, such as the newly created Ministry of Culture and the Ministry of Health; (2) those agencies whose primary tasks are to check up on the economic performance of other ministries and to execute the technical, rather than the policy-making, aspects of drawing up economic plans (for example, the Ministry of Finances, the Ministry of State Control, and the State Planning Commission); and (3) the hierarchy of soviets, extending from the village, town, and city soviets to the Supreme Soviet, which are in essence appendages of the Party organization and also of the ministries in Moscow, although certain minor local administrative functions are carried out with relative freedom from central Party direction.

This threefold system of control—through the Party, the instruments of violence, and the Soviet apparatus—is superimposed on the patchwork of territorial divisions which constitute the USSR: the sixteen Soviet Socialist Republics (sometimes called Union Republics), of which the largest is the Russian Soviet Federated Socialist Republic (RSFSR); the approximately one hundred and sixty-odd *oblasts*, economic regional units into which each Soviet Socialist Republic is ordinarily divided; and the smallest territorial and administrative units, the *raions*, which exist in both the countryside and the city.[2] Unlike many formal provisions in Soviet legal documents on Russian political structure, these territorial arrangements form the basis of real behavior. They are key administrative divisions around which a host of economic and political activities are organized.

The Party organization follows this territorial scheme.[3] While Party communications from the center in Moscow sometimes skip the Union Republic organizations and go directly to the oblast, the Union Republics, particularly the larger ones, are also significant administrative units. At the 1952 Congress, Nikita S. Khrushchev, then on the road to becoming a major figure in Party organizational questions, suggested the inclusion in the Party statutes of a clause to the effect that the *obkom* (Party oblast committee) and central committee in a Union Republic systematically inform the Moscow Central Committee about their work by furnishing it with reports at set intervals. Though such a clause did not appear in the new statutes, it represents standard operating procedure that has existed for some time. Also in the interests of stricter control, Khrushchev suggested the creation of a secretariat, not to exceed three persons in number, in the obkom and central committee of a republic.[4] This provision, which was adopted, also reflects the factual situation that major responsibility for events in a specific area rests on the shoulders of the Party secretary.

Refugees who were in a position to be familiar with these matters report that, as a rule, the nucleus of power at the oblast level is composed of the Party secretary, the oblast administrator for the secret police, and the representative of the economic ministry concerned with tasks in the area in question. At the raion level a corresponding arrangement probably exists, although printed confirmation of this point has not come to my attention. In some areas a military representative may also participate in local decision-making. All such officials are of course Party members.

The functions performed by the three major instruments of control are necessary in any complex industrial society if that society is to continue in existence. The first function, which may be labeled the politically positive one, consists of eliciting the kind of behavior from the population that the regime desires. The Party is the major agent in this area of control. Part of this work is done through formal education, which attempts to inculcate a set of attitudes, as well as to transmit knowledge and skills. Another part is done through the establishing of unequal material rewards or incentives for different kinds of work. Both the educational system and the system of differential incentives are under the close and continuous supervision of the Communist

Party. On a number of occasions the highest Party authorities
have intervened in these matters to establish major policies,
scrapping old ones and adopting new ones that they considered
necessary. Still another part of the politically positive function
is performed by the Party's elaborate propaganda apparatus and
through the control and deliberate manipulation of all media of
mass communication.[5] At the individual level, the Party member
himself is of course supposed to serve as a living model of the
desired behavior in all walks of life. Finally, the network of
Party organizations indicates by suggestion and exhortation, as
well as by direct command, the policy and behavior expected of
organizations and individuals.

By their politically positive pressures the Soviet leaders seem
to be aiming at enough spirited and intelligent support from
the population so that at least minor officials, Party or non-Party,
can be counted upon to do the right thing at the right time within
the area of discretion that must of necessity be left to them. This
hope has undoubtedly diminished with the passage of time and
has been replaced with a more cynical and manipulative attitude,
also a strong tradition in Bolshevik thinking. There are still,
nevertheless, very strong traces in major public statements of
the belief that only a certain irrational perversity, the relic of
capitalist society and capitalist psychology, prevents segments of
the population from accepting socialism with spontaneous enthusiasm. Thus, the politically positive strand of control represents a vast attempt to impose a new consensus, a new set of
ideals, and a new social framework on a structure in which the
sources of cohesion had already been partly destroyed in pre-
Revolutionary times by the forces of industrialism and liberalism.

The positive function of eliciting certain kinds of behavior
shades over into the negative one of preventing people from engaging in other kinds of behavior. Between these two, but closer
to the negative pole, one finds compulsion used to make people
do something, as well as to prevent them from doing something.
The gradations along this continuum involve subtle distinctions

that need not detain us here. Any society has to have negative means to channel and control behavior. Their extent, nevertheless, is an indication of the failure of the positive ones. In the development of the Soviet system, as positive methods failed to produce the required results, Lenin and Stalin found themselves compelled to resort more and more to terror and violence. In this connection it must be emphasized that the choice was not between using terror and permitting the disintegration of Russian society. Rather it was between using terror as a major instrument to create and then consolidate a new social system, or else letting power go by default. By the late twenties the forces of recovery and reintegration were growing stronger in Russian society. Since these forces were growing from the ground up in a way that threatened Bolshevik power, terror had to be used to destroy them and impose a new order, a process most clearly seen in the collectivization of agriculture. Later, terror had to be used within the Party itself, again to consolidate the power of the top leadership, perhaps essentially that of only one man, Stalin himself. A parallel growth of the importance of the instruments of violence may be observed in the Politburo's relationship with the outside world. Communist parties have not come to power anywhere outside Russia itself without prior military action.

The purpose of both positive and negative political controls in the Soviet Union, as elsewhere, is to enforce political decisions. A political decision, like any other, is a choice among alternatives. Can one point to any general criterion according to which the major political decisions made by the Soviet leaders appear to have been made? The maintenance of their own power has been suggested as an answer to this question, particularly by W. W. Rostow in his *Dynamics of Soviet Society*.[6] Such an answer is, I believe, correct as far as it goes. Indeed the maintenance of pure and simple power does appear to have been the overriding criterion of major Bolshevik decisions, to which the leaders have been quite willing to sacrifice any literal adherence to Marxist doctrine. They are likewise relatively little concerned about questions of economic efficiency and general material welfare when such considerations conflict with the demands of keeping themselves in power, though they may continue to claim that, in the long run, their system will produce greater material welfare than any other.

Nevertheless power does not constitute a sufficient answer to this question. Power cannot be pursued as the one and only goal of any ruling group, in isolation, as it were, from other values. In modern times the pursuit of power requires the use of technological instruments that are quite complex. It also requires the creation of very complex human instruments: armies, bureaucracies, industrial systems, and devices for feeding and servicing these instruments. In turn the efficient manipulation of these human groups demands consideration of the forces of traditional beliefs and behavior which impede or resist social changes. Ingrained peasant traditions, as well as the more recently established industrial patterns of evasion and conservatism, constitute factors which the dictatorship cannot afford to ignore. A fuller picture of the role of tradition will be given at later points in this study where its relationship to specific social institutions and to other criteria of Soviet rule can be more appropriately brought into focus.

Both the human and the material instruments have certain minimum technical requirements as to the way in which they must be used. If these technical requirements are neglected by those in search of power, their search will fail. In this respect power is limited by the autonomy of the instruments that must be used in its pursuit. Military strategy has its own technical requirements and autonomy that cannot be neglected by the most brilliant political strategist. Likewise, any industrial system requires discipline and punctuality from its labor force, some regularity in the availability of supplies of raw materials, means for distributing the finished product, and other functional arrangements that turn out to be very much the same in Magnitogorsk as in Detroit. Scientific research also is clearly an activity that has certain technical requirements in its successful pursuit.

For these reasons, even such thoroughly politically minded rulers as the Bolsheviks cannot make all of their decisions according to political criteria alone. Every decision of any consequence must take into account these instrumental or technical requirements as well. In any concrete issue that arises at any level of the Soviet bureaucratic hierarchy one criterion of a "good" decision will of course be: does the decision contribute to the power of the dictator? But another element that the Bolsheviks are forced to consider in trying to find a "good" decision is: does the decision meet the technical requirements of the situation? Naturally the reconciliation of these criteria is often far from easy. The technical requirements of a "good" decision demand therefore still a third instrument of control. The economic and noneconomic ministries, or the "Soviet apparatus," perform this control function. The description of the way in which they operate may be left to later chapters in which certain aspects of Soviet society receive more detailed consideration.

Here it is sufficient to point out certain general characteristics of the control system as a whole. Positive and negative political controls, as well as the technical ones, are by no means clearly allocated to various agencies, all of which stay neatly within their tables of organization. Instead, the system is one in which distinct lines of authority and sharp divisions of function are generally conspicuous by their absence. The confusion and overlapping stem partly from the speed with which the Soviet bureaucracy was constructed. They derive in addition from the dictatorship's need to fragment authority, lest one or the other levers of control develop into a power in its own right.

On this account one finds certain similarities in the structure and operation of a wide variety of Soviet institutions, ranging from a military unit, through a factory and collective farm, to even a scientific laboratory or a university. Three important officials will usually be found representing each of the three control functions. The Party secretary and the secret police officer, with his network of informers, serve as the positive and negative political controls. Technical control functions are performed by the cadre officer in the military unit, the manager in the factory, the chairman in the collective farm (where one or the other agents of political control may be missing), and by the director of a scientific laboratory or the rector of a university.

Such is the basic pattern of the Soviet dictatorship. Are there, however, "built in" tensions and probabilities of change inherent in this system as it has developed during the past thirty years? Stated more broadly, we would like to know whether power is automatically, subtly, and inevitably modified by the mere process of its exercise under the specific conditions of twentieth-century Soviet dictatorship, or whether something approaching an equilibrium point has been reached, at which potentialities for change are somehow kept in check. From this standpoint four major problems of the control system require discussion: the nature of the demands on the top leadership, the relationship between the political and the technical administrators, the forms of organized evasion and techniques for coping with it, and finally the potential role of the instruments of violence, the army and the police.

A dictatorship of the type exemplified by the Soviet variety requires, it may be suggested with considerable confidence, a very energetic and at least moderately competent individual at its head to compensate for the fragmentation of power and responsibility beneath. The leader and his associates at the top must shoulder an exceptionally heavy load. Because of the insecurity and continual cross-checking at lower echelons, there is a tendency to shove responsibility upward. As a consequence, even trivial problems, which in another political system could be solved at a point short of the apex, often find their way into the agenda of the highest Party leadership. In addition, owing perhaps to suspicion of their own sources of information, the leaders attempt to keep open more or less irregular channels of communication, supplying information on events in the USSR and probably also abroad. At the Party Congress in 1952 it was claimed in *Pravda* that all the letters addressed to the Party Central Committee are examined by high officials of the Central Committee's "apparatus" and that some of them form the basis of Central Committee discussions.[7] It is not improbable that a certain number of such communications are also discussed by the Party Presidium. Thus the wide range and variety of problems confronting the dictator and his associates must place a tremendous burden on their energy, capacity, and judgment.

The Soviet system appears on the whole rather well-suited to take care of this problem. At least it has some advantages over a hereditary monarchy, in which biological accident can put a weakling in a responsible position. To be sure, there is occasional evidence of the growth of a *jeunesse dorée* among the children of the high Communist elite. Perhaps in time this tendency could lead to a certain loss of energy and capacity for forceful leadership among the Kremlin rulers. Such a turn of events could take place, however, only if those close to the dictator were, or could be, sure of their position. Instead, at the present time, the dictator's security depends heavily on the insecurity of his associates. Though one would scarcely choose to call membership in the Party Presidium open to merit, since realistic aspirations for inclusion in this body can be held by only a very few persons, it is a distinctly competitive position. With the shake-up after Stalin's death the competitive aspects of the position have probably increased. This may put an even greater premium on the kind of energy and political ruthlessness necessary in any one who might eventually take over Stalin's key role. A sifting process, one may easily infer, takes place that is likely to prevent the emergence of serious political incompetence.

There remains another aspect of the top leadership's problem, the need to find some method for resolving both personality clashes and alternative views in regard to policy. It can be argued that Stalin's forceful and brutal methods, which were applied even to his own associates, have made it nearly impossible for his successors to find some regular and acceptable procedure for handling this problem.[8] On the other hand, the present situation, both inside and outside the USSR, apparently presents fewer major alternatives to the Soviet leadership than was the case during the struggle of the twenties, so that these two factors might cancel one another. In the absence of reliable data so far on the alignment of personalities and policies within the top leadership we are on the edge here of uncontrolled speculation. One can, however, specify the power base that will be needed by any group or individual that endeavors to stabilize its own authority. It would have to be composed of some combination of elements among the following: (1) the Party apparatus, particularly the secretariat with its control of appointments; (2) the secret police; (3) the armed forces; (4) the major economic ministries.

The second problem facing the Soviet dictatorship is that of finding and maintaining an appropriate relationship between the political and the technical administrator. In the early years of the regime this problem was frequently solved according to the pattern of the political commissar in the army: the Party compelled or cajoled some one who had the necessary technical skills to make essential technical decisions, while a Party official stood figuratively, and sometimes literally, with a revolver at his back to make sure that the political aspects of the decisions were carried out. In the factory the "Red director" was assisted by an engineer of considerable experience, but who was not regarded as politically reliable. Similar devices were used elsewhere.

After the Soviet regime had created its own group with sufficient technical skills, the nature of the problem shifted. Under Stalin, much was made publicly of the point that the new Soviet generation of technically trained people was loyal and trustworthy. On the other hand, the elaborate set of checks and crosschecks strongly suggests that the Stalinist regime operated on the basic premise that nobody, not even the most seasoned

Party member, could be trusted. Partly as a consequence of this shift, and partly as a remnant of the political commissar technique, Soviet society still tends to display at many points a double system of status in regard to matters of authority. The person who is technically qualified and who holds the position with formal authority, may be in certain important areas of his conduct subordinate to a Party official without any position of formal authority within the organization. Thus, during the thirties at least, the secretary of the Party organization within a Soviet embassy was superior to the ambassador on Party matters.[9] At times the situation could have ludicrous features, when, for example, a stage-hand with Party status was in some questions superior to the most skilled musicians and actors on the Moscow stage.[10] It is obvious that if the work of the organization were to go on, some feasible arrangement would have to be found in which the scope of political and technical authority received an acceptable definition. This has taken place in wide areas of Soviet life and will be discussed in more detail in later chapters. There remains, nevertheless, a certain fundamental instability in this respect.

This instability may be traced to the following sources. While there is a tendency in a dictatorship to shove responsibility for policy upward, there is also a corresponding tendency to shove responsibility for results downward. Even if the Soviet dictatorship operates on the premise that nobody is trustworthy, somebody has to be held responsible for results demanded by the center. By and large, this somebody has come to be the territorial Party secretaries, at the republic, oblast, and raion levels, in descending order.

Since the Party territorial administrators carry a prominent share of the responsibility for seeing to it that things get done, particularly that economic objectives are achieved, they display a natural tendency to usurp technical roles. Thus they take responsibility away from the technical administrator and tend to become technical administrators themselves. The consequence is that they become absorbed in a maze of local and technical problems and lose sight of political matters. In part this absorption of the political administrator into the role of the technical administrator takes place because the Kremlin, for political reasons, lays such heavy stress on a particular kind of economic result, the execution of the national economic plan.

In his major speech to the Party Congress in 1952 Malenkov asserted that war conditions were responsible for this situation and that, during the war, Party organizations tended to take over administrative work directly. The war may have intensified the situation, but it existed long before. The results that Malenkov pointed to, however, find numerous confirmation elsewhere. "There was created," he said, "the familiar danger of a break between Party organs and the masses, and of their turning from organs of political leadership, from militant and independent organizations, into singular administrative and directive establishments, unable to oppose all kinds of localist, narrow departmental, and other anti-governmental tendencies, failing to notice straightforward distortions of Party policy in economic construction and violation of the interests of the government." [11]

This transformation of the political administrator into a technical one, and the consequent blinding of one of the eyes of the Kremlin, is apparently a matter of great concern to the top Party leadership. It was also the subject of frequent reprimands in the organizational journal of the Party Central Committee, now no longer available in the United States. In Uzbekistan, to cite a case involving an autonomous republic, it was found that the administration of cotton-growing had become entirely concentrated in the hands of the Party's central committee for the republic, and that the republic's technical line of control, the council of ministers, kept away from the problem. The high Party officials went into such detailed questions as the use of a certain type of carburetors on tractors.[12] In another case, the same Party organ observed rather tartly that the head of the Volga Caspian fishing trust always went to the Party oblast committee with his troubles over materials and transportation. People in this area, the report continued, were accustomed to the fact that there was no point in turning to the executive committee of the soviet on such matters.[13] Understandably enough such harassed Party officials have a tendency to become abusive, petty tyrants. "Everybody knows how to swear, but there isn't anybody to show how to organize the work," runs one typical complaint on this score.[14]

No appraisal of the extent of this practice can be made beyond the point of its obvious concern to the very highest leaders of the USSR. The evidence indicates quite clearly, however, that a process is at work, which, if continued unchecked, could leave the central authorities in Moscow with physically the same administrative apparatus on their hands, but without any way to perform the positive political functions, or to oversee the machine as a whole. Other channels of control, such as the secret police or the Ministry of State Control, to be discussed in a later chapter, do not appear capable of replacing this vital function should it wither away.

A certain minimum of regularity, precision, security, predictability, and clarity in hierarchical relationships is of course essential, even in a totalitarian dictatorship. Parts of life have had to be rationalized in this fashion. It is easy to see certain crystallization points in Soviet society, from which the process might spread. One of these is the factory director, and factory relationships generally, about which more will be said in a subsequent chapter. Another crystallization point might be in the military forces, about which, however, we are less well informed. If the Communist rulers ever achieved the degree of regularity and precision in their society that they seek so constantly and vigorously, they would seriously alter and probably destroy the basis of their own rule.

The Party itself shows some signs of strain under the conflicting requirements of being both a rational bureaucracy and an instrument of arbitrary despotism with secular utopian pretensions. Bolshevik organizational principles, along with their well-known stress on discipline and hierarchy, still carry with them a considerable emphasis on camaraderie and equality within the Party, shading over into paternalistic relations with those outside the Party. Even if the relationship is between a superior and an inferior, it must still have a personal touch, like that between a gruff father and a naughty child. Conceivably this aspect of Bolshevik organizational principles is related to widespread traits in the Russian population. There is good evidence, I believe, for the view that a substantial number of Russians shy away from cold, impersonal relationships that involve only a small segment of the personality. They tend to prefer and even demand a commitment of the whole personality.[15]

Such a commitment is ruled out in a full-blown bureaucracy on the model of the Prussian civil service, where the relationship one has to another person depends upon his position in a table of organization, each with its title, grade, and honorific to wall off and protect, as it were, the individual psyche. Lenin, impressed with the reflection of this machine in the German Social Democratic Party, tried to transplant it to Russian soil, where it has never taken full hold. Furthermore it was not desirable, from the Communist viewpoint, that it should take hold too well. Strict bureaucracy implies communication "through channels," step by step, up or down the line. For the Bolsheviks it was necessary to be able to leap into the situation at any point they chose, skipping one or any number of steps, to "shake up the apparatus," as a favorite Bolshevik expression puts it. On the other hand, the Party apparatus displays a continual tendency to shake down into the kind of impersonal, hierarchical, bureaucratic relationships that are necessary to get business done accurately and with dispatch. An individual is likely to maintain a working relationship only with his immediate superiors and with one or two immediate subordinates, who in turn are responsible for the work of some unit beneath them. High Party officials are inclined to disapprove of such limited relationships and to demand of their harried subordinates a cultivation of full personal knowledge about the people whose work they control, as well as an awareness of this work in all of its aspects.

The third major problem confronting the leaders derives from the fact that the Soviet system of centralization is continually breeding its opposite in the form of groups within it that become involved in a network of protective evasions. These groups build walls around themselves that are at least temporarily impervious to Moscow's demands. The basic elements in this frequently repeated situation appear to be the following: Particularly on account of the frenzied pace of economic growth, Moscow puts demands on its servants that are objectively beyond the possibility of human achievement. Moscow also makes the situation more difficult by hedging every responsible individual's behavior with numerous administrative and legal restrictions in order to make sure that this behavior flows in the proper channels. It is therefore often impossible to get results and stay strictly within the law. Hence many successful administrators have some blot on their record that can be brought out against them at any time Moscow chooses. In one respect this is excellent from Moscow's viewpoint, since it means that the central authority has a hold over its lieutenants. From this point of view the Soviet system depends upon giving everybody an impossible job and then threatening them with punishment when they fail to accomplish it.

There are other consequences, however, that are less desirable from Moscow's standpoint. To get results by breaking the law, one official ordinarily has to persuade another one to do him a favor. For this a favor is naturally expected in return. In this way a network of mutual obligations is created among those who have broken the rules. This network of evasions can reach all the way up to a ministry, or involve substantially the entire control mechanism of a Union Republic. Furthermore, from each control center, from the raion up to the Kremlin, there often radiate several spiderwebs of connections. Except of course in the case of the Party Presidium, these spiderwebs extend both upward and downward. Outside the control centers themselves they are also woven horizontally to include people with parallel interests. At their center is usually a powerful and ambitious individual. The key individual in each control center, in order to maintain power, must balance one web against another, as well as endeavor to destroy any that inhibit the exercise of his power.[16]

When the growth of protective cliques occurs on the outskirts of the huge Soviet domain, the regime's difficulties are further exaggerated by regional and national lines of cleavage. In turn, local issues in far-off places become intertwined with the palace intrigues of the Kremlin. The serious nature of these difficulties has been illustrated by a series of events in the Republic of Georgia that preceded the fall of Beriya, one of its most prominent citizens. Without going into details concerning the alignment of individuals on local or Kremlin issues, it is enough to point out that in the course of less than a year the Soviet press has announced two virtually complete overturns of the Georgian leadership and has specifically mentioned the personal intervention of the Kremlin.[17] The report of one of the new brooms, for a brief time chief of the Georgian Communist Party, gives many concrete illustrations of the distortion of Moscow's power as a result of the pressure of local forces and local "connections." In the course of his report this official raised the question of possible consequences if the situation had been allowed to deteriorate further: "If this had happened," he said, "Georgia would have broken up into a number of 'provincial duchies,' which would have exercised the real power, and nothing would have been left of the Georgian Communist Party and the government of the Georgian Republic." [18] In part the remark is undoubtedly an attempt to curry favor with superiors by bragging about the difficulties of the job. In addition, however, it casts a significant sidelight on the nature of some of the obstacles encountered in the Kremlin's efforts to control its subjects. The network of protective evasions arises where the irresistible forces of the center meet the immovable aspects of the populations' desire to live life according to their own group standards as they have been handed down from generation to generation—or in other words, according to tradition.

Moscow is, however, by no means helpless in the face of the traditionalist absorption of the rulers by the ruled or by related splinter tendencies. Instead, the structure is so arranged as to permit, indeed to encourage, higher authority to skip over its immediate subordinates and to intervene directly, where intervention is necessary. Through several alternative lines of authority Moscow can reach down, bypassing the rungs of other control ladders. One such line is the secret police, whose role is hinted at by Soviet press reports on Beriya's part in the Georgian incident. Another line is the Ministry of State Control, to be discussed more fully in Chapter 2. Still another is of course, the Party itself. In tight situations it has long been the practice for the Party to send out plenipotentiaries from the center, armed with strong powers to deal with local questions. Recently, at the 1952 Party Congress, this arrangement appears to have been strengthened by the establishment of plenipotentiaries in the Republic, the krai, and the oblast. These officials are independent of local Party organs and receive their orders from the Committee (formerly Commission) on Party Control, an organ of the Central Committee. The Control Committee, which has had a long and important history, is primarily charged with handling questions of internal Party discipline and morality.[19] Through these devices Moscow can keep itself informed in detail about developments anywhere in the USSR. As is shown by the liquidation of whole republics after the war, as well as a host of other incidents, the central authorities have not hesitated to intervene vigorously and on a broad scale, to make clear where real power lay.

The fourth major problem inherent in the structure of Communist dictatorship concerns the relationship of the military forces and the secret police to one another and to the Party. It is often asserted that the Bolsheviks' increasing reliance on the instruments of violence will inevitably lead to a corresponding increase in their importance in the Soviet state, culminating in the Party's loss of control over them and a consequent shift in the basic character of the regime. For the Soviet leaders the problem is thus part of the larger, ever-present one of devising methods to keep technical experts and associated group interests within the bounds demanded by over-all political objectives that require their use.

How much of a competitor is the army? Its most obvious asset is its direct control over the major weapons of destruction, combined with the expert knowledge of how to use them. Possibly another asset might be that the military forces are not closely identified with the most unpopular and repressive aspects of the regime in the eyes of the mass of the population. Though such an hypothetical asset could not become effective until popular sentiment itself became far more of a political force, it is a plausible guess that a military distatorship might be more acceptable to the population than the Communist one. Finally, one can point to certain experiences of the Second World War as a precedent out of which military control of civilian life might grow. In areas under the Soviet equivalent of martial law, military soviets were established that, according to a recent Soviet source, took over "all functions of government power in the sphere of defense, the securing of public order, and government security." [20] The phrase "government security" is suggestive in this connection, as its maintenance is ordinarily the task of the secret police. Although local political organs continued to function, this source states, they were subordinate and responsible to the local or regional military authorities.

In its briefest essentials such appears to be the strongest case that can be made for the assumption of power by the military in the foreseeable future. It is not a very impressive one and is rendered less probable when one examines the controls over the military exercised by both the Party and the secret police.

Party controls in the army, as elsewhere, are designed to perform the positive function of insuring loyalty to the regime, as well as to nip in the bud any attempt at independent action which might weaken Communist authority. From this point of view, perhaps the most valuable service provided by the Party network is to supply a stream of information on the political mood of each army unit down to the company level, which passes upward through channels independent of both the military authorities and the secret police. The extent to which this arrangement induces positive political enthusiasm for the regime appears much more doubtful.

The relationship between the regular cadre military officer and the Communist official in military dress, first as commissar and later as *zampolit*, has long been a vexatious one for the Soviet authorities. Between 1918 and 1942 six decrees were issued, alternately establishing and abolishing the position of zampolit, three of them under the stress of war between 1940 and 1942.[21] It would therefore seem premature to regard the present situation as stable. Primarily the zampolit is now responsible for indoctrination as well as for reporting on morale. Soviet published sources, though slightly ambiguous, tend to emphasize that full responsibility for *both* military and political affairs rests in the hands of the military commander,[22] which would, if taken literally, render the zampolit somewhat superfluous. As an alien source of authority in the military hierarchy, the zampolit can often be a cause of friction with the military. In particular he can make trouble for the commander by reporting that the commander is neglecting political indoctrination, just as the commander can make trouble for his political deputy by claiming that the latter interferes with necessary military duties. On the other hand, a division of labor and a fairly smooth working relationship can also be reached. Much obviously depends on the

personalities involved in this relationship. By and large, however, it appears to be one in which the Soviet authorities sacrifice some measure of technical military efficiency for the sake
of effective political control.

Much less information is available on the nature of the secret
police controls over the military forces. Some reports indicate
that the secret police has officers for military units down to the
battalion level, and it unquestionably has a network of informers
in all ranks. Like the Party, it has a separate chain of communication and command implanted in the military forces. An unfa-
vorable entry on an individual's police dossier can blight the
career of a regular military officer. Some refugees claim that a
low-ranking officer in the secret police can make trouble for a
high-ranking Soviet general. As a generalization this seems dubious. It is more likely that the situation depends on personalities and "connections" on both sides. A work published by an
officer in the American intelligence services notes the absence of
any signs of defiance of the police at the highest level of the
Soviet army, with the intriguing exception of a marshal who
supposedly beat up a high police functionary in Moscow for
planting a glamorous woman to spy on him.[23] Scattered interview material gives the impression that regular military officers
generally fear and avoid the secret police officer. Some, on the
other hand, may try to ingratiate themselves as a form of self-
protection.[24]

It is much more difficult to appraise the effect of the Party and
the police controls over the military forces under circumstances
that cannot be clearly foreseen, than it is to sketch their structure, even if structure and effect are related. Nevertheless a few
suggestions may be offered at this point. In the first place, the
high proportion of Communist Party and Komsomol membership
among the military officers—86.4 per cent in 1952 [25]—is not necessarily significant. Because a military officer carries a Party card
in his pocket does not mean that he will identify himself with
the Party in every situation. In the second place, it seems at least

conceivable that the zampolit might in the course of time be absorbed into the military forces to an extent sufficient to blind this eye of the Party. In general there is a tendency for the Party man to be absorbed by the organization in which he works. This happens because he faces the choice of doing a good job within or for the organization, or remaining relatively ineffective as a man of words. The Moscow authorities, as we have noted, counter this, by demanding that he retain his Party identity, and by surrounding him with other Party members so that the organization as a whole may remain distinct.

The case of the secret police in the army, as elsewhere, is different. Their job is to spy. Therefore there is not as much of a serious tendency for them to become deflected from their attachment to the police system by the nature of the function they are required to perform. Also the task of spying on one's fellows is not the kind of job that leads to winning popularity contests within a military or any other organization, and it tends to maintain the isolation and separate identity of those associated with this operation. On the whole, then, it would seem that police controls might increase in importance within the military forces at the expense of strictly Party ones. Though our information on this point is extremely scanty, I am inclined to believe that the police are already the more significant agency, and sufficient to paralyze the military forces as an independent political force.

For the military to attempt a Bonapartist coup seems almost out of the question. A marshal or general who risked an open break with the high command of the Party or secret police would have tremendous difficulty in getting his orders obeyed by enough subordinates to give himself or his co-conspirators an adequate power base. This does not, however, rule out the possibility that in the course of time the military forces may greatly strengthen their power position in the top ranks of the administrative system. Thus far no strictly military man, or one who could be identified as an advocate of military interests as such, has achieved membership in either the Politburo or its successor, the Presidium. Voroshilov, a member of the Politburo from 1926 onward and People's Commissar of Defense after 1934, does not constitute an exception, since he rather clearly owed his military position to his long and close connection with Stalin. If a military man on the order of a Zhukov, or another whose rise came about solely through the armed forces, should reach the Party Presidium, it would be a very clear indication that the Party must compromise with the demands and requirements of its military instrument far more than was the case under Stalin.

In contrast to the soldier, the policeman had already reached the highest seat of power some seven years ago, through Beriya's election to the Politburo in 1946. At a lower level the contrast is even sharper. The secret police has its network flung wide throughout the armed forces. No corresponding network exists through which the military forces can penetrate the secret police, though it is a plausible guess that the military forces do engage in some relatively minor espionage and dossier-making activity against a few police figures. This relationship would seem to give the police a very marked advantage in any internal jostling for power.

The power of the secret police has grown rather steadily through the years, though not without interruptions. By 1941 the People's Commissariat of Internal Affairs (NKVD), which, to be sure, included other operations besides the secret police, had become by far the most important economic organ in the whole Soviet Union. Out of the 1941 Soviet budget for capital construction of 37,650,000,000 rubles,* the NKVD was to undertake tasks amounting to 6,810,000,000 or more than one-sixth. The concentration camps alone were allotted 2,675,000,000 rubles worth of construction, an amount exceeded only by the Commissariats of Oil Industry and of Aviation Industry.[26]

Are there any elements in the situation to offset the compara-

---

* This figure does not include capital construction undertaken through the Commissariats of Transportation, Defense, and the Navy.

tively advantageous position of the secret police? What are the prospects that the secret police might emerge from the position of an instrument, where Stalin managed to keep it, to the supreme ruling force in the state? Naturally such questions cannot be answered with scientific precision. Nevertheless, certain considerations may be examined that point to limitations and checks on the police power.

There is fragmentary but convincing evidence that after the war the secret police was not permitted to retain what might conceivably have developed into a near strangle hold on the economy. In January 1946 the NKVD was deprived of what a Soviet source called "functions significant in their extent that belonged to it in the construction of plants in various sectors of the economy." These functions were instead included among the tasks allotted to three new People's Commissariats that were set up at the same time: the Commissariats for the Construction of Heavy Industrial Plants, Fuel Plants, and Military Establishments.[27]

The nature of Party channels into the secret police, particularly at the higher echelons, remains one of the crucial unknowns in any attempt to analyze the position of the police. Formally at least, Party members in the central apparatus of all major administrative organs of the government form a single unit and are required to report directly to the Central Committee and the heads of the ministry any defects in the work of the ministry.[28] Presumably Party units in the secret police are also subject formally to these requirements. It seems rather improbable, however, that high career police officials, all of whom are undoubtedly Party members, would identify themselves with the Party versus the police. This aspect of Party control is perhaps therefore relatively insignificant. Some refugee sources also allege the existence of a super-secret organ, either within the Party or the police, to spy on the police. While the existence of such an organ is difficult to prove or disprove, the matter is of doubtful importance, since the same problem of controlling this police instrument arises as in the case of the secret police as a whole.

More important would seem to be the device of dividing the police against itself. This was particularly important during the time of the great terror in the late thirties. Not only the chiefs, Yagoda and Yezhov, perished or disappeared; the terror also reached well down into the ranks of the NKVD. Not infrequently those who were jailed would find their police examiners as cell mates.[29] In more recent times one can also observe the same process at work. The removal of Beriya from his posts as chief of the secret police and member of the Party Presidium in July 1953 was preceded by press criticism of the police, voiced before Stalin's death, and by other divisive actions taken by the Party.

The basic technique by which the dictator divides the police against itself is evidently the same as that used elsewhere throughout the administrative apparatus. An official is given a task that he must perform, yet one that he cannot execute without violating the rules laid down by the dictator. His violations give his superiors the power to cast him aside whenever it may be appropriate for larger reasons of policy. Moreover, his insecurity is further increased by the loss of protection he may suffer when shifts in power take place at higher levels. The substance of the technique seems to have been carried forward as a legacy from Stalin into the post-Stalin period, though the present regime has been at some pains to convey a contrary impression.

It is doubtful that the police could dominate Soviet society to the point of dispensing with the positive and technical lines of control embodied in the Party and the Soviet apparatus. There appears to be a sort of symbiosis among these three, in which no one of them can do without the other two. This symbiosis does not preclude the possibility of an increase in the power and influence of one of the three major instruments. Without too great distortion one can say that the growth of the Soviet system since 1917 has been characterized by the rise of the technical and politically negative lines of control, with which the politically positive one has had to compromise in order to retain its dominant position. The Party man has had to change from agitator to political administrator and give ground to both the engineer-administrator and the policeman. It is equally apparent that the last two have not been able to shake off the Party any more than the Party has been able to dispense with their services.

chapter 2

THE POLITICS OF
INDUSTRIALIZATION

No one doubts any more that the Soviet Union is a great industrial power. Professional economists, to be sure, differ rather sharply in their quantitative estimates of what has been achieved.[1] As long as the Soviets maintain their policy of secrecy about many essential statistical facts, these differences of opinion are likely to remain unresolved. Yet after full allowance for deception and concealment, the brute fact of Russia's continuing rapid industrial growth, particularly in the areas most relevant to military power, cannot be dismissed.

Economic growth is not purely a matter of natural resources. The rows of statistical columns that reflect greater output in coal, steel, and oil, and all the elements of economic power also reflect the organized activities of human beings. They record the consequences of the numerous relationships into which men and women enter with one another in order to produce goods and services. It is these relationships that will be the subject of inquiry in this chapter.

Given the fact of Soviet industrial growth, one conclusion immediately stares us in the face. The social instruments devised by the Bolsheviks serve the Kremlin well. Such a conclusion does not, however, by any means exhaust the problem. It merely serves as an excellent reminder not to regard the many incidents of local bottlenecks and failures as signs of crucial over-all weakness. Since the Soviet press stresses these incidents as horrible examples to be avoided, and since refugees probably have some tendency to exaggerate them, it is highly desirable to keep this caution in mind. Even if the Soviet industrial machine works in fits and starts, nevertheless it works. Granting this point, we still want to know how and why it succeeds. Further, we want to know if Soviet economic institutions contain any latent structural defects that might cause the machinery to slacken its pace at some future date under altered conditions. For example, does the situation in which these institutions put key individuals, from the Minister at his desk to the worker on the assembly line, serve to motivate them in a way that will keep the system going in roughly its present form? Or is the relationship among the various people who play important roles such that it is likely to generate important changes at some future date? If the latter possibility seems imminent, in what part of the system might the changes begin, and what counteracting forces might also be anticipated? Such questions cannot receive any final and "scientific" answer, yet may be pursued in the spirit of science.

With these questions in mind the following approach appears appropriate. The Soviet economic system, like any other, may be regarded as a set of social institutions regulating the way in which members of the society reach decisions about the allocation of natural and human resources to certain kinds of activity. It provides, for example, a more or less regular procedure for deciding whether steel will be used for tanks or for plowshares. From this standpoint it becomes necessary to find out who makes such decisions and how the decisions are related to one another. Clearly not every such decision can be made by the dictator himself. Nor is it possible to leave them to the spontaneous choice of the individuals immediately concerned without destroying the nature of the dictatorship. Therefore it becomes necessary to discover and analyze the ways in which the dictator can control or manipulate indirectly the situation confronting those who make economic decisions, as well as the response and reaction of the decision-makers themselves. Such analysis involves tracing the flow of decisions from the dictator downward through the various bureaucratic and informal paths in the society, as well as observing the various forces which policy encounters en route. Furthermore, the search for potential foci of change requires that careful attention be paid to the criteria of what constitutes a "good" and a "bad" decision at various points in the economic system, since change by definition implies an alteration in the effective criteria of choice. If a good decision at some point in the system is not one that advances the power of the dictator, his power is automatically weakened or limited in this area. Since, as I have already argued, not every decision can be made on the criterion of the dictator's power alone, conflict and the possibility of change are always present.

Although direct documentary evidence is lacking, it is a safe inference that in the USSR the key economic decisions, or those relatively few choices that influence the majority of other decisions, are made by the men who exert every effort to determine all other aspects of national behavior, the members of the Party Presidium. In the past it has often been a small group or faction within this body that has made the vital decisions, and a similar arrangement may very well prevail now.

The situation that confronts the rulers of the Soviet state, as remarked in the preceding chapter, includes the entire play of social forces within their own society and the world at large. A political appraisal of these forces and agreement on a political objective to be pursued within the framework of these forces constitute the first step in the formulation of national economic policy. "The purpose of the state plan for the development of the national economy of the USSR," says a semi-popular Soviet manual on planning, "is to achieve definite political and economic tasks. Pursuit of a political purpose is a cardinal feature of the Bolshevik plans. . . . A correct appraisal of the internal and international situation, and an analysis of the plan for the preceding period are the starting point for drafting the national-economic plan." [2]

In the light of these general objectives and its over-all appraisal, the Party Presidium has to make concrete decisions determining what proportion of Soviet resources will be devoted to the requirements of the military forces, the police, industry, agriculture, and other needs such as education and cultural welfare. In effect, some order of priority in respect to the various activities of the state has to receive at least tacit agreement at the highest political level.

In this connection the question immediately arises of the extent to which any group interest in Soviet society can make its claims effective in the course of major economic decisions. Does the Party Presidium, in other words, represent the point in Soviet society where conflicting pressures that arise throughout the society find their ultimate reconciliation in some form of political horse-trading? Or does it instead constitute an agency that manipulates the various control levers in order to bring about the kind of behavior that it seeks at all, or nearly all, points in the society? Both elements are certainly present to some extent in the process of making economic decisions at this level. Under Stalin the aspect of manipulative control from above clearly dominated the scene. From the decisions to force the pace of industrialization and collectivization, straight through the postwar amalgamation of the collective farms, the record for more than twenty years reflects a ruthless willingness to impose a new social order and to manipulate its instruments from above. Indeed the whole spirit of Bolshevism is opposed to any conception of the ruler as merely the one who reconciles the demands of active pressures within the society. Concessions have of course been made from time to time. But they were concessions regarded by the Stalinist leadership as the minimum necessary to keep the system going.

Under these conditions a decision on how to allocate resources represents primarily an evaluation of each functional group's minimal requirements in order that the group may make its contribution to the over-all political objective. It is not the outcome of a pluralist conflict of interests. For example, a decision in respect to the level of wages, which are set by the central authorities for the USSR as a whole, does not represent a compromise between the demands of management and labor both pressed insistently before the Party leaders. Instead, it represents a judgment by the dictator and his associates concerning the type of incentives necessary to elicit the requisite amounts of labor power in a program of industrial expansion. Likewise, the decision to allocate more resources to one industry rather than to another does not reflect the desires and interests of those engaged in running this industry, but a conclusion by the Party leaders that it must be expanded for military or other reasons.

Stalin's death may well have removed an essential element from this part of the decision-making machinery. Without a single and generally accepted leader it is difficult to see how the focus of Soviet energies and resources on a single objective could be maintained against the centrifugal pull of special interests. By the fall of 1953 no single leader had distinctly emerged. Such a situation favors the possibility that those who now make national economic policy might become identified with, or even dependent upon, specific group interests, or in effect bureaucratic empires within the dictatorship. Although this is only a possibility, it is worth while pausing briefly to explore some of its consequences.

Two things might be expected to happen. In the first place, the mechanism through which the various parts of the economic system are kept in balance would be seriously impaired. Since the dictator ultimately takes the place of the "invisible hand" of the market in relating various economic decisions to one another, difficulties at the top would spread rapidly to all portions of the system. Compromise and bureaucratic log-rolling are not likely to be sufficient to make sure that all the economically necessary tasks are performed. A ministry whose chief was successful at bureaucratic intrigue, but whose economic tasks were relatively trivial, might get huge allotments of aluminum for making pots and pans, while the producers of airplanes had to skimp. In one respect, of course, this extreme possibility merely represents an accentuation of present difficulties, where certain sectors of the economy are chronically short of the supplies they require. But shortages now are only partly the consequence of bureaucratic intrigue and inefficiency. They are essentially the result of a deliberate decision to allocate scarce resources to armaments and capital goods and to compel the rest of the economy to manage as best it can with what remains. If compromise became the chief element in the decision-making process, it would be very hard to force through any single policy and maintain continuity. In the second place, and as part of the same process, one might expect the disappearance of dynamic expansionism in the Soviet economy. To anticipate later conclusions, there appears to be very little in the situation confronting most people from the ministerial level down to the worker that would encourage economic growth of a spontaneous sort. The pressure to produce apparently originates at the apex of the Communist Party hierarachy and is transmitted downward through a variety of channels.

Some signs have already appeared that point to at least a temporary diminution of this pressure. In a major address on August 8, 1953, Malenkov claimed that between 1940 and 1953 the Soviet output of producers' goods had more than tripled, while the output of consumers' goods had risen by only 72 per cent. This, he announced, was a highly unsatisfactory state of affairs. For the future, he continued, "The job consists of making a sharp turn by producing consumers' goods and assuring a more rapid development of light industry and food industry." He promised that 32 billion rubles worth of consumers' goods would find their way into Soviet trade channels over and above the 312 billion that had been originally planned for the period between April and December 1953.[3] This is a very substantial increase when the price cut of April 1, 1953, roughly 10 per cent across the board, is also taken into account. The Soviet consumer would have reason to rejoice if these promises are kept by the new government. Whether they can or will be kept is of course another question. To carry them out the Soviet leaders would require a reduction in international tensions, which are to a great extent the consequence of Stalinist policies. Though the Bolsheviks have taken some steps in this direction, notably in connection with the Korean truce, it is unlikely that the Kremlin has reached any firm and irreversible decision about the closely related problems of foreign policy and industrial growth.

Before tracing downward the process through which economic decisions are reached, it is necessary to point out certain general characteristics of the instruments available to the Party leadership for enforcing economic decisions, and some of the problems that arise in using them. The impact of these instruments does not fall upon a mass of atomized individuals having no relationship to one another except through the ruler, much as this seems to be the utopian dream of every dictator. The factory constitutes a miniature society in its own right, as do smaller units within the factory, such as the shop and the shop section. Through intermediate administrative levers at his command the dictator attempts to coördinate the activities of all these miniature societies. But these control levers also tend to take on a life of their own. As they do so, they both facilitate and frustrate the objectives of the dictator.

Among the control levers one can distinguish two broad types. In one, compulsion and the giving of direct commands predominate. The direct allocation of raw materials to certain industries and the labor draft are examples of this type of control. The use of forced labor from the concentration camp constitutes its most extreme form. In this chapter, however, the discussion will be limited to the formally free sector of the economy that is evidently by far the more important in industry as a whole. The other type of control lever operates by influencing the economic environment in which an industry has to function. Controls over prices and wages are of this latter type. The actual decision or choice made by an individual is not in this latter instance a form of mere obedience to an order. Instead, the individual responds, and by no means always in the way anticipated by the authorities, to a situation that the authorities have created for him. By giving individuals a certain area of discretion, some elements of risk and responsibility for results can be thrust downward within the society and away from the dictator. The factory director, as will be indicated later, bears a heavy portion of this burden.

Crosscutting the preceding distinction is another one. Certain elements in the control system are intended for different targets in the economy. Some are designed to penetrate and influence conditions inside the factory. Important among the latter are the plant representatives of the police and the Party. Other features of the control system are external to the factory and define the situation within which the basic unit of production, the plant or enterprise, must operate. The direct allocation of some supplies, along with the greater discretion left to the manager by manipulating prices of other supplies and by leaving him free to choose among them, constitute, for example, major features in the social environment of the factory. Elements of direct compulsion and indirect manipulation play an important role both in determining what takes place inside the factory and in giving shape to the environment in which the factory operates.

The steps between the formulation of policy by the Party Presidium and its translation first into concrete quantitative objectives in the form of a national budget and an annual economic plan, and then into the economic realities of steel, coal, and other goods and services, are obscure at certain points, though the main outlines can readily be pieced together. In general terms the process by which any specific decision is reached represents a compromise between two forces: the demands of higher authority backed by political and economic sanctions on the one hand, and opposed on the other hand by the subtle resistance and evasion of those beneath, who have on their side the advantage of knowing concrete circumstances and possibilities and being able to conceal them at times. The Soviet economic system is a form of bureaucratic guerilla warfare, in which the top constantly, and by and large successfully, seeks to drive the lower layers to greater and greater performance, while at the same time the forces of relaxation and evasion spread their network upward, at times brushing close to the apex of the system.

No doubt the process of transforming economic policy into economic reality is facilitated by the fact that certain members of the Party Presidium also hold office as members of the Council of Ministers of the USSR, which includes the major economic ministries. Within the Council of Ministers these members of the Party Presidium constitute a sort of nucleus. In addition to the post of chairman of the Council of Ministers, held by Stalin and then by Malenkov, several members of the Party Presidium hold the title of first vice-chairman in the Council of Ministers and are frequently in charge of a specific ministry as well. In this manner they have direct access to the flow of day-to-day decisions on immediate and concrete questions that constitute the substance of effective policy.

The State Planning Committee (*Gosplan*), attached to the Council of Ministers, provides one of the major channels, though by no means the only one, through which economic information flows upward to the Party's high command. The available evidence indicates that it is a technical instrument rather than a policy-making body. Its main task is evidently the rather unenviable one of reconciling the political demands of the top Party leadership, either in their capacity as members of the Party Presidium or of the Council of Ministers, with the demands for more and more supplies that originate in the factory and are transmitted up the line to the head of each ministry. In this respect the following procedure prevails. The economic ministries and the councils of ministers of the union republics receive drafts of plans from the industrial plants under their jurisdiction. After working over this material they forward projects to the Council of Ministers of the USSR and a copy to the Gosplan.

The latter body coördinates this material "on the basis of directives from the Party and the government." [4]

A similar process of transmitting information upward and coördinating it at the center takes place in connection with the budget. The Soviet budget is the financial counterpart to the plan, but also includes noneconomic operations, such as expenditures on military forces. The coördination is provided by the USSR Ministry of Finances, which draws up the draft of the budget on the basis of the plan for the economy as a whole, the financial plans of other all-union ministries and offices, and certain other data. According to an official source, the Council of Ministers then examines this draft, along with the conclusions of the Gosplan authorities, and resolves any disagreements between the Ministry of Finances and other ministries. [5] Subsequent passage of the budget by the Supreme Soviet is largely a matter of rapidly acted and well-rehearsed routine, though minor changes are frequently made.

Both the Gosplan and the Ministry of Finances constitute agencies through which a political decision, where the primary criterion is the power of the Party high command, becomes transformed into an economic decision, in which the criterion of choice becomes the rational allocation of scarce material and human resources in order to derive a maximum of goods and services. In this transformation the Gosplan and the Ministry of Finances perform at least three functions. Along with other sources of information, they provide the top Party leadership with facts about the existing state of economic affairs in the Soviet Union, thus indicating the limits to political choice that are imposed by economic realities. In the second place, they are technical and drafting agencies that translate political demands into concrete economic choices. As Stalin's last essay, "Economic Problems of Socialism in the USSR," makes quite clear, the highest Party leaders are inclined to intervene directly in these technical matters and are by no means content with merely indicating the general outlines of policy. Finally, the Gosplan and the Ministry of Finance also serve as one point short of the highest authorities where conflicting bureaucratic and economic interests may be ironed out.

In the form that the national budget and the annual plan reach the chiefs of the economic ministries, it represents a set of concrete directives that have the force of law and the might of the dictatorship behind them. These directives specify the kinds, quality, and amounts of goods that are to be turned out by each ministry. At the same time they specify for each ministry the amount and kind of certain basic raw materials and semi-finished products it will receive in order to perform its task. This specification applies only to what is known as "funded" commodities, or those whose distribution is centrally controlled. The list of "funded" commodities is subject to change, but usually covers a substantial proportion of the products required in industry. In this fashion the government allocates directly the most important types of industrial and also agricultural products required by the economy.[6] The economic ministries in turn transmit the plans to the individual factories in their charge. Production tasks are also broken down by geographical areas. Each republic and oblast has its economic share in the over-all program specified in considerable detail.[7]

The necessary exchanges of raw materials and semi-finished products among producers are further regulated by the Soviet version of contracts. As indicated above, certain lists of "funded" materials are set up by the government in accord with the plan. The "fund" represents a right to receive a specified quantity of a certain type of material. The organization that produces raw materials or partly finished goods receives an order (*naryad*) that obliges it to deliver to the organization which will further process these materials a certain amount of "funded" material. On the basis of this order a contract is drawn up between the two parties. Contracts are also drawn up for the delivery of goods not subject to "funded" control, so-called "decentralized" commodities, according to the requirements of their distribution indicated in the plan. Before the war there was also an intermediate category between "funded" and "decentralized" commodities, known as "quota" commodities, but this distinction has evidently been abandoned. The government determines which factories and ministerial organizations must conclude contracts with one another, as well as the more important terms of the contract.[8]

What are known as "general contracts" are drawn up between the central supplying and consuming agencies at the ministerial level. In turn the factories in their charge conclude local contracts that reflect the terms of the general ones. There are also some instances of direct contracts between factories.[9]

At first glance the combination of plan, "funded" commodities, and contracts gives the appearance of an economy entirely controlled by administrative allocation from above. There seems to be no room for discretion either at the level of the ministry or below it. Closer examination indicates that such is not the case.

On general grounds it is obvious that the amount and type of supplies a particular producer will use in turning out a commodity cannot depend upon administrative fiat alone, but will also depend upon the objective requirements of the producer. The method of determining these requirements therefore assumes crucial importance. The prevailing method is for the ministry to draw up a list of its anticipated requirements, evidently with as large a margin of security as possible. This information the ministry gets from its plants, which also draw up their lists of requirements with as much of a margin as they can. In some cases the estimates presented by the ministry are expressed in monetary terms, while in others they are expressed in units of physical goods, tons of steel, cement, and so forth. These estimates are supposed to be ready by December of each year in order to form the basis of the annual contract with the supplying ministry or ministries.[10] Quite frequently, it would seem, the estimates are not ready on time, and the paper work is forced to overtake and cover up, as best it may, the realities of what has taken place. In particular, new construction work often goes on without prior estimates of the material requirements.[11]

The estimates presented by the ministries and their subordinate units are required to be based on certain norms governing the use of each kind of material in the production process. While the norms are expected to reflect scientific knowledge in respect to the efficient use of materials, in practice they are frequently nothing more than the amount of material used during the previous planning period. Even though the officials in the supplying organizations are urged to examine the estimates and requests submitted to them with a skeptical eye,[12] the arrangement is clearly one with considerable potentialities for waste and stagnation in the development of technological potentialities. The norm is an administrative rather than an economic spur to reduce costs and increase efficiency.

Soviet published comment indicates further ways in which the ministry, together with its subordinate units, participates in the decisions concerning the allocation of suplies. The general contracts between consumers and suppliers at the ministerial level are drawn up in accord with what are called basic conditions of delivery. These basic conditions are agreed to by the ministries concerned,[13] although the conditions are subject to review by the government. We also learn that a great deal of "preliminary work" is required in drawing up the terms of the general contract with respect to the quality and variety of the goods concerned. Even though specific details are lacking, these rather broad limits make it clear that there must be considerable informal bargaining among the ministries, in which they try to shove off the more difficult tasks on one another.

One of the major purposes of the contract system is to make sure that the supplier adheres to specifications in regard to the quality and variety of goods that are turned out. Evasion in this respect is very common, according to detailed evidence that appears widely in the Soviet press. The reason for this evasion is easy to see. If one factory on the supply side turns out goods that do not meet specifications, the ministry that produces these goods is likely to force them onto a receiving ministry, that will be unable to object because of the over-all scarcity. Poor quality, according to a semi-official Soviet source, does not ordinarily constitute adequate grounds for refusing to accept delivery of goods or to pay for them.[14] The receiving ministry is therefore apt to unload the inferior goods onto its subordinate plants. They then turn out a product that departs from the exact requirements of the plan. Both the supplier and the receiver will in this way be able to report over-all plan fulfillment in terms of the monetary value of the goods produced. Thus it happens, to cite one example among many, that in 1952 the glass factories of the RSFSR Ministry of Light Industry overfulfilled its plan for salt shakers, for which there is little demand, by 103.1 per cent, and underfulfilled its plan for drinking glasses, where a shortage exists, by nearly 30 per cent.[15] An evasion that begins at one point in the economy can in this fashion spread its effect in widening circles throughout a large sector of industry. For this reason there is a widespread tendency for suppliers and receivers not to sign contracts, as legally required, but to exchange goods without them.[16]

Still another source of leeway in the system of allocation stems from the fact that the estimates of what will be required for the coming planning period have to take into account the supplies that a ministry may have left on hand from the preceding period. Though this kind of reserve can be estimated from previous rates of use, it is a matter of guess work. By demanding more than it may need and by careful husbanding of the allocations it receives, a ministry can sometimes build up substantial reserves in this fashion. For example, the Ministry of Agricultural Machinery managed to obtain an extra sixty tons of steel for the first quarter of 1952, although it supposedly required only twelve tons for this period.[17] These reserves are accumulated largely as a form of insurance against increased demands from above. In this way scarce goods pass out of circulation, and the system of centralized allocation becomes partly self-defeating.

Financial controls complete the system of administrative allocation. The transfer of supplies from one government agency to another is formally regulated through the State Bank, which in the beginning of 1952 had nearly 5,000 branches scattered throughout the Soviet Union. Except for transactions involving less than 1,000 rubles, no government agency has the legal right to provide goods or services directly or for cash to another organization. Instead, all such transactions must pass through the hands of the bank. The extent and nature of the State Bank's credits to various branches of the economy are also subject to plan. They are reviewed on a quarterly basis by the Council of Ministers.[18] Likewise, all such transactions are supposed to take place at whatever price has been established by the government, which is ordinarily one of the terms specified in the contract.[19]

The role of price in the Soviet economy is at first glance rather puzzling. Even those in policy-making positions in the Soviet Union are evidently not altogether clear in their own minds about this question, as shown by Stalin's caustic reference in 1952 to the "muddle that still reigns with us in regard to price policy," because of the ignorance of "our managers and planners with but few exceptions." [20] If the main decisions that allocate supplies among producers are made by administrative order, why should it be necessary to have prices at all? Where price does not serve as a guide for the producer in choosing between more expensive and less expensive elements of production, it would seem to play a merely vestigial role, and perhaps one that only adds confusion to the process of reaching economic decisions.

The solution to the puzzle lies in the fact that price does serve in the Soviet economy both as a measure of existing performance and as an incentive to alter this performance in some of the same ways as in a capitalist economy. The difference lies in the fact that this measuring instrument and incentive is determined by administrative decision in the Soviet economy, whereas in a free economy it is the outcome of supply and demand, or of the economic process itself. Soviet prices serve as a measure of existing performance in that the price of a given commodity is set by the government at a level that ordinarily includes costs, the turnover tax, and a planned amount of profit. Hence price is really a measure of whether or not those in charge of a particular economic operation are staying within the estimates established by the plan. This measure applies particularly to organizations that operate upon what is known as a cost-accounting (*khozraschët*) basis. Such an organization has its balance at the State Bank and is expected to cover operating costs out of receipts. Though Soviet publications frequently claim that most of their economy is operated on their version of responsibility for cost accounting, it is not exactly clear to whom the responsibility applies. Some administrative units within an economic ministry may be on a cost-accounting basis, though it is seldom discussed in this connection in the Soviet press. On January 1, 1949, in connection with a wholesale reorganization of the price system, the practice of state subsidies for heavy industry was eliminated, supposedly resulting in a marked increase in the importance of cost accounting in the economy. Most of the emphasis in Soviet sources lies on the way in which price and cost accounting serve as the framework within which the director of each plant must make his decisions in organizing the work of the plant.[21]

As an incentive to improve performance, price control supplements the allocation of goods among producers by administrative order. Thus we learn that at one time the price of leather was mistakenly set at a level that approximated the price of textile footwear materials. This price ratio provided no incentive, as a Soviet source points out, for making economical use of leather in footwear production. Therefore the ratio was changed by means of the turnover tax, a form of sales tax that is used to manipulate prices.[22] Clearly it would make no sense for the government to alter the price of leather unless the producers of footwear did not receive all their supplies by allocation and therefore had some choice in the kinds of materials they would use, as well as some reason to search out the cheapest method of producing them. Even where the goods are made available by administrative allocation, price manipulation can be used as an additional incentive to persuade producers to use more of some commodities and less of others. Hence it is not quite correct to assert, as Naum Jasny does, that a wholesale market does not exist in the USSR.[23]

Considerable variation prevails in the actual procedure by which prices are determined. In heavy industry, according to a recent Soviet source, there is only the industry wholesale price, for the most part uniform for all plants turning out the same product. This price is based on the industry-wide average unit cost, plus a fixed amount of profit, ordinarily set at 3 to 5 per cent of the plant's income.[24] An efficiently operated plant can of course make more profit than this rate if it is able to reduce costs below the average or if it is favored by natural circumstances, such as nearness to supplies. In some cases, however, the price includes, in addition to unit cost and profit, distribution costs, including those of transportation. In other cases, transportation costs are not included. In still other cases, the cost and price are not based upon an industry-wide average, but upon the unit cost of a particular plant, or for a particular geographical area.

All of these variations must make it extremely difficult to find an objective basis for calculating costs and hence efficiency, either at the level of the central authorities in the ministries concerned, or at the level of the factory itself. Furthermore, as might be expected, the calculation of unit cost is often badly organized from a technical standpoint. Draft prices worked out by certain ministries are considerably altered when they are examined in the Ministry of Finance and the State Planning Committee.[25] It seems safe to assume, therefore, that a "strong" ministry can get a price set for its products that permits considerable leeway for itself and its subordinate plants. It also appears likely that in other cases price represents a routine decision based on the situation for the previous year or the previous quarter. The potentialities for stagnation and "taking it easy" under such a situation are obvious. This tendency is ultimately countered through intervention by the Party Presidium, which may throw out recommendations from below and establish prices directly in order to pursue a policy it believes necessary.[26]

As might be anticipated on general grounds, the Soviet regime by no means relies on economic sanctions and incentives alone to make sure that the appropriate economic decisions are taken by those who must decide among the alternative uses to which material supplies are put. The Ministry of State Control, which performs a mixture of technical, economic, and political functions, evidently enters the situation well above the level of the individual factory, though it is very active here as well. Its functions indeed range throughout the entire economy. A recent Soviet description of its duties declares that this Ministry "(a) [exercises] supervision over the production, economic, and financial activity of state . . . establishments, strictest supervision over the state of the accounts, the safe-keeping and the disbursement of money and material goods in the charge of these establishments and plants; (b) checks up on the execution of decisions and decrees of the government of the USSR; (c) brings to the attention of the government of the USSR special questions having economic significance, which arise out of the materials of its inspections and check-ups; (d) renders to the government its conclusions concerning the fulfillment of the government budget." Among its many present powers is the right to "examine the financial and economic activities of all ministries and their local offices."[27]

The Ministry has its supervisors in the "more important plants, railroads, storage warehouses, military districts, naval units, ports, and certain districts of the country that have special economic

importance." "Supervision is achieved," so the official account continues, "through various methods, the choice of which is determined by the tasks, objectives, and situation of the branch of
the economy. . . ." [28] Except for the somewhat stronger emphasis
on strictly economic tasks, the account of this ministry's functions reads like a description of the duties of the secret police. To
what extent this organ represents an alternate channel of in-
formation-gathering and control to the secret police can only
be guessed.

The all-important responsibility of selecting managerial and
supervisory personnel is divided among the Party, the economic
ministries themselves (in which Party men occupy the key posts),
and the secret police. High ministerial officials are changed frequently by the Party. Notices of such changes in the official
gazette, no longer publicly available outside the USSR, used to
appear over Stalin's signature, in his capacity as chairman of the
Council of Ministers, and that of the head of the Administration of the Affairs of the Council of Ministers. Presumably each
shift represents victory for one faction and defeat for another in
the ceaseless warfare of cliques and entourages that exist behind
the façade of any bureaucratic organization.

Each ministry has its section (*otdel kadrov*) for the allocation
of personnel, although intermittent press accounts indicate that
it does not play a key role. Perhaps this is due to the Party's
continual intervention in matters of appointment. At lower levels
the Party regional and district secretaries appear to be key officials in determining the appointment of plant managers, though
a great deal depends on the importance of the plant. Since the
purges, the function of the secret police appears to be primarily
negative, in that they can veto an appointment if an individual's
background seems to warrant it.

The necessity for regularity and the placing of individuals in
clearly labeled slots with distinct and limited functions, is at
least partly recognized through the activities of the State Staff
Commission, analogous to our Civil Service. This was not estab-

lished until just before the Second World War, on June 5, 1941. On large construction jobs, and presumably throughout much of the rest of industry, the table of organization and the salary scale of the administrative and engineering personnel require confirmation by the Commission. Once confirmed, these facts are registered with the Ministry of Finance.[29] Thus, personal connections, the ability to get results, and political reliability enter as ingredients of roughly equal importance in the choice of industrial leaders from the ministerial level down through the higher supervisory echelons of the plant itself.

Since about 1930 the Soviet state has had at its disposal two sets of controls that could be applied to the mass of its industrial labor force. Their purpose is to produce so far as possible the desired form and intensity of labor at the time and place needed. One set of controls, primarily the determination of wage rates, consists of manipulating the incentives placed before the workers. To the extent that workers are free to choose among alternative kinds of work, this set may be regarded as an indirect form of control. The second set of controls is direct, in that it seeks to compel the worker to behave in a definitely specified manner. Such controls range all the way from rules for factory discipline to the forced labor of the concentration camp. Toward the end of the thirties the significance of direct controls began to increase very markedly.

The incentive aspect may be considered first, along with the decisions that must be made in the course of manipulating the incentives. Presumably the highest political authorities decide the proportion of the country's resources that they expect to devote to wages for a given planning period.[30] There is a good deal of slippage, however, between such a decision and the amounts that are actually spent, which find their way into the workers' pockets. Apparently these unplanned benefits for the worker take place primarily at the level of the individual plant. Former Soviet citizens with experience in these matters often speak of the need to get around the limits on the wage fund at

their disposal in order to hang on to their labor force. Administrative regulations put no great bar in the way of a manager who
exceeds his wage fund for a limited period of time. Indeed, if he
cannot meet the normal pay roll out of current resources, the
State Bank is obligated to pay it for him and without his permission.[31] If he exceeds the allotted pay roll by more than 10
per cent, the permission of the minister of his industry is supposedly required before the bank will release the cash. Generally
the bank is not supposed to release money for wages unless production goals are being met.[32]

At higher levels those who participate in setting incentives
have rather little room for maneuver within the limits set by
the top political authorities. For some industries wages are
worked out by the ministry in charge of a particular branch of
production together with the top officials of the union responsible
for this industry. In others, the All-Union Central Council of
Trade Unions (AUCCTU) participates in drawing up the rates.
In still others, the ministry apparently decides matters on its
own. Increasingly tight control over these matters by the central authorities is indicated, however, in that ever since June 4,
1938, the permission of the central government, presumably the
Council of Ministers or the Party Presidium, has been required
for any alteration in wage scales.[33]

It would be a mistake to confuse the participation of union
officials in the establishment of wage rates with the kind of
bargaining that takes place rather frequently in the West. The
latter is often a genuine test of strength. High labor officials in
the USSR are closely identified with the Party and the government, and their careers depend on executing its will. At the
same time they may furnish the other authorities with some
clues concerning the effect on industrial production of further
deprivation of the workers, or the need to increase incentives by
some improvement in the latter's situation.

Wage scales consist of a minimum rate for a specific kind

of work, together with multiples of this minimum rate for similar jobs requiring increased levels of skill, or performed under more difficult conditions.[34] Several sets of scales may be applied in any large-scale plant. In most machine-making plants, for example, there are from four to six scales in use.[35] The number of steps in a given scale depends upon the type of industry in which it occurs or the work to which it is applied. Soviet comments mention scales with as many as a dozen steps and as few as seven.[36] Before the war, in 1940, fragmentary evidence indicates that the highest rate within a given scale ranged from about twice to somewhat under four times the lowest rate.[37] The differentials evidently increased greatly during the war. Since then Soviet sources assert that the differentials have been reduced to roughly the prewar level,[38] a claim that is hotly contested by Solomon Schwarz.[39] Part of the function performed by wage inequalities is to direct workers into heavy industry and to promote the industrialization of new areas, particularly the Soviet Far East. It is a safe guess that such policies have been decided at the very highest levels.

The widespread use of compulsion and direct controls over labor may be traced to two reasons. One of them is manifested in the tendency of a substantial part of the workers to wander from job to job in a restless search for better conditions. This tendency may have its source in the destruction of social bonds that is part of the rapid industrialization of a peasant country. It is significant that in his major report to the Nineteenth Party Congress of October 1952 Malenkov repeated earlier complaints about labor floating.[40] This is one of the latest indications that labor mobility remains very much of a current problem, despite the system of compulsion. A second reason for compulsion derives from the failure of incentives to attract labor where it is needed. Since the primary economic decisions are not made in terms of welfare, it is understandable that the consequences of such decisions would react back through the economy to produce "bottleneck" situations that have to be handled through compulsion, especially in a poor country with little margin to spare for the redistribution of incentives.

In an impressive chapter of his monograph on Soviet labor, Solomon Schwarz has traced the gradual growth of compulsion in labor relationships since 1930. The system of labor passports, introduced on December 20, 1938, and the rules on tardiness, absenteeism, freezing to the job, and compulsory transfer, introduced on June 26 and October 19, 1940, are the part of the story that is best known in the West. Schwarz's analysis destroys the notion that these measures were emergency devices in preparation for war which lasted into peacetime because of their proven utility. He shows clearly that they were the culmination of a long series of attempts to deal with a severe internal problem.[41] Their effectiveness, however, is a more difficult matter to appraise. Labor floating still exists, perhaps on a fairly wide scale. The use of incentives to induce labor to go into certain kinds of work is clear testimony on this point. Furthermore, refugee testimony indicates that, because of the general shortage of labor, those who hire are frequently not very fussy about the rules or a prospective employee's past history, even though the risk of penal prosecution may be present. The rather widespread practice of forging identification papers may also contribute to the existence of a *de facto* labor market through a substantial portion of the economy.

A major lever of direct control is the system of State Labor Reserves. In essence it is a labor draft. Some months before the German invasion, on October 2, 1940, the government decreed that up to a million young boys would be drafted annually for technical training in workshops, factory, and railroad schools. After the training period, lasting from six months to two years, the boys were to be considered mobilized and obliged to work for four years at whatever government establishments they were sent to.[42] Although urban youths were included in the draft, the major purpose, in the initial stages at least, appears to have been to direct a flow of skilled and semi-skilled workers into the factories, removing them from the farms.[43] The role of the Reserves in the total economy has considerably expanded since the war, though some difficulties have evidently been encountered. The Fourth Five Year Plan provided for 4,500,000 young workers through this procedure, or more than 10 per cent of the number of workers and employees planned for the national economy in 1950.[44] During the first three years of the plan, however, only 2,172,000 workers were turned out by the Reserves,[45] whereas three-fifths of the total would yield an expected figure of 2,700,000 by this date. The Party directives for the Fifth and current Five Year Plan give no figures on this point, confining themselves to a brief sentence stating that the quality of the training is to be improved.[46] A high proportion of those mobilized in recent years have probably been sent into heavy industry. Between 70 and 80 per cent of the new worker cadres in coal-mining, ferrous metallurgy, and machine building were expected in 1949 by one Soviet economist to come from this source.[47]

To sum up the discussion so far, we may point out the kinds of decisions for which the minister must accept responsibility and try to sense the atmosphere in which he has to make his choices. Some of the most important ways in which this atmosphere has changed since Stalin's death remain a matter of guess work. It is of course known that several mergers, amalgamating two or more ministries into one, were put into effect almost immediately afterward, ostensibly in the interests of administrative efficiency. There are also hints in the Soviet press that other changes were made which increased the minister's authority to make decisions in his own right, though the nature of this increase is not specified.[48] Perhaps the most telling atmospheric change is a new sense of uncertainty about where ultimate authority resides and whom it is necessary to satisfy in making a particular choice. But even about this point we cannot be positive, since the answer to the succession problem might easily be obvious to insiders long before it was known to the outside world. Despite these gaps in our knowledge we may learn much by concentrating on the fact that many important decisions must continue to be made every day and that they are actually being made.

If the ministry is an important one, and of course if its chief is also a member of the Party Presidium, he will participate in major decisions affecting the economy as a whole, such as drawing up the list of "funded" commodities to be allocated directly to the economic ministries. Here he may feel the contrasting pull of his departmental interests and the demands of broader leadership. At the same time he has to find out what his factories need, telling them to cut their requirements to the bone. Then he has to sign contracts with other ministries, both to obtain supplies and to dispose of his own department's output. Sometimes this may be a routine matter in which he simply obeys orders. At other times the contract may involve a great deal of tugging and hauling behind the scenes, with the danger ever present that he may wake up one fine day to find his ministry in such an impossible position where it cannot hope to live up to its commitments.

His next task is to decide how to distribute these supplies among "his" factories. Shall he try to raise production in a plant that has a conspicuously weak record and that is giving his ministry a bad name by granting it more materials? Or shall he let them go to a plant with a conspicuously good record that has always made it possible for the ministry as a whole to get under the wire with its production quota? At the same time he must decide if it is wise to squirm a little more elbow room for his ministry by getting his output price raised. *How* one meets the quota is less important than meeting it, and he may not want to hear a blast about seeking "narrow departmental interests." He also has to choose people to run the plants, though the ministry's voice is by means the only one in this type of decision. Finally, if the product turned out by his ministry fails to meet specifications, he may have difficulty disposing of it. Then there may be a test of strength between customer and producer, with the advantage of the rules on the customer's side and the advantages of a scarcity economy on the producer's. In some cases, particularly with regard to consumer goods, however, he may have to resort to advertising to compete for the scarce ruble of the consumer.

Many, perhaps most of the decisions that he makes, are likely to reach him ready-made in the form of recommendations from subordinates in charge of the various chief administrations in his ministry. It is far from likely, however, that he will want, or be able, to accept all of them in the form presented to him. There is constant pressure from below to "ease up," to be "realistic." Since "facts" come from below, the minister has to decide continuously which ones to face as realistic parts of his situation, which ones to change by persuasion, threats, as well as by bargaining with his superiors. He knows that a stream of facts, which may not, and probably will not, tell the same story, are constantly going to those who watch him, the Party, the Ministry of State Control, and the secret police. If he is a powerful figure with good connections in the highest Party circles, he may be able to influence his situation through these channels, as well as those open to him through the machinery of the Council of Ministers. All in all, it appears to be a situation in which the drive for production comes from above and meets its counteracting forces from below. The way in which the ministry responds to these two forces in turn determines a large segment of the bureaucratic environment within which the factory itself operates.

This administrative environment is not of course identical for every factory. There is considerable variation in the extent of centralized control. Local soviets may even set up and administer a plant on their own, serving purely local needs.[49] Presumably the claims of such a plant on local resources are met only after supplies have been sent to other factories in the area that have greater significance to the national economy as a whole. Though there has been considerable variation and experimentation over time, the degree of centralized control corresponds roughly to the importance of a plant to the over-all economy. Furthermore, local organs of authority, in the form of the republic, oblast, and raion representatives of the Party, the ministry, and even the police, tend from time to time to become insulated and form independent foci of power, as was indicated in Chapter 1. In such cases the local authorities become a more immediate and vital aspect of the administrative environment than the distant authorities in Moscow.

The plant, as observed at the beginning of this chapter, constitutes a miniature social system in its own right. Certain characteristics of this system as a whole require comment at this point to aid in understanding the relationship of specific aspects of factory life to one another. Since the main criterion of success in the operation of the factory is the fulfillment of the plan, every person in the plant is under compulsion to behave in a way that keeps the factory going as a coöperative social system. Not only individual interests, but also formal rules prescribed by outside authority, must frequently be sacrificed to the overriding necessity of maintaining the organization as a productive unit. This imperative, imposed by the external environment of administrative demands, may be regarded therefore as the major unifying force in the factory as a miniature society.[50]

At the same time, and by only a superficial paradox, these same administrative demands constitute the central source of hostilities and tensions within the factory. If one examines a series of concrete incidents involving hostile or friendly relationships among two or more individuals in the Soviet industrial system, a general pattern emerges clearly. Hostility is directed upward for the most part against individuals who are felt to be making an excessive demand for effort. Just how standards of acceptable effort arise is not altogether clear, though a few suggestions will be offered in the course of the discussion. Expressions of aggression are frequent against the individual on the spot who represents the demands of the central authority. Naturally these sentiments of aggression and exasperation are reciprocated. On the other hand, harmonious relationships tend to prevail where two or more individuals are either working together on a common task, or else are united in opposition to the regime's insistent demands for greater effort and greater production. To some extent, all roles in the factory are exposed to both disruptive and integrative pressures, though the exposure varies from one case to another.

The best place at which to begin the analysis of the plant is with the position of the director, since he constitutes the chief point of contact between the miniature world of the factory and the system of administrative controls. This set of controls confronts the Soviet manager with a situation that is qualitatively different from that facing his capitalist counterpart, at least under the theoretical conditions of a free economy. In the latter situation the supply of labor, materials, and the price of the finished product constitute given elements which are determined by the play of market forces and to which the capitalist manager must adapt by the efficient organization of production, or face the penalty of the bankruptcy court. In the Soviet situation the supply of labor, materials, and the price of the finished product also constitute given elements in the situation that confronts the plant director. But they are "given" by the will of a ponderous bureaucracy, in which it is very frequently possible to persuade some one to alter a decision. Hence a high proportion of the Soviet manager's energies are devoted to attempts at manipulating his bureaucratic environment. The skills needed are those in dealing with people rather than in dealing with physical objects, though the Soviet director ordinarily has to have considerable technical knowledge as well. The capitalist world, it may be noted in passing, with the growth of large units heavily dependent upon the political climate, is in actual practice developing in the same direction. Except under wartime conditions, when political considerations also dominate the allocative mechanisms of capitalist society, the distinction between the two sets of situations remains, however, very great.

The pressure of the external bureaucratic environment on the director makes itself felt, as already noted, primarily in the form of an insistent demand for plan fulfillment. To be sure plan fulfillment is not always a strictly unambiguous criterion of success.[51] Quality and the assortment of goods, such as the supply of spare parts for machines, may be sacrified to quantity as a result of unrelenting pressure from above. Material stimuli to encourage plan fulfillment exist in the form of a bonus, legally payable only if all the specifications of the plan are met,[52] and in a Soviet version of profit-sharing. Of the two, the bonus appears to be the more important stimulus, according to refugee testimony. It consists of a direct proportional addition to the basic salary. Published figures for one industry indicate that at least a fifth is added for fulfilling the plan, and that the proportion rises very rapidly for overfulfillment.[53]

There are indications from another source of a steady decline over the past half-dozen years in the importance of profitable operations as a stimulus to production. The government has tried to thrust more of the burden of obtaining adequate resources on the plant, through forcing it to use its resources efficiently and thereby stretch the distance they will go. At the same time there has been greater pressure on the plant to contribute more of its own resources toward day-to-day operations. This policy is reflected in a rise in the plant's own contribution to increases in its working capital and a corresponding decrease in the amount allotted to the plant from the budget. For the Soviet Union as a whole, the share in this increase carried by the plant was 36.7 per cent in 1948, rising to 52.6 per cent in 1951, while a still further rise to 57.2 per cent was anticipated by the plan for 1952. In commenting on these figures, the Finance Minister, A. G. Zverev, suggested that assignments from the budget for an increase in working capital ought to be made dependent on the fulfillment of the plan in regard to both physical output and the rate of profit.[54]

There are, however, certain intangible rewards for being an efficient and hard-driving manager. Perhaps the most important among these, that can easily be sensed in Soviet fiction, is the awareness of contributing to the growth not only of a new order but also of a great industrial power. This motivation is in many ways similar to that of the creative giants and captains of industry that played a vital role in the growth of Western capitalism. Even in the fictional sources, however, it is clear that this motivation requires a strong sense of attachment to a particular plant and an identification with its fate.[55] Therefore there are limits to the encouragement of such sentiments. The Soviet system can tolerate this form of plant patriotism only to a very limited degree. Too much of it threatens control from the center. There is also the reward of moving on to positions of ever greater authority, responsibility, and prestige. Full scope for creative managerial talent exists in the Soviet system in the sense that the economy definitely requires this talent. At the same time this factor too is offset by the awareness that greater prestige carries with it greater risk. To many the danger of prominence outweighs its attraction.

One further crucial element in the director's situation remains to be described. As elsewhere in Soviet society, "objective" conditions do not count as an acceptable excuse for failure to live up to the demands placed upon the individual. The actual availability of supplies depends largely upon decisions made in the remote fastnesses of the bureaucracy. But the fact that they were not available, or failed to arrive on time, or that they were of the wrong kind, does not constitute an acceptable reason for failure to get results. On this account, success, and even physical survival, pivot upon the director's ability to influence or evade the administrative controls that determine the task given to his plant.

One interesting response to this situation is the development of the specialized role of the *tolkach,* literally "pusher," who serves the director through cultivating personal connections up and down the bureaucratic hierarchy. The tolkach bears a close family resemblance to the "expediter" who flourished in the American wartime economy. The Soviet expediter, operating sometimes on a commission basis for several firms, and often maintaining headquarters in Moscow, lives by his wits on the fringe of legality, locating scarce materials, persuading officials to put one order ahead of another, all for the service of his director client. By interfering with the intricate system of priorities he perfoms a definite disservice to the regime. On the other hand, by scaring up supplies that may be useless where they are, but are badly needed by his employer, he performs a definite service for the economy. Possibly his positive contributions outweigh his disadvantages in the eyes of the authorities, who therefore continue to tolerate his existence.[56]

Beneath the surface of the external administrative pressures on the director and in the response of many directors to these pressures it is again easy to perceive the potentialities of economic stagnation. Because of the heavy emphasis on plan fulfillment, it is in the director's interest to obtain for his factory a plan well within the plant's capacities. In general this implies a plan as close as possible to the one for the previous year. It also means the avoidance of new products, that may bring with them unforeseen problems, and hence the danger of extreme penalties for failure to deliver the goods. There is furthermore little to be gained by reducing costs below the norm set by the plan, since the norms will then merely be lowered to this level during the next planning period. Likewise, output norms will be raised if the plant exceeds by too great a percentage the output required by the plan, though the system of bonuses partially offsets this factor. If a plant makes a high profit, the ministry may simply take the profits for its own purposes, despite formal regulations to the contrary.[57] Thus the ministry transmits downward the demand for more and more production, while the director frequently pushes for less production and more "realistic" plans.[58]

Within the plant the director's role is a difficult one. If the plant is to succeed, he must somehow or other combine the other important centers of power and authority in the factory into a coöperative group with, at the minimum, an effective working relationship. Although some of the other centers of authority perform necessary tasks in the plant, they also act as agents of the government's control system to check up on the director. Furthermore they are formally responsible to authorities outside the plant. Therefore no relationship is possible that will fully satisfy all interested parties. Some directors try to build up a relationship by cajolery, while others resort to browbeating or a combination of the two. Particularly when a new director is sent into a plant, as happens rather frequently, all of the other plant officials, down to the level of shop superintendents, are likely to be on the alert to smell out any shifts in the internal distribution of power. If the new director does not establish a good working relationship, production will suffer and so will he. If he establishes too harmonious a relationship, the regime loses part of its control over the situation inside the factory and may react with accusations about the disappearance of proper Bolshevik self-criticism, management by family clique, and the like. The director must therefore continually walk a shaky tightrope knowing that one misstep may plunge him into oblivion.

The secretary of the Party organization within the plant, often known as the *Partorg*, constitutes one of the key figures with whom a *modus vivendi* must be reached. Formally responsible to the territorial Party secretary, the Partorg is a major figure in the government's control system inside the factory. Soviet press comment suggests that he is regarded by the authorities as the chief agent of innovation within the factory to offset tendencies toward stagnation. "One of the most important tasks of Party organizations in production," says a Soviet manual on plant management, "is a constant struggle for *technical progress.*

Communists must be innovators in production, and revolutionists in technique." [59] Since the careers of both the director and the Partorg depend on meeting production goals, their relationship is eased to some extent. How the fact that both are ordinarily Party members affects the situation is not clear from the sources. In many cases there may be some difficulty due to the reversal of relationships that takes place behind the closed doors of a Party meeting, where the technical official must yield to the Party official. In other cases, the Party man who directs a large plant may dominate not only the organization within the plant but the district unit of the Party as well. Finally, there is evidence in both published sources and in the accounts of former Soviet citizens that Party channels can be used to get supplies and make things easier for the plant, when other methods fail.*

The chief of the "special section," or secret police unit within the factory, apparently constitutes another major center of power. He remains, however, a rather shadowy figure on the basis of the information so far available. Evidently he is feared, and not easily drawn into the top circle of factory authorities. Through his network of informers he is undoubtedly aware of many of the semi-legal and illegal practices that are generally necessary for the life of the factory. He is also aware of the grumblings of exasperation and resentment that still result from

* A valuable glimpse of the shoving and juggling that goes on much of the time behind the scenes comes from the complaints of a Leningrad deputy to the Party Congress in 1952. An important machine-making factory in his area was ordered almost to double its output without being granted any additional facilities by its ministry. Presumably at the instance of the Party secretary in the factory, protests went all the way up to the Central Committee, and very likely the Politburo, of the Communist Party. The Central Committee instructed the Ministry of Heavy Machine Construction to take care of the situation. As the latter did nothing for several months, the Leningrad deputy registered a detailed complaint at the Party Congress, which was published in *Pravda*, October 8, 1952. Though we do not know whether this criticism of the ministry was cleared in advance with high Party officials, it seems likely that it was. Whenever any such complaint appears in the press, according to a former Soviet newspaperman who claims considerable experience in Kremlin circles, it means that the Party has already decided to deal with the situation.

the frantic pace of Soviet industrial growth. If he takes these too seriously, and tries to initiate legal or police action, he may actually be punished by his superiors for interfering with production. If he fails to do anything, he will be accused of lack of vigilance. The safest course is to gather all the information that he possibly can and send it along to his superior, thus shoving the responsibility for a decision upward.

The role of the head of the trade union committee within the factory is largely a vestigial one, though there were some indications after the war that the regime wanted to give the workers an impression of its revival. No matter what their place had been in industry, former Soviet citizens whose experience antedates the war are nearly unanimous in condemning the unions as one more form of exploitation and as unable to do anything for the workers. Since wages are specifically excluded from the area over which they can negotiate with management, the main activity left for the unions is to press for housing, which is often the responsibility of an industrial ministry and eventually of a particular plant. Under conditions of chronic shortage, however, housing and the amenities are likely to be matters of little urgency for management, no matter how strongly union officials may push their case. Thus the impotent officials are likely to be berated by the Party for inactivity. Furthermore, there is some indication from Soviet fiction that the director will do a number of things for his workers in order to hang onto his labor force, such as sending his agents through the countryside to scare up food from the collective farms. When a director does this, he tries to take the credit himself, both before the workers, the Party, and his administrative superiors, brusquely pushing the union officers aside.[60] Only if the pace of industrialization slackens somewhat to permit turning out more consumer goods and services, such as housing, over which the union can retain control, does it seem likely that the local union official can become once more an important figure.

There are also three officials formally subject to the director, whose relationships with him are likely to constitute somewhat of a problem for both sides. Of these perhaps the least difficult position, at least in its relationship to the director, is that of the chief engineer. In contrast to earlier times, both the director and the engineer are likely to have good technical knowledge, even if considerably greater in the case of the engineer, and to be roughly equally identified with the Soviet regime. Together the director and chief engineer are ultimately responsible for the quality of the goods turned out.

In terms of plant organization, however, the check on quality is made the special province of the department of technical control, which has its own head. Even though it is a technical department, it is not made subject to the chief engineer but, nominally at least, to the director.[61] Refugee testimony indicates that actually the department of technical control serves as a check on the director, and as an additional set of eyes and ears for the ministry concerned.[62] At the same time there are limitations to the rigor with which this check can be applied. If the head of the technical control department becomes too fussy and insistent, the director can accuse him of holding up production, a charge with overtones of sabotage. In such a move, the director may be able to count on the support of his superiors in the ministry, who also have a strong interest in quantitative fulfillment of the plan.[63] The head of the department of technical control is thus compelled to become a relatively coöperative member of the managerial team.

The position of the third official, the chief bookkeeper, is somewhat more difficult. Like the head of the technical control division, he is formally subordinate to the director, but is expected to check on his superior. One informed refugee source asserts that the director cannot discharge his bookkeeper.[64] His major responsibility is to keep the accounts of the firm and insure that no unauthorized expenditures occur.[65] Strict adherence to regulations is frequently nearly impossible, however, if the work of the enterprise is to go on and the plan to be fulfilled.

Though the chief bookkeeper may on this account be brought into the team, he is also subject to controls that originate outside the factory and, more important, outside the plant's ministry. The Ministry of Finance, according to one former chief bookkeeper, inspects plant accounts fairly regularly. In addition, representatives of the Ministry of State Control may descend on a plant without advance notice, impound the books, and give them a thorough going-over. If grounds for legal action are discovered, the case may be prosecuted in the courts.[66]

As we turn to the intermediate administrative level, we find that a good-sized Soviet factory is subdivided into a number of "workshops," each of which is under the direction of a shop chief. The shop itself is a factory in miniature. It has its own bookkeeper, and other administrative units that correspond roughly to those described above for the factory as a whole.[67] In postwar attempts to carry the relationship between pay and performance to its logical conclusion, some factories have experimented with making the shops, and sometimes even units within the shops, independent units for accounting purposes, so that each shop chief would not only see the consequences of his work, but also profit or suffer from these consequences. The experiment runs the danger of destroying the unity of the plant and increasing the amount of paper work that is already a drag on the organization. One writer, associated with one of the largest machine-building plants in the USSR, warned in 1948 that such decentralization put a dangerous limit on the director's power, since it kept him from transferring his technical staff and supervisors from one position to another in accord with the requirements of the plant.[68] The fanfare accompanying the experiment suggests that it was a Party effort to raise production. Though the experiment itself seems to have run its course, the movement indicates that there is still considerable flexibility in Soviet industrial arrangements and a continuing search for more effective forms of organization.[69]

Beneath the workshop chief there are two more layers of

supervisory personnel above the workers themselves. These supervisors are in charge of sections organized around a bank of
machines that perform the same operation, such as the "lathing
section," "grooving section," "gear-cutting section," and so on.
They must make a variety of concrete decisions concerning the
ways in which labor, machinery, and material are to be combined in order to complete that part of the production process
for which they are responsible. Thus we see that within the
factory each supervisory level, from the director downward,
performs the same kind of function and must make the same
kind of decisions, but on a progressively reduced scale.

At the bottom level the supervisors are in direct contact with
the workers and are exposed to their back-pressure against the
demands of the regime. The situation in which they must make
their decisions is a harassing one. It has been vividly described
by a former section chief:

"The norms are impossibly high. The chief of the section must work
to fulfill these norms come what may, or else take the consequences
for being responsible. As a result he not only performs his ascribed
duties, but does everything else possible so that the norms can be
met. . . . He checks the work, he instructs the workers, he puts the
persons where they are best suited for their skill. It is up to me to
determine what methods to use in order to guarantee the quality of
the goods. . . . If the worker does something wrong, the administrator, that is, the chief, gets the blame."
Interviewer: "Well, doesn't the worker get blamed?"
Respondent: "Both share the blame." [70]

The main concern of people in this position, it appears, is to
be known as a "good organizer," both from the standpoint of
management and of the workers. On them ultimately falls the
responsibility of figuring out evasions of the norms for expenditure on labor. Such evasions appear to be rather widely necessary for keeping the plant's force together. So far as possible,
however, supervisors try to arrange matters legally. As another
former supervisor said, in the course of an interview, "I tried to
arrange shifts and divide up work so every one would earn as

much as he could. If I didn't do that I would have been considered a poor foreman and a bad work-organizer." [71]

In the web of Soviet industrial relationships the main decisions open to the worker concern granting or withholding his labor power. The major element in the situation still appears to be a chronic labor shortage, despite the increase in the size of the labor force. The government's attempt to cope with the problem through various gradations of forced labor has not solved this difficulty. The possibility that workers will simply wander off and leave the plant helpless in the face of insistent demands for production evidently forces itself on everyone's attention, from the shop foreman to the top echelons of the Party. Such decisions to move off and seek one's fortune elsewhere appear to be largely individual matters. Reading the life histories of Soviet workers, one gets the impression of much moving about of the kind that does not result in any redistribution of the population.

Other ways in which workers might react to their situation, particularly by any form of effective group action, are almost entirely eliminated under present Soviet conditions. Within the factory there is almost no opportunity for the workers to become a cohesive and organized unit in opposition to management. The frequent occasions that do bring all the workers together are meetings at which they are exhorted or scolded by their superiors. Workers resent them as one more invasion of time when they could rest. In contrast to the situation twenty years ago, clandestine organization appears to be out of the question. Thus the possibility of a political alternative to the present regime arising among the workers is remote as long as the controls from above remain intact.

We are now in a position to see how all the millions of decisions in Soviet industrial life are related to one another and thus form a recognizable and concrete whole. If one begins at the bottom, it is obvious that even the factory worker is faced with the relatively trivial decision to hurry up and get to the job on

time for fear of the severe penalty for tardiness. On higher
levels the supervisory and administrative personnel must make
more significant decisions that affect progressively larger numbers of people. Yet the choices made by the worker and by his
superiors are linked together in a very simple and very important relationship: each decision made in the course of the industrial process must be reached within the framework of another
decision made higher up in the bureaucracy, ultimately in the
Party Presidium itself. Through controls over the allocation of
material supplies, credit, wages, the exchange of finished products, as well as the pace and direction of industrial growth, the
Soviet dictatorship creates the channels through which the flow
of more detailed economic choices must pass.

The dictator does not of course have absolute and unlimited
power. Much more than his will alone enters into the flow of
decisions, even at their very beginning in the Party Presidium.
He and his subordinates have to take into account the requirements of the machine they have created. Some of these requirements are strictly rational ones, in the sense that effective means
have to be found to pursue material ends. A reconciliation has
to take place between the specifications of the engineer and the
specifications of political authority. These technical and rational
requirements also serve to impose at any one time a definite
form and pattern upon the flow of decisions. In addition, the
human characteristics of the machine, for example, those of the
factory as a miniature social system, must be considered in
the formulation and execution of economic policy. All these
requirements involve some delegation of the dictator's power.

In its delegation this power is, however, diffused, fragmented,
and elaborately cross-checked. Provided the source of unity at
the center in the Kremlin holds fast, there seems little prospect
that the machinery as a whole or any substantial segment of
it can act in concert to the point where it threatens those in
ultimate control. If this vital condition prevails, the Soviet industrial machine might continue to run in approximately the
same way it has done in the past for a dozen years, and perhaps

many more. Still another condition for its continuation would be that no external force intervenes to upset or destroy it. The Soviet machine is admirably adapted to a world of chronic emergency short of war, and would have several short-run advantages in war itself.

Yet even if these conditions should be fulfilled, and even if one is willing to grant these elements of at least potential stability, there appears to be one very serious flaw. The drive for industrial expansion, I would suggest, comes almost wholly from the top. Of itself the Soviet economic system does not generate the ruthless energy that has made the USSR a first-class industrial power. For the most part it merely reflects this energy. In the form of prestige, possibilities of advancement, and hence also of concrete material rewards, there do exist at the present time substantial incentives for the economic administrator to reduce costs and increase output. These are, however, political rewards in the hands of the political elite. Beyond the positive political pressure there can be discerned very little in the situation facing the economic administrator that would produce the dynamism that now exists. The Communist elite is in this respect a substitute for the adventurous spirit that built the great industrial and financial empires of the Western world during the nineteenth and early twentieth centuries. Within the Communist Party itself, it now seems that most of this dynamic pressure comes from the top downward. Should the political source of industrial expansion vanish or decline, there is nothing in sight to take its place. From the worker up to the minister, the disappearance of this political pressure would mean the end of that part of his situation which now results in the drive for greater and greater output. Stagnation, as has been indicated at other points, appears built into the structure of the Soviet economy and lies continually just beneath the surface. So far it has not been permitted to develop because of the dynamic leadership at the center. If this factor changes, the entire machine could conceivably grind to a stand-still at a level unsuited to the role of a world power.

chapter 3

THE PEASANTS' ROLE
IN THE WORKERS' STATE

On humanitarian grounds, as well as those of economic efficiency alone, it is possible to make a strong case against the Soviet system of collective agriculture, as does Naum Jasny in his monumental study, *The Socialized Agriculture of the USSR.*[1] The argument that a different set of arrangements would turn out more food and other agricultural products at a lower human and material cost stands, I believe, on very firm ground. Indeed, during the summer and early autumn of 1953 the Communist leaders came close to conceding this point in their promises of at least a temporary new deal for the Soviet peasantry. However, this thesis has only a limited bearing on the problems of potential change and stability in the Soviet system. A negative economic and humanitarian appraisal does not tell us very much about the political services that collectivized agriculture performs for the Soviet regime, or whether it performs these services in a way that is likely to modify the existing system or to maintain it. Political change cannot be reduced to a reflection of economic misery, even if the latter sometimes has an important bearing on the former. The problem posed here is a different one: to understand what political, as well as economic, objectives the Communist leaders sought through collectivization, as well as the inherent tendencies toward change or self-perpetuation that exist in the institutional arrangements devised to pursue these objectives.

For centuries the peasants have been a source of intermittent ferment in Russian society. Though the nature of the "peasant question" shifted with changes in the society, much of Russian history is studded with brutally repressed peasant revolts. Toward the end of the nineteenth century and the beginning of the twentieth, peasant upheavals provided part of the impetus behind a series of reforms that were transforming Tsarist society in the direction of a structure roughly similar at least to Germany, if not to the more liberal "bourgeois monarchy" that stabilized itself in Great Britain and the one that existed for a brief time in France. This development was not permitted to run its course. Instead, the Bolsheviks, after the temporary retreat of the twenties, attempted to "solve" the peasant question once and for all, by speeding up, as they thought, the clock of history and carrying out the most far-reaching revolution from above that has perhaps ever been attempted in the record of human affairs.

With a strangle hold on the food supply, for more than a dozen years after the Bolshevik *coup d'état* the peasants represented, even in their inchoate and spontaneous fashion, a distinct and independent nucleus of power, able to exercise leverage on all other aspects of policy. After some experimentation the present system was adopted in essentially its present form during the early thirties. While a heavy price was paid in human suffering, the main Bolshevik objective was achieved. The economic independence of the peasant was destroyed and a method created for getting grain to supply the cities and industry. A secondary gain was the release of manpower from the rural areas to the cities.

Henceforth the supply of "surplus" grain to feed the cities could be determined by the Kremlin, instead of by the individual peasant and by the automatic working out of economic factors based on millions of personal decisions in the towns and in the countryside. By 1940, with the adoption of the State Labor Reserves, the number of "surplus" men in the countryside needed for industry could also be determined by the Kremlin. In this way, power to shape all the major economic decisions was secured by the dictatorship. It became possible to thrust the heaviest burden of sacrifices on the peasants, including both those due to variations in crop yield and those generated by the demands of high-speed industrialization. The system of collectivized agriculture thus came to constitute one of the key means through which the Kremlin could manipulate the entire society, and especially the relationships between its urban and rural sectors.

The institutional forms that give effect to the Kremlin's power are largely borrowed from the city. In this fact lies some of their potentially serious weakness. In industry the huge monopoly with its rational and bureaucratic internal organization provided at least a rough model and a basic framework suitable for centralized political control, even if the problems turned out to be much more difficult than early enthusiasts imagined. Except for the large estates, already destroyed by the time full-scale collectivization began, no such model existed in the pre-Revolutionary countryside. New forms in imitation of industry had to be invented to serve the purpose. Furthermore, the urban Marxist revolutionary often displayed a simple faith in the liberating and rationalizing powers of secular industrial society as soon as it could be freed from the fetters of private property. With this attitude went a corresponding contempt for the "idiocy of rural life." The peasant family, the basic work unit of rural life, was to be broken up into its component parts, and the job separated from the household, as in industry. The rhythm of the seasons was to be replaced by the rhythm of the machines. The factory's relationship between the individual's contribution to the total product and his material rewards, expressed in wages, was to be forced upon the countryside. Rationality, science, and "improvement," defined largely in material terms, were to replace the static and traditionalist bias of the peasant world, with its heavy reliance on magic and religion to tide the group and the individual over crises. In practice, the compromise with reality has forced the modification or abandonment of those elements in this program that were not essential to the maintenance of the Kremlin's power over the countryside. The consequence has been that a substantial portion of the peasantry has gotten the worst of both worlds. Furthermore, the compromise situation stands as an open invitation to evasion.

As in industry, there is a descending series of administrative organs that influence and permeate the miniature society in which the actual work of production is done. The major form of this miniature society is the collective farm, or *kolkhoz*, a supposedly voluntary union of peasants who have agreed to pool their land and certain other resources in order to realize the advantages of coöperative agriculture. By 1938 the kolkhozes occupied about 86 per cent of the land under cultivation in the USSR.[2] With functions corresponding roughly to those in industry, there is the familiar administrative battery of the Party, the "soviet apparatus" (now consolidated in the Ministry of Agriculture and Procurements), and finally the secret police. There is also a special channel of control through the Machine Tractor Stations (MTS). The end purpose of this apparatus is to make sure that the peasants carry out compulsory deliveries of a substantial portion of their produce to the government. The government pays a nominal price for this produce, a set of figures that is carefully kept out of Soviet publications.

The Machine Tractor Station constitutes a crucial link in the control system, since it supplies the mechanical power necessary to operate agriculture on a collective basis. There is considerable evidence to the effect that the regime has been able to allot only enough resources to mechanization to maintain the essentials of its political controls, and that under the strain of the war it fell short of this minimum objective, with the consequence that the control system disintegrated in some areas. In 1937, the peak year of prewar agricultural output, the tractors and combines in the hands of the MTS supplied only 45.5 per cent of the total power resources of the collective farms.[3] Presumably the rest, or well over half, was made up by horses, which were even then very scarce, and by human power.

The war years took a heavy toll in the destruction and obsolescence of agricultural machinery. Soviet sources claim the total or partial destruction of 2,890 MTS, about 41 per cent of the total number of stations.[4] In the absence of strictly comparable data it is difficult to estimate the extent of postwar recovery. But it seems reasonably clear that mechanical resources, if again adequate for political purposes, were still strained to the limit in 1950 and 1951. According to the Minister of Agriculture, in 1950 each kolkhoz had, on the average, the services of one tractor brigade at its disposal.[5] From a local study we learn that a tractor brigade, composed of four to five tractors, is expected to be capable of handling 800 to 1,000 hectares of sowing and 1,000 to 1,500 hectares of plowing.[6] This is probably a maximum figure that would have to be cut sharply to represent typical operating conditions, frequent breakdowns and the like. A rough idea of the average size of a kolkhoz in 1950 may be had by dividing the total number of farms, 123,000 toward the end of 1950, into the total sown area in 1940, 151.1 million hectares,[7] which is more than fair to the Soviets as the plan for 1950 envisaged an area of 158.6 million hectares.[8] Probably the actual area was somewhere between the two figures. On this basis in 1950 the average farm had more than 1,200 hectares, an area over the maximum that could be handled by sowing and only slightly less than the maximum for plowing. While such an average conceals the range of difference between the remaining small farms and the new giant ones, it strongly suggests that there are still scarcely enough MTS to handle the operations of plowing and sowing under even the most favorable conditions.[9] In 1952 more than half of the tractor stations failed to fulfill their allotted plans.[10]

To a great extent these difficulties are due to the frequent breakdown of tractors manned by inexperienced young drivers. As Nikita S. Khrushchev, the newly chosen first secretary of the Party Central Committee, said, these workers can only sit helplessly by their machine when it refuses to run any longer. To improve the situation the Party on September 7, 1953, ordered a campaign to attract mechanics and engineers into agriculture from industry, a stop-gap measure that can be put into effect only at the cost of skills badly needed elsewhere. In addition, however, the Party also ordered an extensive training program that envisages by 1957 no less than 300 new training centers with between 240 and 270 students in each. Meanwhile for the year 1954–1955 the Ministry of Culture has been ordered to turn out 6,500 engineer-mechanics for the 8,950 tractor stations now in operation.[11] Thus the educational part of the program cannot be expected to produce as many as two new mechanics a year for each station, which strongly suggests that even with the new program the strain will remain severe for several years to come.

The nature of police controls in agriculture is more obscure than in other aspects of the Soviet system. Mention of a special section, a usual feature in the structure of the Soviet factory, crops up very rarely in the accounts of former *kolkhozniks*. With the amalgamation of farms into larger units in 1950 it seems likely that a high proportion of them are now equipped with this ubiquitous Soviet organization, though there is no definite proof on this point. A refugee, who had been a minor kolkhoz official, with whom I had several long conversations, told me that it was quite common for the peasants in his area to gather around the lamp in one of the kolkhoz buildings when the day's work was done and discuss everything under the sun freely and bitterly, a situation which would indicate the absence of a police network in the prewar period. Since peasants as a rule had very limited opportunities to visit the village where the police office was located, it appears that the police in rural areas had to depend rather heavily on the chairman of the kolkhoz for the kind of news they required. As disaffection was, and almost certainly remains, quite extensive among the peasantry, it would seem impossible to maintain as detailed a record of subversive attitudes as is done elsewhere. In the control apparatus itself, particularly the Ministry of Agriculture and Procurements, the secret police undoubtedly has its regular officers and network of informers.

It is quite likely that they extend down to the level of the MTS in many cases. According to one refugee report, whose authenticity cannot be checked, though the account is plausible, there was in Moscow before the war a special department of the secret police in charge of the food industries, set up primarily to insure secrecy in regard to production plans and the political reliability of the more important employees.[12]

In comparison with its urban counterpart the Party control apparatus in the countryside is still weak. As late as 1939, according to a report to the Eighteenth Party Congress by A. A. Andreev, Politburo member and chairman of the Commission on Party Control, only one kolkhoz in twenty had a Party unit. In 1950 the Party high command ordered an amalgamation of the collective farms into larger units, ostensibly on grounds of greater economic efficiency, but probably in order to give the Party and other segments of the control apparatus a smaller number of units with which to deal. From 254,000 collective farms that existed in the beginning of 1950 the number shrank to 94,000 so-called "giant" units in the autumn of 1953.[13] Of these only 76,000 kolkhozes had a Party cell, leaving about one farm in five without this form of supervision.[14] The detailed report on Soviet agriculture by N. S. Khrushchev, published in the Soviet press on September 15, 1953, shows clearly that the amalgamation program has by no means solved the problems of control.

The local Party committee is expected to keep an eye on kolkhoz affairs. In some areas it is the practice of the kolkhoz chairman to make reports in person to the local Party office. In turn, Party officials study his reports, criticize the shortcomings, and try to spread word through the area about useful features in the experience of individual farms.[15]

There is also a tendency, noted elsewhere in Soviet society, for many district Party officials to ignore the Party primary organization in the kolkhoz and to deal directly with the person who has authority, that is, the kolkhoz chairman. It is said to be characteristic for the raion Party officer to make a rushed visit to the kolkhoz, have a brief chat with the chairman, and on his way out the door remember to say, "Tell the Party secretary to give a hand with these jobs." [16]

Since the war the Party has been experimenting with various methods of strengthening its line of control through the MTS. In February 1947 it set up in the stations the new post of deputy director for political affairs. His formal task was to insure correct relations between the MTS and the collective farms, to prevent the mutual concealment of each other's difficulties and to be an active Communist propagandist.[17] The deputy director soon faced the typical problems of combining the roles of administrator and propagandist. If he did a good job in helping out on local production, he ran the risk of becoming absorbed in straightforward economic administration, to the displeasure of his superiors. If, on the other hand, he merely remained a propagandist and a man of words, those who were pressed with concrete difficulties were likely to have little use for him. As one former tractor driver remarked sarcastically, "It would be better if he brought some spare parts" instead of talking all the time.[18] Perhaps on this account the post was abolished in September, 1953. Then the Party tried the new tack of setting up groups of political workers in the raion offices, directly responsible to the Party secretary, who are to be in charge of political work in both the tractor stations and the farms.[19] By removing these political workers one step away from local problems, the Party may reduce the probability of their absorption in economic administration.

The situation in regard to day-to-day supervision over the collective farms is one of too many cooks and even too many broths. As Khrushchev put it recently, "You can say that the secretary of the Party raion committee, the chairman of the raion soviet executive committee, the head of its agricultural section, the director of the MTS, and many others are responsible for the tractor stations and the kolkhozes. But who in the raion is concretely responsible for such and such a kolkhoz? To such a question you won't get a definite answer from anybody." [20] Though the Party Central Committee made some administrative changes in September 1953 to define responsibility more closely, they were largely confined to restating regulations already in existence, and by themselves are unlikely to alter the basic situation.

Both official sources and the descriptions given by refugees indicate a much more detailed supervision over the kolkhoz than over the factory. A considerable portion of this burden falls upon the section of the local soviet, known as the *raizemotdel* (often abbreviated to *raizo*), that serves as the representative of the Ministry of Agriculture and Procurements. It also acts as a link in the flow of communications in respect to planning, and most important of all, as the agency for collecting compulsory deliveries of produce.[21] In principle the kolkhoz, like the factory, is given a certain production task and certain incentives to fulfill this task, which it is then supposed to carry out as best as it sees fit, within the framework set by the law. But perhaps because the vagaries of the weather make exact fulfillment of the plan much more difficult in the case of the kolkhoz, and also perhaps because the temptations to evade agricultural controls are more serious, as will be made plain shortly, the supervision is much closer. Undoubtedly the situation varies considerably from one place to another. Abundant accounts in the press, however, indicate that the district soviet authorities are expected to keep in touch with the farms in their charge on an almost daily basis. Interview materials give the same impression. One former collective farmer reported that the raizemotdel sent directives out to his farm every single day, and that all of its activities were subject in this manner to the most detailed set of norms and controls.[22] Another, who had been a minor official on a kolkhoz, spoke to the writer about carrying sheafs of instructions each day to the tractor driver, with the standing joke between them, "Here's your order of Lenin for today." Particularly at harvest times matters are likely to get into a frenzy, as the Party joins the campaign and the stream of orders inundates the hapless kolkhoz authorities and peasants.

To some extent the flow of frequently conflicting orders to the kolkhoz has been a reflection of confusion and overlapping in Moscow. Since the war, as well as in earlier times, the Party high command has experimented with various degrees of administrative centralization and decentralization, whose details need not be recounted here. It is sufficient to point out that in 1947 there were seven ministries that had something or other to do with agriculture, and whose requirements had to be coördinated in the planning process.[23] In the reorganization following Stalin's death, in the spring of 1953 the Ministry of Agriculture was merged with four other ministries into a single Ministry of Agriculture and Procurements. But old and stubborn problems have not yielded to these measures. In the early autumn of the same year Khrushchev's major report repeated the familiar complaints about overlapping, duplication, and the failure to take local conditions into account when issuing orders from the bureaucratic center.[24] The situation recalls Chekhov's remark that when there is a large number of ways of curing a disease, it is a sign that the disease is incurable.

As in the case of the factory, the impact of the control apparatus does not fall directly upon the individual peasant, but upon the kolkhoz as the social group organized for production purposes. In the internal organization of the kolkhoz the major figure is the chairman. His role is characterized by heavy obligations and limited authority. The key decisions concerning agricultural processes, plowing, sowing, and harvesting, come to the kolkhoz from the outside. The chairman's duty is to see that they are carried out, and that the quota of obligatory deliveries to the government is met. To enforce his orders he has certain powers of punishment and reward, ranging from the authority to order a piece of work done over without pay to conferring prestige and financial benefits on those who exceed the planned quota.[25] There is some evidence showing that the extent of outside control tends to defeat its purpose by destroying initiative among the chairmen. They react by "rolling with the punch," transmitting orders without enforcing them. Many kolkhoz administrators, according to the journal of the Party Central Committee, limit their leadership to the passing out of forms.[26] Possibly the creation of a smaller number of larger farms may render this form of evasion more difficult. Even after the consolidation of the farms, however, the difficulties of the chairman's post have continued to produce a very high rate of turnover in this position. In 1953 nearly a third of them had held the post for less than a year.[27]

In addition to the chairman the kolkhoz may have an administrative board, formally limited to between five and nine members, though the limit has often been exceeded, since people attempt to avoid hard labor in the fields in favor of a relatively well-paid desk or supervisory position. The bookkeeper and various technical specialists, such as the agronomist and the veterinarian, are ordinarily members of this group. Published sources are vague about the duties and functions of the administrative board except to complain about bureaucratic overstaffing on the farms. As a result of an investigation begun in September 1946, 535,000 people were taken out of unnecessary and "dreamed up" jobs and 213,000 removed from kolkhoz payrolls.[28] Even if these are overlapping figures, a point not made clear in the sources, they mean that on an average two people in the administrative staff of every kolkhoz in the Soviet Union were at that time found to be doing a job that the government considered useless. By a decree of September 3, 1948, the government set certain norms of expenditure of farm income on administration, ranging from 8 per cent for the smaller to 3 per cent for the giant farm, now the prevailing kind.[29] Should these norms be adhered to, which appears unlikely, it would mean around ten administrative and technical officials on a farm of three to four hundred kolkhozniks.

This complex administrative apparatus is designed to get the rank-and-file kolkhozniks to grow their crops and, as already indicated, to turn a substantial portion of them over to the government. We may therefore examine what this arrangement means in respect to the concrete situation that confronts the peasant household.

In terms of economic incentive the situation facing the Russian peasant resembles in many ways that of an American share cropper. The desire to produce appears to be rather low in both cases, because such a high proportion of the results of arduous labor disappear almost at once into the hands of higher authority. Uncertainty about the final size of the "pie" to be divided acts to diminish incentive further, though the government has recently promised some improvement. As one kolkhoznik remarked to a member of the Harvard interviewing staff, "For a whole year I did not even know how much I was earning. That is how it is with all kolkhozniks. They work and work and only the next year do they know how much they have earned." [30]

Out of the total production the lion's share goes to the government in the form of what amounts to forced sale at nominal and, it will be recalled, secret prices, payments in kind to the MTS, and payments into the "indivisible" or reserve fund of the individual kolkhoz. The peasants' claim on agricultural production is definitely the last one to be met. No postwar figures have been published on this point, but prewar ones illustrate the relationship. In the bumper-crop year of 1937 only 35.9 per cent of the grain crop was made available to the peasants in payment for their work on the farms, while in 1938 and 1939, years of smaller crops, their share dropped to 26.9 and 22.9 per cent.[31]

The income in cash and in kind that a kolkhoz receives is divided up among the members according to the so-called "labor-day" system. This is an attempt to bring about in agriculture the same relationship among effort, skill, and reward that is supposedly achieved through wage scales in industry. The various jobs on the collective farm are rated according to the skill required. A day's work on some jobs is rated at a fraction of a "labor-day"

while a day's work on jobs requiring greater skill is rated at up
to 2½ labor-days. A decree of April 19, 1948, established nine
grades of pay with a ratio of 5 to 1 between the highest and the
lowest, a slight change over the system set up in 1933 with seven
grades and a corresponding ratio of 4 to 1.[32] In the course of
the year the individual kolkhoznik accumulates a number of
labor-days that form the basis of his claim upon the net income
of the kolkhoz. Thus the labor-day constitutes a unit of income
whose magnitude is unknown at the time the work is being done.
Nobody knows what a labor-day will be worth until the end
of the year. Here is an obvious difference between the system
of incentive payments in industry and agriculture, with a clear
disadvantage to the latter.

In the light of large variations in the crop from year to year, as
well as enormous variations in the income of various farms,
average figures on what a labor-day is worth have but little
meaning. In the highly mechanized grain-growing areas of the
Northern Caucasus, according to a report by Khrushchev in
1953, some kolkhozes managed to make a labor-day worth 8 to
14 rubles.[33] Probably this is a showcase figure. It may be compared with the report of the Ukrainian Party secretary, citing
two farms in his area to contrast their 1951 productivity and
earnings. In the good farm 2 kilograms of grain and 3.10 rubles
in cash were distributed for a labor-day, while in the poor one
the amount was practically half, or 1 kilogram of grain, and 1.60
rubles.[34] No figures are given on the number of labor-days actually earned. These amounts correspond rather closely to the
figures reached by Jasny for the average prewar value of a
labor-day in the USSR as a whole. Between 1932 and 1940 its
value in grain is estimated to have varied between 1.6 and 2.9
kilograms, except for the bumper-crop year of 1937, when the
amount was 4.0 kilograms. Cash income, however, was by Jasny's
estimate considerably less than in the poorer Ukrainian case.[35]
Whatever the exact value of the labor-day may be, it is perfectly
clear that the government is seriously disturbed about the opera-

tion of the system of incentives it has created. At the same time its freedom to alter these arrangements is closely limited by broader economic and political considerations.

The shortcomings of this system of incentives force the government to rely on certain supplementary methods which in turn carry their own dangers. The peasant's chronic shortage of cash compels him to market produce, grown primarily in his private garden plot, on what is known as the open kolkhoz market. Likewise, his shortage of food compels the diversion of energy from the collective to the private undertaking, thus tending to undermine the system as a whole.

Together with the open kolkhoz market, the private plot represents a concession by the Communists to the persistence of the household as the basic productive unit in agricultural life. The private plot is also a survival from the days of the *mir*. In former times, Jasny notes, the land lying under the peasants' dwellings, as well as adjacent vegetable and fruit gardens, were held by the peasants individually and were not subject to periodical redistribution.[36] According to the current rules, collective farmers are allowed to retain between one-quarter and one-half a hectare of land (in special districts an entire hectare of 2.5 acres) for their personal use. In addition, in the basic farming areas the household may retain a cow and certain other specified items of livestock. The economic importance of this concession is shown in the Soviet admission that although the private plots constituted only 5 per cent of the area under collective cultivation in prewar years they accounted for about 20 per cent of the total agricultural production of the country at that time. More than half of the livestock in the country was then in private hands.[37] From the Communist viewpoint, then, it is not too much to say that the private plot represents the difference between scarcity and disaster.

Despite its political disadvantages, it is on this account a concession that the Bolsheviks can withdraw only with great difficulty. Toward the end of Stalin's reign there were evidently some high Party officials who expected that the government would be able to force the private plot out of existence in a not too distant future.[38] After his death these radical proposals were thrust aside. Instead the new regime has adopted exactly the opposite policy and has explicitly stated that it wants to make work on the private plot more attractive. The fact that the amount of livestock in the USSR in 1953 was less than before the revolution, and much less than in the last year of the NEP, undoubtedly constituted a major consideration behind this decision.[39]

On August 8, 1953, Malenkov promised to reduce the government's economic pressure on the private plot by a decrease in the tax burden and in the compulsory deliveries to be made from produce raised by the individual household. Shortly afterward Khrushchev announced large increases in the prices paid by the government for obligatory deliveries of livestock, potatoes, and vegetables, in which the production of the private plot plays a major part. The meaning of the change was partly concealed by the usual device of providing only percentage increases without any reference to the actual price.

Up until the end of September 1953 the Soviet government had not revealed any intention of raising the price for obligatory deliveries of grain, the major product of the collective efforts of the kolkhoz. Unless this price is also raised, there is no prospect of substantial improvement in the economic position of the peasant. The other measures are little more than palliatives. The net effect of the government's efforts so far is likely to be an increase in the attention paid by the peasants to the private sector at the expense of the collective one. Before long the new regime may run into this familiar trouble in an intensified form. The risk, however, is not as severe as it would have been immediately after the war, since the administrative apparatus at Moscow's service is considerably stronger.

The kolkhoz open market is a place to which peasants may send or bring produce and sell it for whatever price it will fetch, with the government's permission, if—in the past at least—by no means its blessing. A Soviet source has reported that there are now more than 4,500 such markets in the USSR as a whole.[40] Evidently the figure includes everything from an elaborate fair to the activities of a few old women selling vegetables from a sack, squatting under the watchful eyes of the police. Since the number of cities and towns was only 3,362 in the USSR in 1947,[41] it is clear that the network of these markets reaches well beyond urban areas and plays a vital role in rural exchange relationships. As part of the policy of concessions to the peasantry, Malenkov also announced in 1953 that the new regime would encourage the widespread expansion of the open markets.[42] A major weapon on which the government depends to prevent these activities from getting out of hand is its own network of government and coöperative retail stores. Since the government obtains food products for these stores under the conditions of forced sale already noted, it is able to keep prices in these stores generally below the level of that in the kolkhoz market. Frequently, however, the government cannot supply products in these stores in sufficient quantity to approach the demand at these prices.

Since work on the private plot yields both more immediate and greater material rewards,[43] there is a strong tendency for the peasants to expand their private holdings at the expense of the land collectively tilled. Andreev's 1947 report, based on a survey of 90 per cent of the kolkhozes, claiming that 2,225 cases of encroachment on collective property had been uncovered, is often cited in this connection, along with the report made slightly later in the same year, that the total area returned to the kolkhozes from illegal appropriations came to 5,780,000 hectares.[44] It is necessary to retain a sense of proportion in appraising this evidence. The number of cases of violation represents an average of only one violation on approximately every hundred farms. Likewise, the area illegally taken out of collective cultivation represents just short of 5 per cent of the total amount under cultivation in 1938 and would represent an even smaller proportion of the amount in 1947, with the addition of new territory. A reliable figure for the land under cultivation at the later date is not available.[45] In addition, Andreev's report reflects the situation shortly after the war and the serious drought of 1946, when the load on the collective farm system was probably at its worst.

The nature of the division of labor within the peasant family must be considered in connection with the strains produced by the private plot and kolkhoz market arrangement. Before the war it was the usual practice for the wife to do most of the work on the household plot, while the husband was the one primarily called upon to furnish labor for the collective enterprise. The women in the household put in about seven times as many days on the private plot as did the menfolk.[46] The war changed this situation sharply. Soviet figures indicate that every corner of rural Russia was drained of able-bodied men during the war. The percentage of labor-days earned by women jumped from 47.6 per cent to 77.9 per cent in the Black Earth belt between 1939 and 1943, and by the same or larger amounts in other agricultural areas.[47] The figure suggests a ratio of about three women to every man during the war years. Dr. Eugene M. Kulischer, a well-known expert on Soviet population, has drawn my attention to a Soviet source that roughly confirms this estimate. It reports that in 1943 women constituted 71 per cent of the able-bodied rural population, as compared with 52 per cent in 1939. Scattered local items in the Soviet press, also furnished by Dr. Kulischer, indicate that the shortage of men in rural areas has continued into the postwar years.[48] Mainly the shortage appears to be the consequence of a tendency to leave the harsh life of the countryside in search of better pay in the factories.[49]

If such a shortage of men exists, it implies a continuing strain on the system of collective agriculture, partly because of the propensity of the women to concentrate on the private plot. The implications carry far beyond the Russian countryside and into world politics. Since it is the countryside that contributes to population growth, the anticipation of a large increase in the Soviet population during the next twenty years may turn out to be incorrect. As this anticipated population growth, along with rapid industrialization, could make the Soviet Union the dominant world power, the political importance of the rural sex ratio is very great. However, further speculation on this point must await a firmer foundation in established fact.

Throughout the experience of collectivized agriculture in the USSR there runs the theme of a subterranean struggle between the traditional peasant work unit, the family, and Communist attempts to impose a new form of organization, which the peasants continually seek to subvert and refashion in the image of the traditional form. Part of this struggle centers, as we have seen, around the private plot. Another has its pivot in the large work unit, or brigade, which the Communists have tried to substitute for the family as the basic institution within the kolkhoz to control the division of labor.

The brigade was not adopted until 1932, when the drive for collectivization had already been under way for two years. Before then the Bolsheviks did not have any very definite ideas about the organization of labor on the farms, except perhaps negative ones. Jasny quotes one writer who asserted in 1931 that "the peasant household represents a relic of serfdom which must disappear. There is no place for a household as the primary unit in the socialist economy." Likewise the 1930 version of the Model Statute for collective farms provided for individual rather than family membership.[50] In order to raise the level of individual responsibility and individual incentive, the brigade was soon subdivided into "links," or squads of five to seven workers. This step was first ordered for sugar beets in 1933. During the thirties it spread to other technical crops and to grain. Just before the war the link system received the official blessing of the Party in a resolution of the 1939 Party Congress calling for its widespread adoption, which appears to have been carried out in the course of the year.[51]

At this Party Congress, Andreev criticized the "depersonalization under which the collective farmers working in large brigades are not held personally responsible for the quantity and quality of their work" and praised the squad arrangement for the fact that "in this way every piece of sown land in our collective farm has actually a master of its own who takes care of it." Under the new system, Andreev continued, "The results of the harvest are reckoned by teams [squads]," labor discipline had improved and output increased.[52] Similar arguments remained part of the official orthodoxy and were repeated in numerous discussions of farm labor through 1949. In 1950 the policy was suddenly reversed, except for technical crops where squads continued to be the approved form, and Andreev's words were flung back in his teeth by *Pravda*.[53]

As Harry Schwartz has suggested,[54] the reason for this reversal is very probably to combat a *sub rosa* revival of household farming that was favored by the legal protection of the squad system. In particular, the wartime destruction of the Machine Tractor Stations must have both weakened the government's control over the collectives and compelled the peasants to fall back on their own resources. This interpretation is strengthened by the fact that the regime waited until the supply of machinery for the MTS and the number of stations had approximately reached the prewar level before curbing the squads. It is also significant that the official rationalization for the new policy is that the squad makes it impossible to use the MTS machinery efficiently. Thus it is clear that the regime faces an important dilemma in the organization of labor on the farm. If it tries to copy industrial methods to the point of approximating piece-work incentives for small groups of workers, it runs the risk of encouraging the revival of the household as the primary economic unit in the countryside.

Before the amalgamation of the collectives into larger units, each kolkhoz had on an average two field brigades. Slightly less than a quarter of the farms had other brigades engaged in specialized tasks.[55] Local figures suggest that, after the amalgamation of the farms into larger units, sixty to seventy persons now constitute a common size for a brigade, and that it must take care of some 600 to 800 hectares of land.[56] The same piece of land is assigned to a single brigade for the entire period of the agricultural cycle. Husbands and wives are frequently assigned to different brigades with the consequence that the family is reunited only when the day's work is finished.

Like the kolkhoz as a whole, each brigade is expected to have an annual work plan.[57] In accord with the annual plan for the entire kolkhoz the brigade receives a plan for the expenditure of labor-days on each crop. In addition to this annual plan they are given special work plans for special jobs such as the spring sowing, the autumn harvesting, and the like.[58] Both the expenditure of labor by the brigade and its productivity is controlled by norms. The government sets model norms, raising them whenever possible, while each kolkhoz sets for the brigade the norms that supposedly correspond to the individual conditions that it faces. In turn the raion organizations check up on these individual estimates.[59] The whims of the weather must frequently play havoc with all of this careful planning, even though some flexibility is permitted by allowing the individual farm to participate in establishing its own norms. Generally the penalty for poor organization is likely to be that the government takes its quota anyway and the peasants are left to make out as best they can on whatever provender remains. The defense of the kolkhoz officials is to persuade the village authorities to look the other way, while they in turn have to persuade their superiors to overlook dereliction from duty. In this chain of evasions all of the officials are aided by the fact that paper forms and reports can be made into a convenient substitute for unpleasant realities. Thus ruthlessness is partially mitigated by corruption.

If the Soviet regime chooses to devote a greater share of its economic resources to the peasantry (a point to which we shall return), the brigade might conceivably be able to replace alto-

gether the peasant household as the primary cell of rural economic life. Other functions are performed by the peasant family,
however, which Soviet society could not dispense with, or dis-
place by a substitute form of social organization. As in any other
human society, the Soviet peasant family plays a major part in
regulating the relationships between the sexes and the training
of the future generation. But certain aspects of the way in which
these functions must be performed under present conditions
have negative political consequences for the existing regime.

To meet the situation created by drawing large numbers of
women into production the Soviets have tried to supplement the
family by setting up crèches, where the children may be left during
working hours. Ordinarily these nurseries take children up to the
age of three. In the rural areas so-called "field crèches" are set up
at sowing and harvest time. In the Ukraine in 1950 about 1,300,-
000 children were cared for in this fashion during the time of
heavy work in the fields.[60] Since the rural population in the
Ukraine already numbered just short of 20,000,000 in 1939,[61] this
would mean there were in the neighborhood of 2,000,000 or more
children under three years old in the prewar period,[62] and probably more at the later date. Therefore only one youngster in
three could be taken care of by this Soviet version of baby-sit-
ting. Presumably the rest remained in the hands of other family
members too old or too young to be active in the fields. The facts
suggest that even auxiliary arrangements provided by the government are scarcely more than the minimum necessary to make
the system of collective cultivation work.

In regard to older children, the impression I have derived from
refugee interview material is that the family provides the major
channel for the transmission of anti-Soviet values and beliefs.
This point deserves much fuller investigation before its significance can be appraised, although the bias in our sample limits
the possibility of achieving conclusive results. In this respect
the family faces an important competitor in the state-controlled
school system, where Communist indoctrination begins in a

simple form at the kindergarten years of three to seven. However, the kindergarten network does not extend very far into the countryside.[63] Furthermore, in the countryside, where the harshness of Soviet reality is more immediately apparent than in the city and where the memories of forced collectivization are strong and bitter among many parents now only in their early forties, it seems likely that the family viewpoint would usually overbalance school indoctrination. In both the country and the city, the transmission through the family of older patterns of belief about the actual and the desirable nature of human relationships serves in a significant manner to prevent the internal acceptance of Communist values.

In particular, the family represents the most important agency for the transmission of religious belief, not only in the countryside, but also in the cities. During times when religion has been driven under cover the family has been a major element in keeping religion alive and perpetuating it from one generation to another. Now, as part of the uneasy truce between the Russian Orthodox Church and the Bolshevik state, there may be some 33,000 priests in 22,000 to 25,000 parishes, serving to maintain, and possibly even extend, religious tradition.[64]

The importance of organized religion in the countryside, however, may be described as latent rather than actual. Reading the accounts of former Soviet peasants, one comes across very little evidence to the effect that formal religion has a significant place in the Russian rural scene. The priest, if there is one, does not constitute a part of the political and economic control system to which the peasantry is compelled to adapt. Nor are there any festivals that play an integral part of the agricultural cycle in which religious symbolism can attract attention. Even if police and Party controls are less widespread in the countryside, they seem sufficient, along with the advantages obtained from the concordat with the regime, to prevent the priest from becoming a focus of discontent and opposition to the government. Furthermore, the sheer pressure of the cruel struggle for existence, combined with the limitation on opportunities for contact with organized religion, has dulled religious sentiment among many younger peasants. As one recent escapee put it, "In general I didn't believe in God. I just forgot about it. There were no churches and no priests, so you lived according to your education." [65] Another youngster, in whose village the church had been reopened after the war, said, "Our attitude toward religion is very weak. Besides we just don't have any time for it. We have to go to work; when should you go to church?" [66] Such attitudes are characteristic of the younger recent escapees from rural areas.

Even if organized religion despite its partial recovery still remains reduced to a vestigial role in the countryside, under altered conditions the situation might change rapidly. Religious symbols are at least loosely associated with the parents' efforts to inculcate a set of moral standards that are often remembered with both affection and respect. The existence of icons in the home as a symbol of opposition to the Soviet regime recurs as a continuing theme among the memories of peasant lads. The mother, it may be noted, appears frequently in such descriptions to have been the more actively religious member of the family, though the father is usually described as a genuine and practicing believer. An undercurrent of religious sentiment probably prevails in Russian peasant culture that could come to the fore in a crisis situation. The government's wartime decision to permit a wider degree of religious activity in order to draw on sentiments that would aid in the defense of the homeland provides sufficient testimony on this point. It will be difficult for the present regime to withdraw these concessions even if it should wish to, which seems unlikely in the near future, as it has made a point of presenting itself to the populace as milder than the Stalinist dictatorship. Finally, if the contemporary authorities should lose their grip on Russian society, organized religion might remain as one, and perhaps even the major, going concern and unifying force amid chaotic disintegration.

In appraising the Soviet peasantry in respect to Bolshevism's political future, the key point is the regime's inability to allocate sufficient resources to the peasantry in order to make collective farming attractive. In the short run at least, Moscow cannot give more to the peasants in the way of additional equipment for the MTS, more consumer goods, or higher prices for compulsory deliveries of produce, without at the same time taking something away from the armaments or industrialization programs. On this account the Kremlin is forced to rely on the peasant household to supplement the kolkhoz in economic matters, and in order to raise the next generation. But at the same time the peasant household also undermines the kolkhoz, partly through the private plot and the open market, and partly through the transmission of anti-Soviet values and attitudes. The nature of the relationship between the two sets of institutions is one of armed truce, in which any weakness in the set of incentives influencing behavior in the collective sector is likely to be followed by increased vitality in the private sector.

The conflict is not, however, one that is necessarily or inevitably irreconcilable. If it became possible for the regime to satisfy a substantial part of the peasants' economic wants, there is no inherent reason why the household might not be permitted to continue to exist as a subordinate and supplementary economic unit and to perform its other vital functions in the society. Resistance would remain, arising both from the strong remnants of peasant hostility to new social arrangements, and possibly from some new sources, such as an ever-rising hankering after the fleshpots of industrial society. Such disruptive forces could probably be kept under control much more easily, however, than is the case at present.

Now the peasant displays a strong tendency to revert to the household as the primary social and economic cell of rural life. This tendency is only kept in check by forceful administrative methods. The over-all instability of the situation is reflected in the degree of administrative experimentation, ranging from the brigade-squad question through the amalgamation policy, up to the organization of the central administrative organs themselves. Even though the basic features of agricultural policy have remained constant since 1930, there have been more changes in the economic and administrative devices used to pursue this policy than in any other aspect of Soviet society.

If this analysis is correct, five major possibilities are theoretically open to the Kremlin leadership. One of them, the outright abandonment of collective agriculture, may be rejected as a practical possibility for the foreseeable future, except as a desperate last-minute grasp for popularity in the midst of a severe internal upheaval. Such an eventuality cannot be completely ruled out, but now seems highly unlikely.

Only four possibilities are therefore likely to receive serious attention by the men in the Kremlin. One of these is to keep the system as it now exists, through applying sufficient administrative force. The second is to take enough resources from other parts of the economy to strengthen their hold over the peasants by meeting more of the peasants' economic demands. Such a policy would require the sacrifice of other political and economic goals, particularly a diminution of the armaments program as an instrument of an expansionist foreign policy. For the present at least this is the solution that is being explored by the new Kremlin leadership. Still a third program would be to increase the total output of the economy so as to be able to take care of *both* the peasant question and other problems, a long-term rather than an immediate solution. As a fourth program they can try to end present contradictions by imposing the urban pattern on the countryside in a thoroughgoing fashion. Such a policy would imply doing away with the private plot, and paying the peasants in cash instead of labor-days. In addition, they might try to herd the peasants together into "rural cities," where they could be more closely watched through police and Party controls, though such a step does not necessarily constitute an essential part of the program. The ground pattern for the fourth policy is visible and available in the *sovkhoz*, the giant "factory in the field," operated by hired labor. However, this form proved inefficient long ago, and by 1938 was restricted to about 9 per cent of the land under crops.

The first two possibilities represent in the Bolshevik political spectrum a conservative solution of the peasant question, while the last two fall into the pattern of a more radical "left" solution. By choosing, at least for the moment, the conservative solution, the new Kremlin leadership runs the risk of permitting an increase in traditionalist forces in Soviet society that have an important center in the peasant household, and whose further growth could ultimately threaten control from the center. This danger is hardly likely to escape the attention of the more radically inclined members of the Party leadership. The elements of totalitarian control and of technical rationality, both symbolized in the tractor, still dominate the present situation. The control levers are available and in use, should other hands press for their more vigorous application. Whichever tack the Party leadership takes, the situation is such that the peasant question is likely to remain a running sore, continually generating differences of opinion at the highest level on how to cure it. On this account agriculture provides one major focal point over which the leadership will have to settle its differences if it is both to remain united and keep its hold on Soviet society.

chapter 4

COMMUNIST BELIEFS
ON SCIENCE AND ART

The problem of incorporating the intellectual into a larger social fabric is not unique to the Soviet Union. It has plagued much of Western civilization since the days of the Greeks, and finds its analogues in other cultures as well. The difficulty probably does not arise from any especially cantankerous or individualist qualities in the biological make-up of those attracted to intellectual life. Rather it derives from the nature of intellectual activity itself, particularly as this activity has developed in our dynamic and at times rapidly changing civilization. When it becomes the full-time occupation of special groups of people, intellectual activity tends to generate its own distinctive goals and standards of achievement. Particularly in science, each new discovery opens up new areas that appear to the scientist as the natural field for further inquiry. The same tendency also appears in the development of artistic styles. The next step in the exploration of new patterns in art or science appears as a demand upon the creative faculties of the intellectual, particularly one whose entire energy is absorbed in his chosen field. As such goals and standards of achievement develop, they may easily become incomprehensible to the larger public. In some societies, particularly in the Orient, this development has resulted in the elevation of the intellectual to the high priesthood of a theocratic state. Some aspects of this trend are present in the Soviet system and also occur in Western society, as, for example, in the Catholic Church.

Under other circumstances, the goals and standards of intellectual life may clash directly with important beliefs that prevail among influential groups in the larger society, or even the society as a whole. This tendency toward conflict does not by any means imply that all intellectuals gravitate toward opposition movements. Intellectuals are the officers and subalterns of all arms and all armies, as one student of their history tartly observed. Where conflict has arisen, different societies have developed a variety of ways to cope with the problem of maintaining some degree of unity in the larger society. The intellectual has seldom, if ever, been a completely free agent. The patronage of the wealthy and powerful, and later his dependence on a commercial mass market, have limited his freedom of action. Likewise, in their different ways, the struggle of the universities to maintain independent standards of intellectual inquiry, and the social isolation of the artists' Bohemia, have served as important social mechanisms to diminish internal friction.

Even if it is not unique in the Soviet Union, the question of the intellectuals is especially acute, since in this society the rulers require at least outward adherence to a very specific, if by no means inflexible, belief system. In its current form the portion of Communist doctrine that applies to intellectual life may be reduced to five major theses. These apply equally to the creative artists and the scientists, as well as to those who disseminate, use, or criticize the achievements of these two. For our purposes all such persons may be considered intellectuals, although this chapter will concern itself primarily with the creative intellectual.

Since Soviet doctrine suffuses all of intellectual life in the USSR, it is necessary to spell out its primary assumptions. Such comment is essential, because the doctrine raises certain genuine issues that cannot be dismissed with easy phrases about the revival of authoritarian obscurantism. Furthermore, the Soviet premises are closely intertwined with a number of articulate and inarticulate assumptions governing much of intellectual life in the West. Although this is not the place for an extended critical analysis of both traditions and their interrelationship, nevertheless the position taken in respect to Western and Soviet premises inevitably influences any interpretation of Soviet intellectual life that goes beyond the crudest level of factual description. There is no easy out through the lazy assertion that "there may be something to Soviet ideas." For one who is not a professional in these questions, all that is possible is a conscientious attempt to make the position adopted as reasonable and explicit as possible.

The first Communist premise may be labeled materialism, an ancient doctrine with many varieties. To distinguish it from others, the Soviets, as is generally known, call their version dialectical materialism. Since its formulation by Marx and Engels there have been a number of brief expositions of this doctrine, which renders superfluous any such attempt here. For our purpose the significant point is the metaphysical assumption that the external world exists independently of the human mind.[1] The appropriate task of science is to study this external reality. Though absolute truth exists, science can approach it only through a series of successive approximations, each one of which contains some facet of this elusive, ultimate reality. So far the Marxist position is indistinguishable from the working or "common sense" philosophy of many contemporary natural scientists. Non-Marxist scientists, however, would reject the Hegelian dialectic, or the continual fusing of opposite ideas into a new synthesis, as an adequate or necessary description of the way this approximation proceeds.

The materialist assumption of an external and objective reality also forms the philosophical basis of contemporary and official Soviet aesthetics. Art is called upon to give a "truthful picture of reality, a perception of social life," in a way that, to be sure, differs from science yet resembles it. The artist, from this standpoint, ought to transmit the emotional feelings aroused by reality, while the scientist records its objective characteristics. Thus statistics may tell us something about the proletariat, while a novel portrays the emotional sensations.[2] The distinction between the artist and the scientist tends to be blurred at this point in Marxist philosophy, just as it does in contemporary positivism, the dominant view among Western scientists, insofar as the latter are explicit about the philosophical assumptions with which they work.[3]

In other vital aspects of the relationship between "ideas" and "reality" the positivist tradition and current Soviet doctrine are sharply opposed. The key issue is the degree of freedom that scientists and artists ought to enjoy in selecting and even creating the intellectual tools with which to analyze or represent their subject matter. Marxism adheres to the view that truth is a representation of some physical reality that may be difficult to grasp because it undergoes continual change, but which definitely exists outside the human mind.* The opposite view, subscribed to by positivism and many outside its ranks, is that scientific theories are to a great extent the free and spontaneous creations of the human mind, the product of creative imagination.

It was just this standpoint that Lenin attacked at the turn of the century with all the forces at his command, and which is still the object of attack in the Soviet Union today. The purpose of Lenin's attack was crystal clear: the admission that scientific laws are a creation of the human mind, he argued, opens the door to idealism and cuts away the ground from materialism. With the disappearance of the materialist basis of science, the way would be open to a *rapprochement* between science and religion. In turn the smuggling in of religious views, he concluded, favors the forces of political reaction.[4] Current Soviet polemics may be motivated by the same fear that intellectuals, and through them the entire political order, might be subverted by a competing philosophy.

* Marxism does not hold to a simple copy theory of truth, as is sometimes supposed, although Lenin's position is difficult to distinguish from the copy theory. Professional Soviet philosophers have their own view as to how concepts develop genetically out of human experience. For a survey of these views see Gustav A. Wetter, *Der dialektische Materialismus* (Vienna, 1952), pp. 522, 555–566. This study by a distinguished Jesuit scholar (not available until most of the present chapter had been drafted) provides a detailed exposition of the history and content of the formal philosophy.

The next point in Soviet doctrine, its hostility to abstract symbolism, or "formalism" as they often call it, is intimately connected with the materialist assumption and the denial of creative imagination. Indeed, it is scarcely more than an extension of this denial to both the arts and the sciences. Insofar as science does not create something new, but tries to represent reality or some portion thereof, the complex theoretical flights of the scientist with a "creative imagination" frequently arouse the suspicions of an intelligent Bolshevik scientist. He is inclined to suspect that such solutions may be purely verbal or the juggling of abstractions unrelated to reality.

Behind this hostility to formalism appear to be both genuine and spurious intellectual issues. The Communist objection to abstract thinking in science is partly spurious in attributing to Western scientific thought the view that pure mathematics and logic make assertions about the real world. The contrary is heavily emphasized in positivist writings. Thus both the Communists and the positivists agree in substance about the nature of abstract and theoretical statements. The real intellectual difficulty occurs in how these formal statements are to be connected with observable reality. On this question some earlier Western writings assert that when two sets of formal theories lead to deductions that correspond equally well to observations at a given state of knowledge, it is merely a matter of convenience which one is used. Although the Bolsheviks' own theory of how to select among differing theoretical viewpoints is very similar, as we shall soon see, they reject any "convenience theory" of truth or any strictly pragmatic position. To one who is not a professional philosopher the problem of discrimination among theories does not appear to be solved, nor does it seem as clear-cut as it does to either positivists or Communists.

The problem appears both more simple and more complex than the "convenience theory" would indicate. As the positivists themselves point out, the criterion of verification, as a means of choosing between theories, requires prior agreement on the rules by which verification will be carried out. In other words, the operations must be indicated, a point familiar under the name of operationalism. But this specification merely pushes back one step the question of how agreement is to be reached. To assert that the theories must lead to deductions which eventually match our sense impressions is perhaps a satisfactory working position for the scientist. The convenience theory is, however, a confession that this rule will not always yield a decision. In this respect it is scarcely more than an evasion. Furthermore, as Lenin insists, the requirement of agreement with sense impressions leads to a solipsist conclusion: namely, that the self knows and can know nothing but its own modifications and states. Some Western philosophers, it may be noted in passing, are quite willing to accept this implication and to regard the existence of the external world as merely a fiction necessary for communication.[5]

As an amateur in these matters, I am inclined to accept the position taken by Morris Cohen on the relationship between abstraction and reality. Criticizing the notion of fictions, he accepts the reality of both the external world and of the abstractions expressed in logic and mathematics, declaring that the latter are merely expressions for *relationships* that do exist in nature. Even abstractions "contrary to fact," such as frictionless movement, may be said to express relationships that exist, though never in isolation from other relationships that are abstracted in a different manner.[6] Many philosophers today will reject this solution. This is not the place, however, to pursue the problem further. Enough has been said to indicate that many intelligent men see here a difficult problem and that the Communist position cannot be contemptuously ruled out of court.

Anti-abstractionism, anti-formalism, anti-symbolism also occupy a prominent place in official Soviet aesthetic judgments. According to the Academy of Sciences' recent volume on historical materialism, the separation of form from content in the arts results only in sterility and decline.[7] On the grounds that

taste can be explained but not appraised,* I shall refrain from
any discussion of Soviet aesthetics on its merits, so to speak.

The Communists' own view as to how human notions of truth
can be verified may be taken as the third point in their set of
basic assumptions. As has just been pointed out, Lenin emphati-
cally rejects the convenience theory of truth, while his present-
day followers reject pragmatism in even more vitriolic terms. As
materialists, they also reject the contemporary positivist solution,
which holds that sense data constitute the basic elements of
reality. This solution, Lenin pointed out in a quotation from
Mach, leads to the result that the "wildest dream" becomes a
"fact as much as any other." [8]

Quite possibly this rejection is related to a psychological desire for a more secure and absolute basis for the Communist
system. In the nineteenth century many persons thought that
science did provide such an absolute and that it would replace
the declining authority of religion. It was only toward the beginning of the twentieth century that educated opinion forsook the
search for absolutes through science and turned to the view
that science as such must be content with more modest goals.
In their hostility to the positivist view, the Communists take a

---

* I am perfectly aware that these grounds are not impregnable, and that
a great deal of intellectual energy has gone into various attempts to construct logically self-consistent systems of aesthetics. Unless the premises of
the system are granted, it falls to the ground. Obviously aesthetic premises
vary tremendously from one epoch and culture to another. It will be replied
that such variations are irrelevant to a search for the "correct" aesthetic
premises. But I fail to see how the premises can be regarded as correct except in terms of other premises. Anthropologists can try the opposite tack
of demonstrating common elements in the explicit or implicit aesthetic
premises of all cultures, as they have attempted for ethics and morals. If
such elements were discovered, they would carry no logical compulsion for
any individual who chose to reject them. *Logical* compulsion to choose between two or more alternative assertions, as distinct from a choice based
on *force majeure*, requires an agreement on premises. The only reason it is
possible to go some little distance, and precious little it is, in the direction
of developing a universal scientific method (i.e., a logic of choice among
procedures in the investigation of our surroundings and ourselves) derives
from whatever agreement we are able to reach about the premises of
science.

position that is very hard to distinguish from pragmatism. Marx, in his notes on Feuerbach, remarked: "The question whether objective truth can be attributed to human thinking is not a question of theory, but is a practical question. In practice man must prove the truth, i.e., the reality and the power, the 'this sidedness' of his thinking." Marx further observed, "Social life is essentially *practical*. All mysteries which mislead theory to mysticism find their rational solution in human practice." [9] To this position Lenin returned in his attack on early positivist doctrine. As the position taken by Communists today, it is very close to the Western scientist's frequently expressed opinion that the proof of an idea lies in the results of an experiment. The difference is in the fact that an empirical scientist is not likely to be philosophically very much concerned with whether his experiments reflect a manipulation of sense impressions or a manipulation of some portion of the external world, or a combination of the two. For the Communist this is a vital question. For him it is essential to uphold the point that proof lies in a successful manipulation of the external world. As it turns out, success tends to be defined in political terms.

In the domain of the arts the Marxist criterion of practice has led to a judgment of art largely in terms of its political consequences. Stalin's reference to the writer as an "engineer of human souls" often serves as the starting point of Soviet literary and artistic criticism. By the mid-thirties, and partly at Zhdanov's behest, this familiar idea of the social responsibility of the artist was worked out into a definite system of aesthetics, known as socialist realism. This is by no means realism as the term would be generally understood in the West. The emphasis lies instead on the socialist message that must be conveyed. From this standpoint Communists cannot believe that an artist may be apolitical, no matter how much he may wish to be. Since in their view a work of art is bound to have political consequences, it is understandable that, as the Communist rulers of Russia, they want to control these consequences. Hence they demand *partiinost* in art.

Partiinost (whose literal translation is the awkward "partyness") carries all the overtones of enthusiastic, intelligent, loyal, and yet essentially uncritical acceptance of the Communist belief system.

By the same token, convinced Communists do not believe that it is possible for science to be non-partisan and put the same demand for partiinost on the scientist. Lenin's *Materialism and Empirio-Criticism* declares: "That science is non-partisan in the struggle of materialism against idealism and religion is a favorite idea not only of Mach but of all modern bourgeois professors who are . . . 'graduated flunkeys who stupefy the people by their twisted idealism.'" [10] The inevitable partisanship of science can be regarded as the fourth basic assumption in the Communist outlook.

To Westerners soaked in the conception that science per se is neutral in political questions and value judgments, the Leninist position seems merely bizarre. It is easy to dismiss it as a crude barbarism, along with the Soviet epithets that run counter to the folkways of intellectual discourse in Anglo-Saxon countries. Likewise, the spectacle of a distinguished Soviet scientist recanting his scientific beliefs, because, as a member of the Party, he can no longer hold views counter to those pronounced by the Party Central Committee, seems both horrible and pathetic. Since many Soviet scientists, particularly those of the older generation, are heavily imbued with Western scientific ideals, such tragedies are no doubt frequent and very real. Nevertheless, there is an argument here that requires examination before Soviet behavior can be understood properly.

The issues can be made clearer by returning for a moment to the Western view of science. Two points are fundamental. One is that science, as such, is neutral in political conflicts and conflicts of value. There are at least two possible meanings to this first statement. It can mean that scientific knowledge will be effective irrespective of who uses it. Thus a gun will fire under the proper conditions, whether it is aimed by a policeman or a thief. Another possible meaning is that the results of science are equally available for anybody to use for any purpose. The Bolsheviks have a great deal to say about this second meaning, to which we shall return in a moment, and next to nothing about the first. The other fundamental point in Western doctrine is that scientists, as such, are the only persons competent to judge questions of truth or falsehood in their special field of inquiry. In the West the corollary follows that on this account interference with such judgments by a political or any other authority is unwarranted.

The Communist viewpoint, insofar as it relates to these matters, is a contradictory one. But the contradictions do not mean that it is altogether illogical, or that it fails to draw attention to significant matters sometimes overlooked in the West. Communists may deny that science is neutral. Nevertheless their acts give eloquent assent to the proposition that scientific knowledge is effective irrespective of its user. Espionage directed towards American atomic secrets is sufficient evidence on that point. It is perfectly clear that at least in this sense the Western view is correct and that Communists know it.

The situation is quite different in regard to the second interpretation of the neutrality of science, its availability for any purpose. To say that science can be used for any purpose is not the same thing as to say that under a given set of concrete social circumstances everybody has equal access to scientific knowledge or scientific instruments for achieving their ends. Furthermore, as long as scientific knowledge grows, it is certain to become available to some people sooner than to others. On this account it is bound to upset existing power relationships. In the twentieth century it is scarcely possible for a rational person to deny that scientific discoveries have political consequences. In this sense the Communists are perfectly correct in their assertion that science is partisan.

It is possible to concede some further ground to the Communist position. In addition to denying that science is neutral, Communists also argue that economic and social conditions generate the ideas of a society, including its scientific and artistic doctrines and concepts. No one is likely to quarrel seriously any more with the view that social conditions are likely to affect the intellectual climate and the theories which scientists and other creative thinkers produce. The exact nature of the relationship, however, remains obscure, and perhaps cannot be settled by any over-all single formula. In this sense it may be granted that science in different countries and, to a greater extent, the arts will show distinctive characteristics.

Since the Second World War, however, Party enthusiasts have hammered away at the theme that Soviet science, engendered by a socialist society, is something of a different order from bourgeois or Western science. Taken literally, this is of course pure nonsense. Even the most fervent Communist would have to concede that socialist water will freeze at the same temperature as its most bourgeois counterpart. It is worth noting in this connection that Stalin's last major ideological pronouncements on linguistics and the economics of socialism reasserted the possibility of scientific propositions that do not have their base in a particular form of society.

As to the second fundamental point in the Western credo, the autonomy of the scientific professions in matters within their sphere of technical competence, Communists give formal and verbal agreement. Lenin asserts that scientists can make enormously valuable contributions within their own field, but that they are not to be trusted one iota when it comes to the philosophical implications of these matters. The distinction between matters of purely technical fact and matters of philosophy, however, is not one that the Communists have sought to maintain in practice. Within the past few years the Party Central Committee, or Stalin himself, has issued pronouncements on matters of fact in such varied fields as genetics, linguistics, and history.

The distinction between scientific fact and philosophy brings us to the fifth basic point in Communist doctrine, the procedure through which it allows for its own modifications and development. Marxism shares with much of Western intellectual heritage a common source in rationalist doctrines, devoted to change and opposed to authoritarian fetters on intellectual inquiry. Some traces of this parentage. remain in Marxism. Even in its present Soviet version, the official interpreters deny that it is in any sense a dogma, but declare that it must be revised from time to time in the light of new experience. What distinguishes the Communist position is that the right to make such revisions is in effect reserved to the top political leadership, and actually to one man throughout most of its history. At the moment no such final arbiter of doctrine has emerged to replace Stalin. Important elements in the more permanent features of Bolshevik doctrine and political behavior may produce difficulties if no arbiter arises.

One reason for the existence of a single arbiter derives from the fact that Russian Marxism, both before and after the November revolution, developed and grew in a social environment where popular sentiment was unlikely to follow its lead. Lenin was quite aware of this. In his voluminous writings he constantly displayed a fear that not only the workers, but also other intellectuals, might make the "wrong" deductions from experience. Hence he fought with every device at his command for the adoption of his own deductions. Running through Lenin's writings, and current Soviet ones as well, is the horror, which to a Westerner seems distinctly paranoid, lest one small ideological slip lead to a catastrophic tumble into a yawning pit of political error. Under Bolshevik assumptions ideological error automatically and inevitably leads to political disaster. The consequence has been the development of strict central control over vital questions of doctrine. As one authority has put the matter, Bolshevism is an intellectual system in which the theory designates the authority, who is in turn empowered to designate the theory.[11] In this fashion the possibility of change is in fact incorporated into the system, even if in a manner very different from that of science.

The criterion of practice also enters in quite consistently as the basis for deciding what new ideas will receive the accolade of orthodoxy. More precisely, one might say that the choice is based upon a calculation of the services that a new idea can or cannot render to the regime. In the arts this calculation is explicitly stated as the basis of Soviet aesthetics. The same situation appears to prevail in science. Thus, in the choice between two or more competing versions of scientific truth, such as Lysenkoist or Western theories about the inheritance of acquired characteristics, the choice will not necessarily fall upon the one that is most congruent with previous Marxist thought. The reintroduction of Aristotelian logic by order of the Party Central Committee in 1946,[12] apparently because of dissatisfaction with the ability of Soviet youth to reason properly, provides clear evidence on this point. The basic laws of Aristotelian logic are incompatible with the dialectical method of reasoning, the foundation stone of dialectical materialism. To Soviet professors of logic has fallen the unenviable task of making some kind of a reconciliation. Their predicament is the expected by-product of a situation in which decisions affecting intellectual viewpoints are reached on the basis of political considerations.

In this respect there does not appear to be any significant difference between a decision in regard to scientific orthodoxy and a decision on foreign policy or domestic politics. The reintroduction of formal logic appears analogous to decisions reintroducing the traditional study of history, the tightening of divorce laws, the open acceptance of wage differentials, and the rejection of petty bourgeois equalitarianism. All have a basis in the leadership's appraisal of what is necessary to keep their system going. The same is probably equally true of the genetics decision in 1948. That such an appraisal can be thoroughly mistaken goes without saying. So are many appraisals and decisions in foreign and domestic policy. Communist doctrine can take care of this situation too. When a policy proves unworkable it can be reversed, again by the highest authority, and appropriate scapegoats found. This has happened in history, and more recently in linguistics. There is every reason to expect that the policy in genetics will be reversed if it fails to produce results. The zealots of today are the saboteurs of tomorrow.

Another aspect of the provision for change inherent in Bolshevik theory is its own rather special variety of antitraditionalism. No Western scientist could go further than the Soviet press in some of its condemnation of the dead hand of the intellectual past. The authority of great names must not be used to prevent fresh minds from questioning their conclusions. During the last years of his lifetime Stalin himself was often quoted to reassert the theme that science cannot advance except through open, free, and creative discussion. Combined with this antitraditionalism is, at least as far as the words go, an exuberant and turbulent optimism. There are no intellectual fortresses that a Bolshevik cannot conquer, no problems that a Bolshevik cannot someday solve. The same tone prevails in official comment on the arts. "Soviet art is suffused with optimism, cheerfulness, belief in the bright future of the people, in the victory of Communism. It is an art with an affirmative view of life, like all of Soviet ideology." [13] So runs a comment that could be duplicated profusely.

It is easy enough to dismiss these words contemptuously, as a rather clumsy attempt to cover up a thoroughly authoritarian practice. The Western rebuttal can be phrased in roughly the following terms. While Soviet scientists may be free to reject "bourgeois Western authority," in its place they must often accept as scientific truth the Party's dictates, or the views of an antiquated Russian authority. As for contemporary Soviet art, it may be cheerful enough, but it too has by this time become thoroughly stereotyped and traditionalized.

Largely true, the Western rebuttal overlooks at least one significant aspect of the Soviet situation as well as our own. By pointing out the areas where Western and Soviet systems differ, it glosses over some common elements that could conceivably lead to similar results in the West. Soviet antitraditionalism and optimism have their origins in the same rationalist viewpoint that suffuses so much of Western thinking.[14] They are not therefore to be brushed aside as merely clumsy propaganda. Likewise out of this rationalism has come the Marxist belief, also widely held in America, that science can provide the final answers to problems of human happiness. Unlike another great and more tragic stream of Western thought, the Bolsheviks do not, and perhaps cannot, fully realize the instrumental nature of scientific knowledge, since they try to make science the anchor of their total belief system. In this blind spot the Communist viewpoint is no different from that of its more simple rationalist critics.

This sketch of the official doctrine may be concluded with a comment on its vein of xenophobia and often ludicrous praise of Russian and Soviet intellectual achievements.* In its extreme form these were postwar phenomena and may have represented part of an attempt to harness the upsurge of Russian nationalist feeling that played a prominent part during the war. Before his death in 1948, Andrei A. Zhdanov provided the seal of authority for these views in a series of speeches attacking "decadent Western bourgeois cosmopolitanism," though his statements were slightly less extreme than those of minor Party zealots. Such statements continued with increasing intensity, until Stalin's death in March 1953. Some of them contained overtones of anti-Semitism through the identification of individual Jews with official policy. After Malenkov, Zhdanov's former rival, succeeded along with his associates to Stalin's former posts, the situation changed sharply. The anti-Semitic note was in effect repudiated as an attempt to "inflame feelings of national hatred deeply foreign

---

* Boasts of Russian superiority are in part a reaction from the time when it was necessary to stress openly the need for learning from the West. As late as June 23, 1936, the Party Central Committee and the Council of People's Commissars issued a decree criticizing the "extremely inadequate output" of specialized scientific literature in translation. See M. I. Movshovich, compiler, *Vysshaya Shkola: Osnovnye Postanovleniya Prikazy i Instruktsii* (Moscow, 1945), p. 10. There is now a carefully organized system for abstracting foreign scientific literature and making its contents available to research and applied scientists. A description may be found in *Current Digest of the Soviet Press*, vol. V, no. 3 (February 28, 1953), condensed from *Vestnik Akademii Nauk SSSR*, no. 8 (August 1952), pp. 41–45.

to socialist ideology." [15] Insistence on the superiority of Russian intellectual achievements disappeared from *Pravda* editorials.[16] In a manner parallel to the conciliatory line toward the Western powers taken by the Soviet rulers, the president of the Academy of Sciences, A. N. Nesmeyanov, suddenly announced a reversal of the previous policy of suspicion and exclusion. As in many such dramatic reversals, the announcement tried to make it appear that the old policy had never existed, while the Soviet reader must have rubbed his eyes at the vanishing act. "Believing that mutual understanding and businesslike scientific relationships between scholars of various countries can develop independently of social structure, political convictions, and religious beliefs," Nesmeyanov declared, "we gladly accept foreign scholars among us and send our representatives to foreign congresses and conferences called even in capitalist countries. During the summer of this year delegations of the Academy of Sciences of the USSR will take part in the sessions of the XIXth International Physiological Congress in Montreal and the XIIIth International Congress of Theoretical and Applied Chemistry in Stockholm." [17] How much further the reversal may go in practice remains to be seen. As this rapid change demonstrates, the spirit of super-nationalist xenophobia can be turned off and on in accord with the Party leadership's appraisal of the political requirements of the moment.

Such, then, are the articulate major premises of the Soviet system in regard to the place and activities of the intellectual, as they have developed up to the present time. To put them into practice is no easy task. It demands an elaborate system of both formal and informal controls. Here the system runs into counter pressures from below, generated by the requirements of effective scientific and artistic work and by the force of past traditions and habits. The conflict between the demands of the dictatorship and the intellectuals' striving for autonomy will be examined in the next chapter.

chapter 5

SCIENTIST AND ARTIST
IN THE POLICE STATE

The mechanisms through which the intellectuals are partially integrated into Soviet society are of two major kinds. One of these forms part of the over-all system of organized social inequality characteristic of any complex society. Soviet intellectuals, if the term is defined broadly enough, may be found on nearly all rungs of the various ladders of prestige, authority, and economic inequality. But the creators of new cultural products are concentrated near the top. Their greater prestige and access to more material goods and services help to tie them into the larger social fabric. Not relying solely upon these devices, the regime also depends upon the second mechanism of direct administrative control.

Precise data on differences in income and access to material goods are generally hard to find for present-day Soviet society. Enough information is available, nevertheless, to suggest the style of life at various levels among the intellectuals. At the top is a very small court group, able to live in luxury even by capitalist standards, who mingle on intimate terms with Kremlin chieftains. The famous author, Aleksei Tolstoy, could have a town house and country estate, staffed with numerous retainers; collect expensive furniture, art objects, and a large library; give fine dinners; and generally behave like a Western aristocrat with a marked weakness for the bottle.[1] At a slightly lower level, actors in one of the great Moscow theaters are able to enjoy a summer vacation on a fine estate, with access to yachts and other features of capitalist resort life.[2] Members of the Academy of Sciences can be placed on approximately the same level. From this position alone in 1949 they each received a salary of 5,000 rubles a month.

Many of them hold other positions as well.[3] A rough guess might be that there are not more than a thousand intellectuals in this elite group.

Persons at the very top of the academic hierarchy, including those in scientific research institutes, may approach this standard of living, which drops rapidly from this point downward. At the outbreak of the war the academic hierarchy was made up of 5,000 professors, 13,000 docents (roughly the equivalent of associate professors), and 32,000 assistants and teachers, adding up to a total of 50,000. Nearly 14,000 of these were victims of the war, which struck most heavily the younger ranks.[4] By 1951 the number of professors and doctors of science had reached 10,000.[5]

Differences in academic rank are reflected in the standard of living. Eric Ashby, a British scientist with rare opportunities for first-hand observation, reported that in 1945 assistants received in the neighborhood of a third to a half the salary of a professor.[6] In prewar days a professor might have a servant, a rare item in the household of his American colleague. On the other hand, he lived in very cramped or crowded quarters unless he had a good connection with the Party. Clothing, to judge from the accounts of refugees, presented quite a problem, in the sense that it did not come up to what academicians felt was appropriate for their status. A new suit, obtained with great difficulty, could cause quite a sensation in the lecture hall.[7] From the professor downward, the standard of living drops until that of a rural teacher is scarcely distinguishable from the situation of the peasants around him.

Even if much better factual information were available on differences in income and standard of living, we would still be in the dark about their importance in tying various groups of intellectuals to the regime. Extended acquaintance with a few former Soviet scientists and other Soviet intellectuals, along with a considerable body of interview material, has given me the strong impression that, although many Soviet intellectuals resent material privation and take on extra jobs to diminish it, they do not work primarily for material rewards, any more than do American scientists and artists.

Soviet intellectuals hold their relatively privileged position on the condition of outward political conformity. The higher one's position, it appears, the more important this condition becomes, while at lower levels it can be discharged through routine rituals. Though there are occasional signs in the Soviet press that the government is trying to make more room for younger scientists through cutting down on multiple job-holding by their elders, there is no clear indication of an "over-production" of intellectuals with its associated lack of opportunity. To the extent that pressures for change from below can be effective in the Soviet system, they do not seem likely to come from this source. One point, however, does stand out reasonably clearly. The system of differential rewards is inadequate, from the government's standpoint, to attract youthful talent where it is needed. Since 1933 the government has required all graduates of higher educational institutions and those of technical schools * to accept jobs for a three year period in whatever part of the country they were sent.[8]

Direct administrative control of intellectual life is exercised through three channels, in a manner almost identical to that over the factory, the collective farm, or the military forces. As might be expected on the basis of their philosophical premises, the Soviets make no attempt to conceal the dominance of the Communist Party and political criteria of behavior in the life and work of the intellectual. From the viewpoint of a convinced Communist this dominance is normal, necessary, and desirable. Disturbance and uneasiness find expression, therefore, only when Party control seems to be not strong enough. It would be a serious mistake to view this political control solely as a stream of detailed directives concerning what to think as each problem arises for the artist and scientist. Such directives may well exist to some

---

* The Soviet technical school (*tekhnikum*) ordinarily takes students at the age of fourteen. After a three to four year course they may go on to a university.

extent behind the scenes, emerging into public view only in moments of crisis. But there is clear proof that they do not constitute the major technique of control in the numerous instances where prominent intellectuals, even those near the center of power, publicly commit themselves to viewpoints that are shortly afterwards condemned as serious doctrinal errors. If the control system provided more continuous and detailed supervision than is actually the case, it would make some aspects of life easier for the intellectual by furnishing clear and unambiguous signposts and eliminating some sources of apparent capriciousness.

But for creative intellectual work, even if the word creative is defined generously enough to include a substantial portion of hacks, completely detailed supervision is impossible without acquiring all of the intellectual's skills and knowledge. Therefore the Party, for the most part, restricts itself to defining the political goals of intellectual activity and the limits within which variation and autonomy may exist. These limits differ greatly from one field of intellectual endeavor to another. Cramped and narrow though they often seem to a Westerner, they still contain enough ambiguity to permit frequent "errors." Furthermore, these limits have a way of contracting suddenly, in a manner often unpredictable by the intellectual immersed in his specialty or committed publicly, and often irretrievably, to a given position.

Administrative controls impose narrower limits of permissible variation on the artist than they do upon the natural scientist. Yet there is a mild paradox in the fact that the arts are less thoroughly incorporated into a series of bureaucratic controls than is science. So far there is no such thing as a Five Year Plan for the arts, which exists, on paper at least, for science. Numerically speaking, to be sure, the larger proportion of artists, namely those who work through some medium of mass communication such as the movies, the radio, and the newspaper, find their place in a bureaucratic organization. The same situation prevails in the West, with the important distinction that here there are a number of competing bureaucratic systems with widely differing viewpoints and assumptions. But the position of what we may somewhat unfairly call the creative Soviet artist, in contrast to his brother at work in some area of mass communications, recalls in some respects the free professions in earlier capitalist society. Often Soviet artists and writers do not have a regular employer, in the sense of an organization for whom they must perform stated tasks during specified hours. Instead they work on their own, frequently at home. They bear the responsibility for choosing their subject matter and the techniques with which to treat it, though they usually receive very broad hints on these points through Party channels and know that their product will never find an outlet unless they conform. There are also situations that contain elements of both self-employment in a free profession and employment by a bureaucratic organization. Important newspaper correspondents, for example, are paid a general retaining fee no matter what they write, and special fees for individual articles. They do not receive assignments or "deadlines" for writing up specific incidents. Their work is one of producing essays on themes of their own choosing, according to accounts of former Soviet newspapermen.[9] An artist may also accept a temporary or fairly extended commission from the government, with some latitude as to the way it will be executed. Soviet controls over the arts, effective though they are, to judge by the uniformity of the product, appear somewhat loose and sporadic, when contrasted with those in science.

A significant role in the control over the arts is played by the personal tastes and whims of the Soviet rulers. Under Stalin this "court influence" became more important than under Lenin, partly because Lenin was busy with the attempt to establish control in more crucial areas. Both Lenin and Stalin displayed the tastes of a moderately well-educated and conventional individual, very much opposed to those of the sophisticated Bohemian intellectual. Nevertheless, and although Lenin occasionally objected to the café intellectual and bitterly resented his lack of discipline, until the late twenties experimental Bohemianism formed an important part of Soviet literary and artistic activity. As a revolutionary group, the Bolsheviks brought to power with them a few intellectuals opposed to traditional currents. Under Lenin these were allowed to continue. In the early thirties they were pushed aside or compelled to mend their ways, when a series of new organizations was set up to extend official influence into the arts. Stalin, perhaps for political reasons, made much more use of pomp and circumstance than did Lenin. His tastes ran to a mixture of the monumental and the genre. In this respect they happened to be quite suited to the consolidation, as opposed to the initial phases, of the dictatorship. Above and beyond this, his personal idiosyncracies, particularly in regard to music, made themselves felt in official policy. His dislike of jazz, for example, came close to eliminating this musical form in the USSR.[10]

At the center of the formal control system over intellectual life in general is the Party's famous Department of Propaganda and Agitation (*Agitprop*), one of the subdivisions of the Central Committee's secretariat.[11] Corresponding organizations exist at each level of the Party's territorial units, down to the city and district committees. At the local level, as well as nationally, Agitprop bears responsibility for all public opinion media, from movie films to the publishing of textbooks. Although it has been most active in its attempt to secure mass support for the Party line in the general cultural fields, it has a special Science Section concerned with the indoctrination and utilization of scientific personnel.[12] On the whole, most of Agitprop's effort is positive, in that it tries to make certain that the "right" ideas reach the Soviet public. On occasion, however, it must also perform negative tasks as well. For example, the Agitprop of the Turkmenistan's Party Central Committee recently received a verbal lashing in *Pravda* for its failure to take timely measures in preventing the appearance of a history book published by the Turkmenistan Academy of Sciences.[13] When ideological problems, however, take on the aspect of broader policy questions involving administrative and personnel decisions, such matters are likely to be removed from Agitprop's hands and decided by some other administrative section of the Party.

In addition to the day-to-day control exercised by the extensive Agitprop apparatus of the Party, there is also a characteristic parallel organ in the government itself. For supervision over literature and the arts, a Committee on the Arts was established on January 17, 1936,[14] some four years after the Party had carried out a thorough overhauling of literary and artistic organizations. Attached to the Council of Ministers, of which its chairman was a member, the committee had local representatives, down to the level of the larger cities, on the executive committees of the local soviets.[15] Its decisions, issued in the form of orders by its chairman, were obligatory for all government and public organizations in the USSR that were active in the theater, music, and representational arts.[16] During the thirties, and probably still today, its most important power has resided in its right to appoint personnel to various posts in the capital and throughout the Soviet Union. "With a single stroke of the pen," writes a former prominent musician, "[the head of its personnel section] could appoint or dismiss any theater director, symphony conductor, or conservatory professor." [17] In spite of the fact that the chairman of the committee was a member of the Council of Ministers, this control organ was under frequent fire in the postwar Soviet press for such varied reasons as inadequate attention to dramatic repertoires [18] and failure to keep pianos in proper repair.[19] Since March 15, 1953, as part of the administrative changes following Stalin's death, the committee has been merged with the Ministry of Education, Ministry of Labor Reserves, and other agencies into a single unit, the Ministry of Culture.[20] Although a number of important changes may have occurred that were not publicly announced at the time of the merger, it is very likely that the major functions of the committee continue to be performed by some subdivision of the new ministry.

In addition to Agitprop and the Ministry of Culture's control organ, which represent direct political control, there is also a series of quasi-autonomous organizations, nominally operated by and for artists, but thoroughly permeated by the Party. The most important of these are the Union of Soviet Writers, the Union of Soviet Composers, and the Union of Soviet Artists. These unions were established by a Party decree of April 23, 1932, as part of a thorough reorganization and coördination of intellectual life. They are the successors to a variety of literary and artistic organizations, reflecting Bohemian-proletarian and other currents of opinion, that the Party summarily disbanded at that time. In 1940, one of them, the Union of Soviet Writers, had more than 3,000 members, of which nearly half belonged to non-Russian nationalities.[21]

Less influential is the Academy of the Arts, founded in 1757 in St. Petersburg. It supposedly contains the leaders in painting, sculpture, the graphic arts, as well as the leading art historians and critics.[22] In addition to organizing major exhibitions, its work is evidently concentrated on teaching. This function has recently undergone considerable overhauling, with numerous staff changes, in order to increase the influence of Marxist-Leninist doctrine and the official canons of taste.[23]

By these means the Party has absorbed the organized centers of literary and artistic life. Within these centers it tries with varying success to make its influence felt through the individuals who are members. Ordinarily they form a unit subordinate to some higher echelon in the Party. Thus the Party Committee of the Union of Soviet Writers reports to the Moscow City Party Committee, which recently instructed it to intensify its supervision of Party units in a series of publications and in the Soviet Writers' Publishing House.[24] In their efforts to promote Party interests and insure the dominance of political considerations where they conflict with strictly artistic ones, Party units run into frequent difficulties. For one thing, the Party unit may be composed of relatively minor individuals, sometimes not even artists at all. In other cases, where the Party has succeeded in attracting talented writers and artists, the situation still produces problems that have their analogues elsewhere in Soviet society. In theory the Party unit is supposed to provide comradely advice, encouragement, and criticism—that is, to act the role of the elder brother. As in family life, however, it is difficult to combine brotherly relationships with fully candid criticism. This unstable combination tends to develop in either of two directions. One of them is toward formal, impersonal, administrative relationships, stigmatized by the Party as "bureaucratic." The opposite direction is toward an "unprincipled" clique of mutual admirers, praising and promoting each other's work. Both occur frequently and form a major topic of denunciation in the Soviet press.[25]

Through such devices the Party does its best to influence the working atmosphere and conditions under which art and literature is produced. On what may be called the "consumption" side, the Party also exercises direct and indirect influence over the artist's relationship with the various segments of the public and over his sources of economic support. Here the artist faces a delicate problem, in that he must please two masters, whose tastes can nullify one another. Political acceptibility is no guarantee of public success. Yet failure to achieve at least some measure of public success is likely to lead to reproach from the political authorities. It is also an economic sanction in its own right. Many artists live from the sale of their works.

The situation is further complicated by the fact that in itself Party influence over the production of art and literature does not in the least guarantee that any given work will be even politically acceptable by the time it makes its appearance before the general public. It is by no means uncommon for a literary work, to choose one example, to pass through the gamut of publishing and other controls, only to receive scathing criticism in the press. From the artist's point of view, this possibility constitutes one of the most capricious and unpredictable aspects of the system. Such a blast of Party-inspired criticism can wither a promising career, or break one in mid-passage. In the days of the great purges criticism might be a prelude to imprisonment. Today this does not appear to be the case, and recovery is by no means out of the question. Nevertheless, a negative reaction by the Party is likely to close off temporarily the offender's access to the public. From politically tainted sources publishers refuse manuscripts, producers refuse plays, orchestras refuse scores. By its control over the outlets the Party largely eliminates any possibility for the artist to establish a basis for independence through his relationships with the public. At the same time there are limits to the Party's freedom of action, since it cannot foist on the public unadulterated political exhortation without some touches of artistic sugaring and without some appeal to sentiments that have their origin outside politics.

The world of Soviet science differs from that of the arts in that the process of bureaucratization and the elimination of the remnants of the free professions has reached a more advanced stage. The individual scientist working on his own no longer exists in the Soviet Union. Instead, scientific activity is organized under three types of institutions, along roughly functional lines of pure research, applied science, and higher education. In recent years the boundaries between these areas have become blurred, as increasingly heavy emphasis has been placed on the applied aspects of all scientific research.

The academies of science stress theoretical investigations and come as close to the pursuit of pure science as is possible under Soviet conditions. The Academy of Sciences of the USSR, founded under the inspiration of Peter the Great's Westernizing policy, is the core of most of the academies.[26] There are also certain academies devoted to special fields of knowledge, such as the Academy of Medical Sciences and the Academy of Pedagogical Sciences, which do not form part of the Academy of Sciences of the USSR but come under the jurisdiction of a particular ministry or of the Council of Ministers. Contrasted with the academies are the research and technical institutes of the various ministries, such as the Central Aero-Hydrodynamic Institute, and similar organizations. Their task is primarily one of applied science and technology. The research activities of institutions of higher learning occupy a position half way between the academies and the technical institutes, and may take primarily either a theoretical or a practical turn. Higher education is in turn under the administrative supervision of the newly established Ministry of Culture.

These three types of institutions, the academies, technical institutes attached to a ministry, and higher educational organizations, together with the ministerial agencies in which each of the three types is embedded, constitute the technical line of control for science. Within this line the scientist can exercise a very considerable influence. As elsewhere in Soviet society, however, the technical line is subordinate to the political one, represented in its positive and negative aspects by the Party and the secret police. It is likewise characteristic that the boundaries between these three aspects of the control system are far from distinct. Perhaps the best way to capture the atmosphere and situation within which Soviet science works is to begin with the scientists' own organizations, or the technical line of control, and note the extent to which various kinds of political pressures impinge on it, both at the higher levels and at the level of the working scientist or the laboratory itself.

The regime's control over the Academy of Sciences of the USSR was established only gradually, and by means that deserve further investigation. Not until the early thirties was it even formally required to give lip service to the methods and viewpoints of dialectical materialism in its scientific investigations.

In 1935 it adopted a new statute that defined as one of its major functions the rendering of expert scientific advice "to the highest ruling organs of the USSR." [27] Now the Academy is directly responsible to the government of the USSR. Its expenses form part of the government's budget,[28] and it constitutes a fair sized agency in terms of staff and expenditures. In 1941 the Academy's staff included slightly less than eleven thousand persons, with a budget of more than 96 million rubles.[29] While S. I. Vavilov, the Academy's president from 1945 until his death in 1951, managed to stay out of the Party, the present president, A. N. Nesmeyanov, joined the Party in 1944 shortly after winning a Stalin prize in chemistry.[30]

The presidium of the Academy constitutes its powerful administrative nucleus, and within the presidium its chief learned secretary, A. V. Topchiev, seems to be a key figure. Formally, the assembly of all honorary and active members elects the presidium, sets the basic line of scientific work for the Academy and its subordinate institutions, and decides the more important organizational questions. The size of the Academy's regular membership, 146 in 1949, is enough to indicate that it cannot play an active and continuous role in administration, a task delegated to the presidium.[31] In scientific fields where the Party has expressed a definite point of view, the presidium has the task of attempting to put these views into effect by reorganizations and changes of personnel. Thus it ordered the liquidation of the Pacific Institute in 1950 and the transfer of its personnel to the Institute of Oriental Studies, which was ordered to move from Leningrad to Moscow. New section heads and a new director were appointed. The latter official was required to submit his research plans for 1951 to the Bureau of the Department of History and Philosophy to make sure that contemporary problems received adequate attention.[32] Similar upheavals have taken place in linguistics and physiology.[33]

After the war the regime made a concerted effort to tie the Academy's activities more closely to its arrangements for planning in science. Since the notion of planning in science, particularly in research directed toward the discovery of unknown facts and principles, seems to many a contradiction in terms, it is appropriate to pause for a moment to consider the question in general terms. Basically, the Soviet plan appears to be a far from completely successful device through which the government tries to keep the scientist at work on questions that for its own reasons it regards as significant and to prevent him from pursuing ideas and problems that are of interest to him as an individual scientist. Thus planned research is the logical outcome of the emphasis, especially strong in the USSR, on practical results. Parallel problems exist in American science, where there is also, in certain instances, a strong demand for concrete results. In 1946 S. I. Vavilov gave the Soviet rationale behind scientific planning. Scientific investigation, he said, resembles a journey through mountainous country, in which from time to time the traveler reaches a peak from which he can view the road ahead for a long distance, and plan his journey accordingly. Such peaks, Vavilov continued, are the great scientific discoveries, such as Darwin's theory of natural selection, or Mendeleev's periodic law in chemistry, or Pavlov's theory of conditioned reflexes, which set the path of future research for a considerable period of time. In purely technical matters, he added, the possibility of planning is even more apparent and reasonable. An airplane designer knows, for example, in what ways the speed of an airplane may be increased, and approximately how much this speed may be expected to increase from year to year.[34] In his assertion that certain theoretical viewpoints tend to dominate scientific investigation for considerable periods of time Vavilov is of course correct. But if for any reason such views dominate scientific thinking completely, and no possibility exists for exploring the implications of either alternative views of variations on the accepted doctrines, scientific advance would by definition come to a halt. In several fields the regime has tried to impose very strict limits on exactly this kind of exploration. Such attempts, however, are carried on outside the administrative machinery for scientific planning and will therefore be discussed separately.

Formerly the Academy of Sciences of the USSR worked out each year a plan of research in consultation with its own subdivisions, other scientific institutions, and various government agencies.[35] To a great extent this plan appears to have been based on requests by the highest government authorities to investigate certain matters, combined with suggestions made from below concerning problems in which particular scientists and laboratories were interested. For example, in an institute under the direction of the Academy, described by one refugee, the various academicians made proposals that had to be approved by the director of the institute, the Academy administration as a whole, and finally by the Central Committee of the Communist Party. On occasion these research proposals had to be radically modified in the light of instructions from above.[36]

In 1950 the government introduced a series of measures aimed at a closer direction and coördination of research. For the first time the Academy's research plan was to be confirmed by the government. The next year, Topchiev, presidium secretary, announced somewhat ominously to the annual meeting that such confirmation made the Academy's work an integral part of the state plan, and therefore bound the members to fulfill it undeviatingly as a state law. He also declared that to insure compliance there would be a check-up on the work and the personnel in the Academy's establishments. Other measures were promised to make certain that directives issued by the presidium were actually carried out, while a further veiled threat was contained in the promise of "discussions" at future sessions of the presidium. Such "discussions," as in the Lysenko affair, constitute a major device for the imposition of the Party viewpoint on matters of fact and theory in science.[37]

Somewhat before this, perhaps at the suggestion of high Party officials, the Academy drew up for the first time a plan for feeding its completed research into the production processes of the economy. This plan called for the introduction of 335 such research projects during 1950.[38] Since then this aspect of the Academy's work has received increasingly heavy emphasis. The 1953 plan anticipated four times as much applied research as that for 1951.[39] Possibly some work that is actually pure research has simply been reclassified under some applied category. Yet the evidence strongly suggests that the Academy of Sciences may be well on the way to becoming little more than a center for the coördination of applied research on problems selected by the Central Committee of the Communist Party.

For the Soviet Union as a whole an important part of the liaison with industry and its requirements appears to be maintained quite largely, if not always effectively, through the Academy's division of technical sciences. In turn this division is in touch with the ministries in charge of industrial production.[40] At the local level individual plants may make arrangements with institutes carrying on the kinds of research in which they are interested. By the end of 1950 it was claimed that nearly all the Academy's institutes had socialist contracts on mutual aid with particular plants.[41]

There is an important difference between issuing a set of decrees and getting them obeyed, between praising the coöperation between science and industry in general terms and finding arrangements that will make both the controls and the coöperation effective. Clearly the Soviet leaders remain very dissatisfied with the results they have thus far achieved. Toward the end of 1952 the Academy's president complained that the "planning and coördination of scientific work in our numerous scientific establishments, including the Academy of Sciences of the USSR, still remains in a bad condition." [42] Shortly afterward, *Pravda* in its editorial columns castigated the Academy's division of technical sciences for failure to make sure that research kept in touch with practical needs. Other units, including the division of physico-mathematical sciences, were subjected to similar criticism, in some cases on quite detailed matters.[43] At the 1952 Party Congress a delegate from Leningrad, Moscow's rival as the chief center of scientific activity in the USSR, observed sarcastically that the hand of the Gosplan could not be felt in his city's scientific research establishments.[44] Although allowance must be made for extremes in Soviet criticism as much as in Soviet boasting, this evidence suggests that planning in science is very far from complete or effective, and that the Soviet scientist still retains a substantial degree of autonomy in selecting and following up his own research interests.

Considerable evidence points to the conclusion that formal controls and informal pressures within the system of higher education have more of an influence than planning on the substance of Soviet science. This influence is one exerted on the career prospects of the Soviet scientists, and particularly his choice of subject matter and research topic.

As elsewhere on the European continent, the Soviet system of higher education is highly centralized. This has come about gradually and by steps that need not concern us here.[45] Most institutions of higher learning are either directly or indirectly under the administrative supervision of the Ministry of Culture that absorbed the Ministry of Education during the large reorganization that followed almost immediately upon Stalin's death. Since 1944, at which time there was only an All-Union Committee on the Affairs of Higher Education, the central administrative apparatus has included the ubiquitous *spetsotdel*, or secret police unit. Very likely there was one much earlier. It is interesting to observe, however, that Soviet published sources in 1945 listed the spetsotdel as a unit coördinate with such major subdivisions in the ministry as the administrative sections in charge of universities and of military higher educational institutions.[46]

The ministry is responsible for confirming appointments to the research and teaching staffs, and as we shall see shortly, confirmation has at times been refused on political grounds. Otherwise, scientists and other scholars choose their own colleagues in a manner not very different from that which prevails widely in Western countries.* For department heads and some lower positions, when a vacancy occurs, it is announced as open to

---

* The Soviet university, like others in Europe, is much closer to a graduate school than its American counterpart. It is divided into a series of chairs (*kafedry*), or departments, of law, medicine, chemistry, etc., to which the student is expected to devote his full time.

"competition" in the scholarly, and perhaps also the local, press. The director of the institution appoints a committee to examine the materials submitted by each candidate, which include his or her major scientific works. The committee is ordinarily made up of two or three professors under the chairmanship of the director's assistant, a post roughly corresponding to that of provost in some American universities. The committee's recommendation is then acted upon by a majority vote of the institution's council, composed of the administrative officers, senior faculty members, and a few other individuals, serving as Party, Komsomol, and trade-union representatives.[47]

As we turn now to the beginning stages of the scientist's training, to examine the situation confronting students in their career and research choices, the point most likely to strike an American reader is the weakness of any notion of either equality of opportunity or equality of sacrifice as the basis of government policy. Though these ideals still receive a certain amount of lip service, they have had to be thrust into the background under the relentless pressure of circumstances and the extreme shortage of valuable skills. At a number of points in its history the regime has taken steps toward the creation of a privileged group out of those who chose scientific careers. One was the abandonment in 1931 of preference for the children of workers and peasants in admission to higher educational institutions. Another was the introduction of tuition fees in these schools in 1940. The same trend is reflected in the government's decree, issued at the height of the war on September 1, 1943, which deferred from military service all students in a specified list of higher educational institutions, as well as those in technical schools.[48]

Some measure of centralized control over the budding scientist's choice of research topic is imposed through the Academy of Sciences and the Ministry of Education. On December 11, 1948, a *Pravda* editorial declared that a list of appropriate research topics ought to be presented to students who were to write dissertations. The Academy of Sciences, the Ministry of Education, and the scientific establishments ought to work out such a list together, the editorial suggested in rather strong language. Previously an arrangement had been in effect, set up on November 4, 1947, through which some individuals were assigned by research agencies within a ministry to do work toward a doctorate with the Academy of Sciences. This appears, however, to have been a relatively minor operation, and one sabotaged by the ministries, which used it as a channel for unloading their less talented research personnel.[49] By 1950 a system was at least formally in effect for "planning the dissertation themes of graduate students (*aspiranty*) and candidates for the doctor's degree" in some areas under the jurisdiction of the Academy of Sciences of the USSR. In these cases the Ministry of Education did present a list of recommended dissertation themes, and dissertations were regarded as planned scientific undertakings of certain institutions within the jurisdiction of the Academy.[50] It appears, however, that these arrangements were largely confined to the social sciences. Even in this field there is evidence, in the form of letters to the newspapers, to indicate that the system of assigning dissertation topics has failed to take hold.[51] So far the system of centralized allocation of research topics can be written off as a failure.

Much more effective appears to be the government's power to decide which kinds of research will be rewarded upon completion and which kinds will in effect be penalized. The immediate point of impact is upon the career expectations of advanced students, as well as upon mature scientists who want to move up the ladder of rank and prestige. Since some calculation of these factors must be made on a realistic basis by even the most idealistically motivated scientists, the force of these controls extends backward to an early stage in the scientist's career when he is at the point of choosing which field to study. Only by the time that he has reached the closing period of his graduate studies, however, will he know whether or not he has placed his chips wisely.

In this area of overt and formal controls over the advanced student the Supreme Certifying Commission, part of the former Ministry of Education and presumably still active under the Ministry of Culture, exercises important functions. The approval of this commission marks the final stage in awarding the degree of Doctor of Science, a much more advanced title than our Ph.D., as well as the titles of Professor, Docent, and Senior Scientific Worker. The number of those who fall by the wayside for either strictly technical or purely political reasons is relatively small. In itself this small number is probably an indication of the effectiveness of the formal and informal system of prior selection. Nevertheless the political, as well as the technical, aspects are heavily stressed at the time of this rite of passage.

In 1948 there were 557 persons who defended dissertations for the degree of Doctor of Science, and 4,000 for the degree of Candidate of Science. The Commission refused to confer the doctorate on seventy persons, and overruled seventy-eight decisions of academic boards of institutions conferring the candidate's degree.[52] In 1951 the Commission's secretary reported that during the previous three years it had refused 10.7 per cent of the doctorates.[53] No indication is available of how many of these refusals are based upon strictly political grounds. But the reports, which receive wide publicity in the central newspapers, usually select several cases of refusal on political grounds to serve as examples for Soviet scientific youth. Thus in 1948 the Commission refused to confer the title of Professor upon a Doctor of physico-mathematical sciences, V. L. Ginzburg, because he had, even in his popular works, circumvented the achievements of Soviet science and displayed obvious servility toward foreign achievements. The 1951 report stressed the case of an engineer who was refused his doctorate because of a display of "bourgeois objectivism" in the analysis of certain American industrial techniques.[54]

There is evidence that students in calculating their chances for a career tend to choose for their dissertations either a subject in which the Party has laid down a clear and definite line, or else one about which the Party has expressed little or no opinion. They tend, in other words, to congregate at the poles of the control system, and to avoid topics in which the line to be taken has not yet crystallized. Thus students avoided writing dissertations on genetics before the Party finally proclaimed Lysenko's views to be the correct ones for Soviet science, a decision that was not reached until after a series of minor forays by the Party into this area. Three years before the Lysenko decision a high Soviet official complained that dissertations in the field were becoming so rare as to be almost unique events.[55] But in history and philosophy, about which the Party made a series of pronouncements after the war, there was a sixfold rise in the number of dissertations, while the total increase in all fields during this period amounted to only 34.4 per cent.[56] No corresponding figures are known to have been published for students in those natural sciences where controls are as yet relatively weak. But a clue to the general distribution of interests is provided by some recent elections to the Academy of Sciences of the USSR. Twenty-nine fields of knowledge were represented in 1950, with a total of 362 candidates for the position of member and corresponding member. Of the 362 there were 87 candidates in the physical and mathematical sciences, 101 for the division of technical sciences, and 76 for the division of chemical sciences.[57] Thus these three fields of knowledge account for more than two-thirds of those regarded as the most eminent Soviet scientists.

In this connection it is worth drawing attention to the fact that the Soviets, even at this late date, depend rather heavily upon their pre-Revolutionary intellectual capital, at least for general guidance and administrative work, a major task among Academicians. Only somewhat more than half of the "new generation" of Academicians received their scientific training after the Bolshevik Revolution.[58]

Within the university, technical institute, or research laboratory, where the actual scientific work is done, one finds the same set of triple controls and the corresponding cast of characters that are found in the factory or collective farm. The centers of administrative power are the Party secretary, the director (rector in a large university), and the head of the *spetsotdel*. A fourth, but usually inconsequential nucleus of power, is the trade-union organization.[59]

The Party members within a scientific organization are responsible to the district or city committee of the Party, in the same manner as a corresponding Party organization in a factory or a collective farm. Administrative posts are as far as possible confined to Party members. There is now in all probability much less of a problem in finding Party members with adequate professional competence for these posts than there was in the early thirties, since the Party has since absorbed much of the intellectual elite. Nevertheless, one gets the impression, at least from refugees whose experience antedates the war, that a person with strong scientific interests will try to avoid membership in the Party and contact with the more active Party members. The dedicated Soviet scientist seems to share with his Western colleagues an impatience with administrative matters, some inability to understand the need for them, and a mixture of repugnance and contempt in his opinion of people who engage in them. To this natural and perhaps inevitable antagonism there is added, in the Soviet case, a much greater element of fear. The administration, including both the Party and the secret police organization, is often lumped together as an amorphous "they," to be avoided as much as possible. On the other hand, friendly contacts may often exist with people who are scientists first and Party members second.

Before the war Party members were as a rule a small minority in most universities and research establishments. With the enormous increase in the size of the Party this situation has undoubtedly changed to a considerable extent. In one borough of the city of Moscow, where there were many research institutes and higher educational institutions with over 4,000 students and teachers in active scientific work, nearly one-third, or 1,250 were Party members in 1949.[60] Since the concentration of Party membership is extremely heavy in the city of Moscow, this is the highest ratio one would be likely to find. In the provinces it probably drops precipitously. There Party members are probably still for the most part confined to administrative positions or to the teaching of subjects whose political content is regarded by the Party as crucial, such as the obligatory course on Marxism-Leninism.

Since the Soviets place a very high value on certain kinds of scientific research and technical training, local Party units do not ordinarily interfere in routine matters. In fields where the Party has not issued a pronouncement, the scientist can set his own standards governing the appraisal of evidence and reasoning in research, and corresponding standards for the qualifications of his students. By the late thirties it became possible for a teacher to fail a Komsomol or Party member who was clearly incompetent, though the teacher might have an anxious moment in the process. As long as no pressure is exerted from the outside by some higher echelon in the Party, the tendency of the Party organization in a scientific organization is to let well enough alone. The same is ordinarily true of its immediate superior, the local Party committee. The propagation of Marxism-Leninism-Stalinism tends to be reduced to a formality, accepted as a boring necessity by all concerned. In this fashion the Party reaches a compromise with the requirements of scientific activity, similar to the compromises reached in the factory or the collective farm.

There are two main types of situations in which the local Party organization may be expected to intervene. One of these results from the promulgation of a new doctrine on scientific matters by the top Party authorities, as in the case of genetics or linguistics. Then the district committee of the Party and the Party organization in the university or research establishment may play an important role in the reshuffling of personnel. If highly trained scientists are scarce, however, there may be a considerable time lag before the local Party unit intervenes. Intervention also occurs when something "goes wrong," in the looser sense of unsatisfactory conditions or political mistakes which have come to the attention of higher echelons in the Party. Often the Party decides to deal with such situations through criticism in the press. Such criticism unconsciously reveals both the expected and the actual relationships between scientific workers and the Party. Thus *Pravda* criticized the Communist organization in the Lvov branch of the Ukrainian Academy of Sciences, as well as the city and district committees of the Party, for inattention to political indoctrination, remarking that these committees "should constantly follow the work of the Lvov institutions of the Ukraine Academy of Sciences." [61]

The Party organization and the Komsomol also play an important part in the daily life of the students through a special form of group organization. In their structure and relationship to the teaching staff these student groups reflect two contrasting forces. One is the characteristic totalitarian need to atomize and fragment all social units for the sake of political control. The other is the need to find methods of encouraging students to conform to the requirement of disciplined application to their studies and avoid spending too much time on extra-curricular political ceremonial. By and large, the latter tendency has won out.

Entering students are divided into groups of twenty to twenty-five persons. Each group has a chief, known as the *starosta,* appointed by the director.[62] The starosta is directly responsible to the dean of the faculty. According to a refugee source, the director, along with the secretaries of the Party and Komsomol organizations, and the secret police officer, work together in setting up these groups, paying close attention to their composition. The main task of the starosta is to keep track of the members' adherence to routine academic discipline. He must report to the dean any absence from lectures or laboratory sessions on a daily basis, along with the reason for the student's absence. Failure to keep up with academic studies and political mistakes both lead to a "working over" of the student by the Party or the Komsomol organizations.[63] The Party's emphasis on the primacy of academic work is further underlined in decrees of December 13, 1948, and August 4, 1950, which criticized the Komsomol for overloading school children with outside political activities "contrary to elementary educational requirements." [64] Though the decrees refer to Komsomol units in the schools and not in institutions for higher education, where such measures may not have been necessary, they reflect the views of the highest Party authorities on this question.

The secret police representative, the head of the *spetsotdel*, has, as a rule, a more negative role than the Party. His intervention is largely limited to matters where political disloyalty is suspected. He can more readily veto an appointment or prevent some administrative action than he can initiate policy. With a broad and often elastic definition of political loyalty, this role can nevertheless be crucial. During the great purges in the thirties the head of the spetsotdel is said to have been one of the most important figures in a scientific organization. He has his network of agents that report to him on the activities and attitudes of all persons connected with a scientific institution.[65] The extent to which this situation results in an atmosphere of mutual suspicion varies a great deal in both time and place, as is indicated by the varying comments of former Soviet scholars and scientists. But it is clear that both pride and pleasure in one's work frequently survive under conditions that appear paralyzing to one who has not experienced them directly.

The description that has been given up to this point applies with rather minor modifications to all fields in the natural sciences. It is important to recognize that within this general situation there are wide differences from one field to another. In science the impact of totalitarian controls is still very uneven. There is, so to speak, a fluctuating and ill-defined boundary, a sort of no man's land, between the area of politically determined truth and the area of scientifically determined truth. Since the war there has been a very noticeable tendency for the political area to expand. The discussion of genetics in the summer of 1948 is the incident in this expansion that has attracted the most attention in the West. This discussion was only one part of a much larger movement. Philosophy, biology, linguistics, physiology, cosmogony (the theory of the origin of the earth and the universe), and chemistry have to varying degrees felt the impact of such discussions. Others have been promised for mathematics and physics, where certain preliminary flurries have already taken place.[66] Since less is generally known in the West about Soviet developments in physics, chemistry, and mathematics, the treatment here may be confined to these fields in the form of very brief case studies.[67]

First, however, a word is necessary about the general pattern of a Soviet "scientific discussion." So far as can be inferred, what very often happens is roughly the following. The Party, probably through one or more of its own intellectuals, finds an opening for intervention either at some point where a genuine intellectual issue exists among scientists, or where an individual is anxious to climb into favor over the mangled reputations of others, or a combination of the two. Needless to say, such openings are probably fairly frequent, as they would be in any society in which science is actively pursued. There ensues a struggle for the ear of the Party by competing intellectual factions. A large-scale public discussion is ordinarily, but not always, the final stage of this competition, at which the Party publicizes the view that it believes ought to be the controlling one, at least until the next time the Party line changes. Not every discussion, however, ends in complete silencing of the losing faction, perhaps partly because the losers may still be able to maintain connections with powerful Party circles. Another possible reason may be that the Party may wish to maintain a certain level of factional dispute in order to keep the possibilities of an opening for further intervention. The possibility of a united scientific front against the Party must always be guarded against. The net effect of the situation is to throw the determination of truth into the hands of political officialdom, rather than into the hands of scientists joined with educated laymen, who, in the democratic state, determine the "consensus of professional opinion."

In physics, chemistry, and mathematics, there is, I think, a genuine intellectual issue. Soviet scientists and philosophers are not the only ones to express a certain uneasiness about theoretical developments in these fields, particularly in respect to quantum theory and the theory of relativity. Scientific theory, it is felt in both Soviet and some Western non-Marxist circles, seems somehow or other to be getting away from its firm base in the natural world, to be becoming a matter of mathematical equations and formal, logical manipulations. The possibility of direct knowledge of a universe existing outside of ourselves seems to be disappearing more and more the further science advances. Instead, the human mind looks as though it were becoming a law unto itself. Perhaps most Western scientists are unconcerned with this problem or would deny that it exists. The Soviets, on the other hand, partly on account of the Marxist heritage, seem to be acutely sensitive and suspicious of this drift of opinion.

One of the first postwar attempts on the part of a Soviet scientist to grapple with this issue was an essay by a physicist and philosopher, M. A. Markov, who endeavored to reconcile the implications of quantum theory with the materialist view of the world.[68] S. I. Vavilov, then president of the Academy of Sciences of the USSR, and a distinguished physicist whose achievements are widely recognized in the West, wrote a brief introductory note, expressing the hope, vain as later events proved, that Markov's article might prove the starting point for a serious discussion that would not result in the "pasting on of stigmatizing labels." [69]

Not all of Markov's complex argument need be reproduced here. Two aspects of his treatment, however, deserve attention. One is the note of freshness and courage, with which the article opens, and which may have contributed to his being silenced later. Soviet philosophers, he charged, have dodged the issues posed by quantum theory, asserting that the theory is too new, and that unclear aspects will disappear as the theory develops. Thus, Markov remarked sarcastically, all the difficulties are put upon our descendants. Meanwhile the theory has already existed for a quarter of a century and is based in a brilliant manner on experiment. On this account, Markov maintained, it would be a great disaster to overlook the materialist content of the theory simply because it is covered with some accidental idealist decorations.

The second point, that Markov apparently failed in his task, is one that I make with considerable diffidence as a layman in these questions. Quantum theory, Markov says, merely tells us that the electron upon which we perform an experiment to get one kind of knowledge—say, its velocity—cannot be the same electron as the one upon which we perform a necessarily different experiment to obtain a different kind of knowledge—for instance, its location. He therefore argues: "In the first case, as in the second one, realities exist objectively, independently of the knowledge of the physicist himself." [70] Hence, Markov concludes, no new philosophical or epistemological problems arise. Dialectical materialism, which holds that the observer is part of nature itself, remains triumphant. It appears, however, that Markov has merely pushed the point of inevitable ignorance from the place where Heisenberg left it to another realm of the intellect.[71] He is in the peculiar position of being compelled to posit the inevitable existence of something about which he admits that we human beings must remain inevitably ignorant. This is also the position, it may be noted, that Sir Herbert L. Samuel, British Liberal Party leader and a philosopher by avocation, arrives at in an attempt to save materialism by another and completely non-Marxist route. Sir Herbert is compelled to posit the existence of a two-stage ether. About one of these stages we can never know.[72] Markov tells us essentially the same thing: that as human beings our knowledge is limited to certain forms and types. Dialectical materialism in Markov's argument seems little more than the expression of a pious hope that some day matters may be otherwise. In this sense it is merely an accidental decoration on Markov's scheme.

Markov's opponents were quick to sense his failure to preserve the flag of dialectical materialism and rapidly gathered to the attack. He was defended at first by the editors of *Voprosy Filosofii*, an action that they soon had cause to regret, and by other physicists, as well as by his students. The attack soon found other targets, including two of the most prominent Soviet physicists of the older generation, Ya. I. Frenkel and V. A. Fok, both of whom are described as outstanding theorists in research on problems of atomic structure in a prewar survey of Soviet science by a rather pro-Soviet British scientist, J. G. Crowther.[73] Early in 1948 the Party Agitprop evidently intervened and changed the editors of *Voprosy Filosofii*. The new editors published an abject apology for allowing Markov's views to reach the public and thereby failing to lead Soviet physicists and philosophers "along the road pointed out by Comrade A. A. Zhdanov," who had issued some materialist pronouncements on physics some time previously.[74] There the question has rested, so far as physics was concerned.

It may occur to the reader at this point that, after all, these are rather finespun philosophical controversies that do not necessarily affect the work of the Soviet scientist. What does it matter if the popularizers and the Party hacks quarrel over meaningless metaphysical obscurities? Cannot the Soviet scientist pay lip service to this nonsense and continue basically undisturbed in his work? There is considerable substance to this interpretation. But in as crude a form as this it represents, I think, a serious misapprehension of both the importance of philosophical assumptions in modern physics and related areas, as well as the dynamics of totalitarian society.

There can scarcely be any doubt that the Soviet physicist uses quantum theory as well as relativity theory, also recently under attack,[75] in his actual work. Western scientific studies are available to the Soviet scientist in abundance. Several are cited in Russian translations in the article on the atomic nucleus in the *Bol'shaya Sovetskaya Entsiklopediya* published in 1950, which makes merely a perfunctory bow to Marxism. Moreover, two years after the attack on Frenkel and Markov, Frenkel was able to publish a work on the principles of the theory of the atomic nucleus. Nor is there any doubt that the Soviet scientist working in these areas retains a very substantial intellectual autonomy. In contrast to semi-popular and popular literature, Soviet scientific journals are almost entirely free of the familiar clichés about bourgeois idealism, abstract formalism, cosmopolitanism, and the rest. A fairly intensive search through postwar issues of several such journals revealed few items of this nature.[76] Nevertheless, the fact that such items do occur is in itself significant.[77] It also seems very likely, in the light of evidence cited earlier in this chapter, that ambitious students would be inclined to avoid politically charged topics in physics.

An attack in a scientific journal served as the prelude to the formal condemnation of the application of quantum theory in the closely allied field of physical chemistry. As in the case of genetics, the disagreement was resolved by a formal "discussion." During the spring of 1950 two articles appeared in the Academy of Science's *Zhurnal Fizicheskoi Khimii,* criticizing the concept of resonance, particularly as developed by the American chemist, Linus C. Pauling, whose work and that of others had recently been translated by Soviet scientists and published in Russian. This concept is a mathematical hypothesis, based on quantum theory, which describes certain aspects of atomic structure in a manner that accords with a number of experimental findings. The translators, Ya. K. Syrkin and M. E. Dyatkin, were accused in the pages of the Soviet journal of being concealed agents of idealism and Machist philosophy.[78] The next step came shortly after the accession of Nesmeyanov, reported to be an advocate of the anti-Western view in chemistry, to the presidency of the Academy of Sciences of the USSR in the spring of 1951. In June of that year the Academy of Sciences held a conference on the chemical structure of organic compounds, attended by 400 scientific workers in chemistry, physics, and philosophy. At the conference, according to the account in *Pravda*, the "pseudo-scientific essence of the theory of resonance was exposed and unmasked to the end," and all chemists and physicists were called upon to "root out the remnants of [this] mistaken concept." [79] Thus the Academy of Sciences itself was forced to put the stamp of disapproval on the use of quantum theory.

In mathematics, as might be expected, Party-inspired attacks have directed their fire against the formal and abstract character —in other words the essence—of mathematical theory. They do their best to preserve the materialist premise by insisting, as did Engels, that all mathematical knowledge is ultimately a reflection of human experience in a real world. Except for scattered statements by prominent mathematicians promising that idealism would be rooted out of Soviet mathematics, perhaps issued in the hope of self-protection, and vague threats of a general "discussion," [80] the weight of the Party attack has been directed against the theory of probability and also against certain aspects of applied statistics. Though the defenders have made important concessions, by the spring of 1953 they had not made full retractions, nor had they been completely silenced. Other areas of mathematics so far remain undisturbed. But there is nothing in the nature of mathematics itself as a subject matter that would somehow make it immune to demands for political conformity, as some Western mathematicians claim.[81] If anything, the formal and "impractical" nature of pure mathematics make it a natural target for zealous Communists.

The course of events to date in the statistics controversy may be sketched briefly before inquiring into its theoretical and political background. In the spring of 1948, no doubt as a sequel to the attack on the economist Evgenii S. Varga for presenting too rosy a picture of capitalist prospects, the institute of economics in the USSR Academy of Sciences undertook to question in writing a large number of Soviet statisticians on certain matters of theory.[82] On the basis of the results, members of the institute's executive committee, including Varga, worked out a series of theses to serve as the basis of a broader "discussion." It is clear that the intended victim was V. S. Nemchinov, a specialist on agricultural statistics. In his opening speech before the learned council of the Academy, Nemchinov unexpectedly stood his ground firmly and turned to the attack in his closing remarks. The consternation that this must have created seeps through even the stilted language of the official report. "The speaker defended his view, which had already been rejected by the committee for working out the theses, that in the USSR it was necessary to set up [the study of] 'econometrics,' i.e., to import onto Soviet soil the arch-bourgeois school of mathematical statistics." [83]

Nemchinov's defiance may have been due to his membership in the Party and to the protection of influential figures in the Party. But it is also clear that he is a man of extraordinary courage, willing to speak his mind freely on occasions when others keep silent. During the summer of 1948, in what must have been an even more tense and dramatic moment, he defended the geneticist Zhebrak against the onslaughts of Lysenko and his allies at the gathering where Lysenko's views triumphed officially. At that time he was director of the Timiryazev Academy of Agricultural Science, where Zhebrak was carrying on his investigations. In the course of defending his subordinate he had the temerity to declare that he did not regard the Mendelian law as a piece of idealism. Ending his remarks on a note of defiance, he said: "Personally I regard such a position [i.e., such a criticism of Mendel] as a wrong one, and that is my point of view even if it doesn't interest anybody much." The stenographic report records a brief commotion and even laughter in the hall at this point.[84] This defiance could not be completely maintained. More than four years later, after a series of further attacks on his theoretical position in regard to statistics, Nemchinov conceded that his defense of Mendel had been without foundation.[85] Nevertheless, he reasserted in ringing phrases the demand for objectivity in statistics and scientific work generally. "In order that separate statistical data and various statistical indices can be used in the scientific investigation of social life they must be objective, truthful, reliable, and scientifically founded." [86] He also maintained the substance of his original defense of mathematical theory in statistics, cleverly turning some of Stalin's statements against his critics, and elsewhere conceding mistakes on basically scientific grounds. Though his future fate is uncertain, it is remarkable that he has survived this long unsilenced.

Others have not been so fortunate. In February 1950 a two-day Conference on Methodology was held at the Central Statistical Administration of the USSR in Moscow, at which several statisticians found it necessary to recant their earlier views. The conference announced a new textbook on statistics, for use in the special statistical schools of the Central Statistical Administration. In the new textbook, as a member of the conference explained, '

in contrast to former syllabuses it is above all stated that statistics is a social science, class conscious and Party conscious. This disposes of the bourgeois statement . . . that the subject of statistics is mass phenomena of nature and society. In this connection it is necessary to recognize as entirely erroneous the statement that the central thesis of statistical science and the basis of its methods is the mathematical law of large numbers. . . . The scientific basis of statistics is historical materialism and Marxist-Leninist political economy." [87]

In the case of statistics purely practical considerations converge with those derived from the Marxist hostility toward formal abstractionism to produce the intervention just described. The Soviets require a large number of people with statistical training. There is clear evidence that the demand for these skills, even at a relatively low level of technical training, still outruns the supply. For example, it is rather surprising to learn that in the course of the past twenty years the Soviets have been unable to make, apparently even for official purposes, any detailed comparative surveys of agricultural output for the country as a whole that would show variations in yield from one district to another.[88] Given the pressure to turn out large numbers of statisticians who can carry out relatively simple accounting operations, it is easy to understand that there should be complaints about "overloading textbooks with general mathematical formulae that are seldom applied in practice."[89]

There is also a genuine intellectual issue involved. Many statistical calculations are based upon a concept of chance that has certain ambiguities and is liable to misuse in unsophisticated hands. In their simplest form the assumptions underlying certain uses of statistics may be stated as follows. Under certain conditions, which require careful empirical examination to determine whether or not they exist in the material to be studied, no single event is determinate. The classic illustration is the toss of a coin. In the second place, under these conditions, no single event determines what takes place in regard to other events. One toss of a coin does not affect the next toss of the same coin, or the outcome of simultaneous tosses of other coins. Nevertheless the results of all these independent events present a predictable pattern. This is the basis of the simpler forms of probability theory. The pattern can, in the case of coin tosses, for example, be represented by what is known as the normal or bell-shaped curve, if plotted on ordinary graph paper. If ten coins are tossed 10,000 times, there will be very few cases of all ten coins turning out tails, while there will be nearly 2,500 cases of five heads and five tails. Variations from the normal or bell-shaped curve are frequently used by statisticians to determine whether or not the results they have obtained from a series of measurements can be attributed to chance, or whether some other factor or cause is at work. In the words of a famous Soviet statistician, A. N. Kolmogorov, whose work is highly regarded in the West, the law of large numbers is a "general principle as a result of which the simultaneous action of a large number of accidental factors leads, under certain completely general conditions, to a result that is almost independent of chance." [90]

To a Communist this viewpoint is almost automatically suspicious. The idea that the output of one kolkhoz could be treated as if it were indeterminate smacks of both heresy and absurdity. The Marxist view emphasizes, furthermore, that social events do not occur independently of one another, but represent a coherent pattern. "The point is," as one of Nemchinov's critics put the matter, "that the premises on which the conclusions of the theorems of probability theory rest, known by the law of large numbers, have nothing in common with the laws of social development, whose representation in figures is given by statistics. Society is not a mechanical aggregate of elements, in which any combinations are possible." [91] Such a viewpoint is unquestionably mistaken if erected into a universal principle. There *are* social events that, so far as we know, take place independently of one another. As Nemchinov pointed out in his defense, the logical implication of the elimination of probability conceptions would be the abandonment of statistical checks on the quality of goods being turned out on the assembly line, insofar as these checks depend upon sampling theory.[92] Nevertheless, as some Western social scientists have indicated, there are areas of human behavior (and there may be areas in the natural sciences as well) where statistical methods are inappropriate. Language, for example, in the words just cited, is not a mechanical aggregate of elements in which any combination is possible. Instead it is necessary to search for patterns of relationship through other intellectual procedures.[93] The methods of pure mathematics might conceivably help to discover and interpret such patterns of relationship. This point, I suspect, a Communist might concede in a moment of candor. But with emphasis on the concrete, he would be likely to add that the explanation cannot stop with this discovery of formal and abstract relationships, but must proceed to statements about what takes place in a real world outside our own minds. With this position a good many Western scientists would be likely to agree.

Just as there is variety in the extent to which political controls permeate and influence different fields of intellectual activity, so also is there considerable variation in the response of Soviet intellectuals to the situations that confront them. Part of this variation is due to differences in the outlook and personality of the intellectuals themselves. There is a clear distinction between the diminishing number of intellectuals educated in pre-Revolutionary times, now in their late fifties or older, and the more distinctly Soviet products that have been turned out in rapidly increasing numbers for more than twenty years. The relationship between these two types forms a frequent theme in Soviet fiction. On the whole, the older group tends to adhere to older intellectual ideals that transcend political boundaries and are shared by intellectuals through Western culture generally. Some of this influence has been transmitted to the younger generation through the home. The Soviet product, nevertheless, is likely to be somewhat narrower in outlook, more of a technician, and less of a humanist. In this respect the impact of Soviet totalitarianism may be said to have greatly accelerated trends visible elsewhere in modern industrial society, without altering their nature in any fundamental manner.

A second major difference among the intellectuals themselves derives from nationality. Despite the very real increase in educational opportunities for intellectuals who are not of Russian nationality, there are limits to the meaning of such opportunity. Though the degree of touchiness has varied, the central authorities in Moscow have always been sensitive to any expression of non-Russian traditions and culture that carried any implication of independence in regard to the essential political and economic controls. Toward the end of Stalin's reign this sensitivity increased to include a wave of propaganda attacks on the expression of so-called "bourgeois nationalism" among the non-Russian nationalities. Their history was required to be rewritten in such a manner as to praise their conquest by the "progressive" Russians and to show that their national epics were the expression of an essentially "reactionary" spirit. This involved a reversal of the policy of exposing the evils of Tsarist expansions, that had been official as late as 1934.[94] These and similar actions by the Moscow authorities seem to reflect an almost paranoid fear of any symbol that might serve as a rallying point among the various nationalities. Reliable evidence on the actual outlook of non-Russian intellectuals today is almost wholly lacking. That some resentment exists against the Soviet form of "Russification," and that this resentment is concentrated among intellectuals, seems quite a safe inference. It is also probable that the resentment is considerably stronger among writers and artists than it would be among natural scientists, who have received the concrete benefits of laboratories and jobs as a consequence of Soviet policy. Finally, those who hold this resentment are not likely to make very sharp distinctions between Moscow as the center of Russian encroachment on their culture and Moscow as the source of Soviet authority.

One general type of group response to the demands of the Soviet system on the intellectuals is the spontaneous creation of informal cliques dedicated to the pursuit of strictly intellectual interests. Ordinarily these are small groups of people who have come to know one another through continual personal contact in their work. They may be found in all fields of intellectual life, from the theatrical world to the scientific laboratory. Similar cliques abound through all of Soviet society. What distinguishes those among intellectuals is the survival of a combination of guild and professional solidarity. In other words, a person's acceptance into the group does not depend on the kind of favors that might be performed or upon the accidents of congeniality, though these elements enter in, so much as upon the ability to carry out a certain kind of intellectual task. Little groups of this type are able at times to wall themselves off from the demands of the Soviet regime. One of the most striking examples was a coöperative housing development on the edge of one of the largest cities in the USSR, built by a small group of successful artists who were close friends. All were in spirit, if not in strict chronological age, members of the older generation of the intelligentsia. For several years they succeeded in maintaining their unwritten rule that no Party member would be allowed to join their community.[95] For a time such cliques may remain virtually impenetrable to the regime's political controls. When they exist in a large organization, such as a hospital or a scientific research unit, they may contribute to its effectiveness and remain unmolested by the local authorities. But the Soviets, like other totalitarian regimes, are generally suspicious of such groupings and as a rule do their best to destroy them. They tend to prefer a society broken into atomized units. At some point in the history of such a clique professional jealousies, personal rivalries, or the overdevelopment of nepotism are likely to provide an entering wedge for the Party or the police. Then the authorities can break up the clique by transferring some of its members to a different part of the country or by more drastic methods.

No precise information is available concerning the way in which nationality cleavages, or that between the generations, cut across the informal ties of professional solidarity. At the level of individual behavior, on the other hand, it is possible to distinguish certain recurring patterns of response to the situation confronting Soviet intellectuals, and to make some rough inferences concerning their distribution.

One conceivable response is direct and overt opposition to the controls and even to the Soviet system as such. Rare though they are, such cases do occur. Nemchinov's defiance at the time of the genetics conference and also when the statisticians gathered in the pack to pull him down has already been mentioned. If a person's achievements are sufficiently famous and valued by sufficiently powerful individuals, he may get away with occasional defiance.

A second reaction can best be described as careerism and

wangling, or, in more neutral terms, the effort to manipulate the Soviet system for personal or group advantage. In any bureaucratized society this type of behavior is imposed by the requirements of the situation on the chiefs of administrative units, or those who carry on their shoulders responsibility for the survival and continued operation of the group they lead. It may therefore be more common among such persons than among those engaged more directly in intellectual work. Occasionally the two qualities are combined. Thus the famous theatrical director Stanislavsky is reported to have been one of the few people who had Stalin's telephone number and was free to call him if trouble developed at the theater.[96] Soviet society abounds in opportunities for the ambitious, if they are not overburdened with sensitivity and are willing to face the risks of eminence. From refugee accounts, as well as from Soviet fiction, one may draw the inference that a key element in success is the ability to attract the attention of a powerful patron, in which respect the Soviet situation is of course far from unique. The difference between the American or British situation and the Soviet one appears to be one of degree. Under the Soviet dictatorship an artistic career, and to a lesser extent a scientific one, depends more on the unpredictable fortunes of a patron, while professional talent and skill do not provide as much of an independent source of security or achievement.

A third form of behavior is escape into one's work. This type of response appears to be quite widespread, judging both by the accounts of former Soviet intellectuals and the complaints about it that appear in the Soviet press. Probably it is an avenue that is more readily available to natural scientists, with their frequently well-equipped laboratories and generally unfamiliar activities, than it is to other intellectuals. Where this kind of response results in intense effort on the job, as is often the case, it may help rather than hinder Bolshevik interests, even though this effort is combined with a good deal of passive evasion of the control system. In other cases, however, where the escape tends to be a private affair, or a form of "inner emigration," as many refugees refer to it, that does not result in the publication or communication of results, the consequences go against the interests of the regime.

It should be noticed in this connection that apathy, in the sense of a low level of effort, appears to be quite rare among Soviet intellectuals. Political apathy, in the sense of a desire to avoid involvement in current Soviet politics, is almost certainly rather widespread for a variety of reasons. Other elements in the situation, particularly the need to hold more than one job in order to approach the intellectual's customary standard of living, seem to diminish apathy in the work situation. Pride in the sheer amount of effort expended is very often expressed by former Soviet intellectuals, including the most anti-Soviet ones. Much more information would be necessary to reveal the real extent of this effort. But there is considerable reason to believe that it is one of the important factors that help to get things done in the Soviet system and in this fashion serves to maintain it.

The last variety of response is enthusiastic acceptance of the Soviet regime and active conformance to its requirements. In the light of the general situation described in this chapter it would seem that this reaction is increasingly rare. It is perhaps most likely to occur among the younger generation of natural and applied scientists, and then in the earlier stages of their career. The superficially antitraditionalist animus of the official doctrine may help some scientists with really creative and original ideas to overcome vested intellectual interests and make a meteoric career. Such is the model held up in Soviet fiction. Stalin prize winners may in some cases approximate the reality, though sampling of the announced awards strongly suggests that they ordinarily go to mature individuals with an extended record of achievement behind them. In any event it seems unlikely that a truly creative person could function for long in the Soviet system without discovering that the antitraditionalist doctrine is a veil for another and harsher form of authority, and without encountering some fairly serious frustration of his or her intellectual drives.

At both the group and the individual level, the recurring theme in the intellectuals' response to the Soviet system is the search for some minimal degree of autonomy within the system. On the Soviet scene there is no sign that the intellectuals can provide either the leadership or the symbolism for the overthrow of the Soviet dictatorship. Rather their efforts are directed toward squirming as much room as possible for themselves, as it were, within the existing system. Over time this pressure could conceivably lead to a large-scale transformation of the Soviet system, through more or less peaceful internal changes. So far as Soviet intellectuals appear to have a common aim, it is to pursue their activities in a way closer to autonomous intellectual and professional standards. When they object to the Soviet system, frequently it is not so much in terms of abstract criteria of political freedom, as on the grounds that the existing dictatorship is bad for music, or for literature, or for biology, though they may have some vague and diffuse hostility that extends beyond the interest closest to their hearts. In turn the dictatorship, because it needs their services, finds itself compelled to grant them status and some portion of autonomy. At the same time it tries to prevent intellectual autonomy from endangering its overall political control, and to reserve for itself matters of ultimate or political truth, whose symbols only the supreme authority is free to change. The net result is an unstable compromise—the resolution of tensions that might profoundly modify the form of Soviet society should either the rulers or the intellectuals be able to push their demands successfully.

chapter 6

THE IMPACT AND FUNCTION
OF TERROR

Anyone who has studied the Soviet Union for more than a few years is likely to be aware of considerable change in the kinds of statements about the USSR that require or do not require extensive proof. The shifts in what is taken for granted, even among professional students of Soviet affairs, derive only partly from the increase and diffusion of firm factual knowledge. They reflect also the changing tides of public hopes and fears about this huge power. Both factors are extremely influential in any attempt to assess the part played by organized terror in the Soviet system. It also happens that in recent years both factors have tended to push judgments on this question in the same, and possibly an extreme, direction. The tense rivalry for world leadership, together with the stream of new information from Soviet refugees, tend to produce a Western image of the Soviet system in which organized terror is seen as the chief driving force and the main source of motivation in the daily behavior of every Soviet citizen. Because of the still fragmentary nature of the evidence any appraisal of this major factor must face very great difficulties. Here we shall try to examine the terror primarily with two problems in mind. The first is to discover, so far as possible, the significance of terror in the daily life and ordinary actions of Soviet citizens. The second is to ascertain to what extent, if any, mass terror represents an inherent and inevitable feature of the socialist organization of society generally, as well as of the rather special forms that socialism has taken in the Soviet Union.

To comprehend the importance of terror for the rank and file of the Soviet citizenry it would be quite useful to know the proportion that has actually felt the weight of this instrument through the experience of arrest. The burden of the evidence now available indicates that the threat of arrest occurs as a very real possibility to a substantial portion of Soviet men, possibly as many as one in five, at some point in their lives. This estimate must remain, however, a very rough guess.

Two types of evidence may be offered in support of this guess. Naum Jasny, who certainly cannot be accused of partiality to the Bolsheviks, has called for a sharp downward revision of the number of concentration camp inmates that had been previously suggested by students of this question. On the basis of the secret 1941 Soviet economic plan, cited earlier in this book, he arrives at the relatively modest figure of three and a half million able-bodied workers in the camps, which he points out is only a rough approximation.[1] Since most of the camp population apparently are men, and as there were only 45 million men between the working ages of 20 and 50 in the USSR at that time, his figure yields a proportion of about one person in thirteen. Since there is some flow in and out of the camps, the proportion would have to be increased in order to show how many individuals were likely to be affected over any given period of time. Also not all those who are arrested are sent to camps. Hence the figure of one in thirteen is almost certainly too low as an index of those men likely to be directly affected by the repressive organs of the dictatorship. While this figure may do service as a lower limit, the one reached by a statistical study of the experiences of Soviet refugees, carried out by the Harvard Project on the Soviet Social System, probably represents an upper limit. Out of a group of 1883 refugees who filled out questionnaires, about one-third (33 per cent) of the 1290 men in this group reported that they themselves had undergone the experience of arrest. Slightly more than half (53 per cent) reported the arrest of a member of their immediate family. Of the 593 women, on the other hand, only 5 per cent reported individual experience with arrest, while 75 per cent reported arrest for a family member.[2]

This impression of mass terror is somewhat softened by the finding that 30 per cent of those who were themselves arrested said
that they received no sentence. There is no way of knowing
whether the group interviewed by the Harvard Project is a representative sample of the refugee population, far less of the
Soviet population itself. Even though the sample is by no means
a collection of those who were misfits in Soviet society, partly
because a high proportion of the group were sent to Germany
more or less involuntarily as forced workers, it very likely has
more than a representative share of those who had trouble with
the Soviet authorities in the course of their lives. A proportion
of one in five stands at the half-way point between the figure
based on Jasny's calculations and that taken from the study of
the refugees. In itself it cannot be taken with great seriousness.
But it is one way of saying that the thrust of the terror is not
confined to the remnants of former intellectual classes or the
Communist Party itself, as some students were inclined to believe before postwar evidence became available.

Even if every Soviet citizen knew accurately the number of
people arrested each year in the USSR for political reasons, it
is hardly likely that individual conduct would be based on this
fact alone, any more than an American's behavior in crossing the
street is influenced by a careful study of the statistics on traffic
accidents. Particularly in the case of such a phenomenon as
terror, popular beliefs about its impact are likely to be more influential in determining actual conduct than the objective facts
themselves. Refugee testimony reflects a wide variety of notions
about the ways in which the lightning strikes. Some of these are
quite contradictory. The sentiment is frequently expressed that
no Soviet citizens, not even the highest officials of the secret
police and certainly not its ordinary servants, are safe from arrest
and possible execution. On the other hand, it is sometimes asserted that the sons of high officials can get off more lightly than
ordinary folk if their offenses are not regarded as serious political
ones. Yet again, it is said that the Communists are held to stricter

standards of behavior than ordinary citizens. Sometimes the same individual will make both observations in a single breath.[3]

To many Soviet citizens the impact of the police state appears highly capricious. The areas of prohibited behavior expand and contract with dramatic suddenness following each change in the Party line, in a manner that often bewilders the person who has to give full attention to the demanding task of earning a living. To be sure, most people learn at an early age that overt criticism of the Soviet system as such is fraught with danger. Yet one gains the clear impression that a large portion of the population fails to sense any clear connection between a specific act and the dreaded descent of the secret police. Particularly during the *Yezhovshchina,* as the great purge of the latter thirties became known after Yezhov, then head of the police, quite a number of people were certain that their arrest had been a mistake—a stupid slip on some part of the bureaucracy that would soon be put to rights by getting in touch with the responsible officials. Convinced of their own essential loyalty, they could not understand why they found themselves in jail. This kind of reaction appears to have been rather frequent among educated people. It can be interpreted as a failure to understand the real nature and political dynamics of the regime. In other cases, the appearance of capriciousness stems from both hostility to the Bolsheviks and the impossibility of accepting their aims. A peasant lad could hardly be expected to perceive why the Bolsheviks wanted to eliminate the kulaks by police measures. For him such a policy would seen not only brutal but incomprehensible.

From the rulers' standpoint, on the other hand, terror is a means to an end, a rational device, to be used "scientifically." Aside from individual instances, there is very little cruelty merely for the sake of cruelty in Soviet terror.[4] The categories of victims are worked out by a crude but nevertheless rational procedure of deciding what groups in an area are to be considered politically reliable and which ones dangerous. These categories are drawn up according to a combination of Marxist and more rough-

and-ready, common-sense premises, as may be seen from police documents that have fallen into Western hands and the evidence of former police officials.[5] In this regard they are similar to lists of suspects drawn up by police and intelligence agencies anywhere in the world.

Victims who do not regard their arrest as either a fortuitous accident or a rank injustice may be, as Arthur Koestler suggests in *Darkness at Noon*,[6] largely those who both understand the workings of the Soviet system and share to some extent the values of its rulers. Among such persons there may also be a feeling that the regime is capricious, but in quite a different sense. They are aware that for its effective functioning the system requires frequent violations of both the spirit and the letter of the law. Hence they know that the secret police has a more or less permanent hold over them. Arrest is no surprise. As long as they continue to get results, they may be safe. But if they fail, for reasons that may be beyond their control, that can be the end. Those who fear to take the risks avoid responsibility. Those who work their way to the top are likely to be thick-skinned and able to repress doubts and insecurities. This process of selection is a factor that would tend to maintain the stability of the system. Whether there is a net gain or loss in over-all efficiency cannot be determined in any convincing manner.

An important sociological consequence of the system of organized terror is the partial atomization of Soviet society. The regime deliberately seeks to sow suspicion among the population, which to a marked extent results in the break-up of friendship groupings, in the work situation and elsewhere, and the isolation of the individual. The regime tries to destroy all social bonds except the ones that it has itself created, and through which it can manipulate the population. As many writers have pointed out, this process of atomization and the destruction of social ties takes place in the course of industrialization and urbanization. It is by no means a consequence of totalitarian regimes alone. Nevertheless, closely similar processes may be observed in many nonindustrial societies where a strong central authority has attempted to bring about a new social integration.* In the Soviet situation, where rapid urbanization has been accompanied by the attempt to impose a new totalitarian integration on Russian society, the process of atomization may well have gone further than in any previous society in human history. There are, however, limits to the process of atomization, discussed at another point in this chapter, beyond which it defeats the objectives of the dictatorship.

In implementing part of this policy, the MVD relies on masses of informers scattered widely through the population, rather than on a small number of skilled agents located at strategic points in the social system. This part of the government's intelligence network relies on quantity rather than on quality. To be sure, the population undoubtedly exaggerates the number of informers and is encouraged in this exaggeration by the MVD. Yet there is enough evidence from persons who have been associated with the secret police, either as victims or officers, to indicate clearly the reliance on quantity. One may reasonably infer that one consequence is a considerable overloading of the system. Probably there are many more reports coming in than can be adequately evaluated and digested, choking the control apparatus from time to time to the point where it ceases to be effective.

The Soviet authorities display some awareness of this disadvantage. Clever persons who wish to deflect attention away from themselves can start a cloud of rumors and denunciations sufficient to cause temporary paralysis of the local police apparatus. Occasionally the Soviet press runs a series of semi-fictional, sarcastic accounts of such incidents. In one account, a Deputy Minister of Machine Tractor Stations in an outlying province returned from his vacation to find all his friends thinking he had been in jail for embezzling funds. The source of the rumors was

* The Younger Pliny tells in his letters of the Roman emperor's disapproval of the formation of a voluntary fire-protection group in a distant provincial town, for fear that the firemen might be a nucleus of sedition.

a finance inspector with a court record for libel. As long as the inspector continues his slanders, said the account, "his superiors do not dare to sign the order for his dismissal, lest people might say that he was fired for criticism." [7] In another incident, a man wanted to engage in apartment speculation, which involved marrying an elderly lady, the possessor of a large apartment, who died soon afterward. Faced with an eviction order, he counter-attacked with a stream of accusations against the Moscow soviet, Party, and trade-union organizations, persuading his friends to write signed letters beginning, "Help an honest man to obtain justice." Numerous investigations were made that found no confirmation of his accusations. The account ends with the re-mark that investigators representing the Moscow city public prosecutors had to question about two hundred people on the basis of this complaint, twenty court sessions were held, and for two years dozens of different organizations had been "wast-ing their energy, time and money investigating all manner of ly-ing complaints." [8] A follow-up of one such incident announced that certain persons had engaged in systematic slander and were sentenced to two years' deprivation of liberty.[9] Though the MVD is not specifically mentioned as playing a part in such affairs, one can be reasonably certain that it does.

There are obvious limits to the distance that this process of atomization and the institutionalization of mutual suspicion can go without seriously weakening the entire social fabric. In ad-dition to the danger of paralyzing the administrative services, the regime runs the risk of weakening or destroying social group-ings and institutions that it must rely on for other purposes. To take care of the problem of regulating relationships between the sexes and the socialization of children, for example, the regime has found it necessary to come to terms with the family. Fur-thermore, the terror sets in motion various forces that counter those of atomization by promoting the growth of close personal relationships. There is some evidence that the experience of arrest increases the cohesiveness of the Soviet urban family.[10]

Thus terror both destroys and creates personal relationships, friendship groupings, and protective cliques.

Many such interlocking networks of personal loyalties germinate and develop under the circumstances of the work situation. These groups, like the family, are to a considerable extent also essential to the continued functioning of the regime. Their importance is perhaps clearest of all in the army, where comradely feelings and loyalties may, under combat conditions, be the major factor that keeps an isolated group of men from panic in the face of certain death for some of the group's members. Similar groups grow up in field, factory, and office and play a vital role through all of Soviet society.

Ideally the Bolshevik leaders would probably like to see an intelligent and convinced Communist as the nucleus of each of these groups, guiding its activities for the greater glory of the USSR. This, however, is impossible, not only because there are not enough Communists to go around, but also because these friendship groupings at times develop and focus around interests that in part go against the interests and desires of the regime. One of the foci around which they form, for example, is resistance to the demand for more strenuous effort. Since these cliques cannot be entirely Communist-led, the Bolsheviks also depend on forcing one or more members to become informers and spreading the notion widely that such might be the case. The resulting suspicion and loss in voluntary support is balanced by an increase in the degree of control. Not a few hard-headed Communists probably reason that this is the only "realistic" way that control can be maintained.

From the point of view of the rulers a "good" friendship clique is one that aids in the execution of a policy, while from the viewpoint of the population a "good" clique is one that aids in the evasion of policy. Frequently the same clique does both. In a centralized bureaucracy that controls the allocation of goods, services, and manpower under conditions of scarcity there is a premium on pull and clique connections. This is all the more the case because people are called upon to perform the impossible. Pull and connection may enable one to get the demands scaled down, or to get the assistance of the competent and the energetic in meeting the demands, drawing them away from some one less skilled or less fortunate, who will suffer for failure. Stories about *blat* and the manipulation of the Soviet system for personal advantage are rife in refugee circles, and must be treated with reserve because of the human tendency to exaggerate in retrospect one's success in outwitting authority and evading regulations. Nevertheless *blat* undoubtedly plays a vital dual role, at times maintaining and at times altering the system.[11]

Whether a person sees or makes use of opportunities to manipulate the system depends both upon the individual's personality and his position within the system. The Soviet Union evidently has its share of rather fussy and timid individuals, who never dare to break a rule, as well as its picaresque characters who live by their wits, penetrating all the chinks of a not so monolithic state. Both the "operators" and the timid may turn up at any level in this hierarchically organized society. However, the awareness of the possibility of manipulating the levers of Soviet society appears to be rather unevenly distributed. Preliminary inspection of the refugee interview data suggests that intellectuals, especially those highly placed in the system, tend to see abstract possibilities of manipulation in both legal and semi-legal fashions. The same appears to be true of workers, when asked about typical difficulties of daily life and how one might get out of them. The peasants, on the other hand, give the impression of feeling that manipulation and evasion is possible for other people in Soviet society, but very difficult or next to impossible for themselves. But one must be most cautious in making such inferences about subjective feelings, since they would undoubtedly vary a great deal from one concrete situation to another in the same individual.

What is much clearer, and fortunately more relevant for the immediate purpose at hand, is that popular notions about the possibility of manipulating the Soviet system nearly always stop short of the MVD. In all the accounts of evasion examined the writer has come across only one account claiming that it was possible to get around the MVD through bribery.[12] Unlike the rest of Soviet officialdom the MVD is widely regarded as incorruptible. It is mainly viewed as something feared and apart, not something that can be wheedled or manipulated. Clique lines seldom cross the barrier that separates the MVD from the rest of the population.

To the extent that there are exceptions to this generalization, it appears that they occur close to the apex of the Soviet social and political pyramid. In the early days of the regime it was not uncommon for an irate commissar to telephone Dzerzhinskii, head of the Cheka, and demand in no uncertain terms the release of a valued specialist or other worker. The writer knows of no authentic parallel cases from recent times. But at least some persons close to the center of power appear to feel that, in case of arrest, their wide circle of influential acquaintances is useful, and may succeed in bringing about their release. For the rest of the population, there exist two possibilities. One is appeal through normal legal channels, which on occasion does result in acquittal and release. The other, perhaps used more in former times than now, is a direct appeal to the fountain of authority. M. I. Kalinin, Chairman of the Supreme Soviet, in his lifetime was the individual to whom such requests for justice might be directed, and on occasion they too were successful. Now that he is dead, there does not seem to be any such popular figure to whom one can appeal. Stalin too was occasionally described by refugees as playing the role of a benevolent despot in cutting the Gordian knots of Soviet red tape. But since he was also rather widely regarded as the source of all that seemed cruel and harsh in the Soviet system, the idea that an appeal to him might be effective was rare and usually the product of desperation.

Quite a variety of beliefs and attitudes concerning the MVD informer is reflected in the statements of Soviet refugees of all ranks of life. There are, of course, wide degrees of sophistication on how to separate trustworthy members of a group from the informers. Some refugees claimed that in any tightly knit group people soon acquired this ability. A young soldier, on the other hand, declared that there were informers in every army unit and simply no way to spot them.[13] Few were as naïve as a young peasant, interviewed in 1950 before he had come in contact with other refugees, who asserted, as a rule of behavior, that "we would never tell a political joke in the presence of a Party man."[14] Very sophisticated individuals might be quite systematic about deciding who had become an informer. One highly placed intellectual, passively anti-Soviet in his general attitudes, periodically reviewed with his wife their circle of personal friends to decide who was still trustworthy.[15]

How accurately the population can smell out an informer in actual fact is very hard to tell. There are some reasons to suspect that people generally overestimate their ability to spot informers, a tendency which plays into the hands of the MVD. Being forced to become an informer is widely regarded among educated people as both shameful and tragic. Workers and peasants may have a somewhat more matter-of-fact attitude. Though the misfortune may be confessed to an intimate friend in a moment of stress, it is naturally not something to be discussed or widely circulated. Hence the population can seldom have accurate knowledge of who has been caught in the net and who has not. To be sure there are some ways of behaving like an agent provocateur that are sufficiently unsubtle to arouse suspicion. But, on the whole, one gets the impression that many people confuse the convinced Communist, or someone who acts like a convinced Communist, with the ordinary informer. The confusion may be partly due to the fact that one of the duties of a Party member is to be "vigilant" and report suspicious actions or attitudes to the secret police. On general grounds, nevertheless, it is difficult to see what identifying characteristics an informer would be likely to display.

There are no indications that the MVD has any difficulty in recruiting informers. The opening gambit in ordinary cases is for the MVD officer to ask an individual if he wants to help the Soviet regime. To refuse this lofty appeal is of course dangerous. Hence many persons are caught at the outset. Clever ones can think up stratagems of evasion, as did an actress who claimed she was too much of a chatterbox ever to be able to keep a secret. Many others can be forced to serve by threats or by hints that the MVD knows of unsavory incidents in their pasts.

At the same time, an unwilling informer is not necessarily a useful one from the MVD point of view. An engineer, who had spent three years in jail as a result of a denunciation, observed that friends who were compelled to act as informers developed ways of protecting one another and of limiting their serious accusations to Communists whose conduct made them vulnerable. In this manner the weapons of the MVD can in some cases be turned against the regime itself.[16] Other informers are more likely to be forced out of sheer desperation to invent imaginary hostile remarks among their acquaintances, which, as we have seen, tends to overload the system with relative trivialities. To make peace with their consciences, unwilling informers, beset with increasing demands for denunciations, frequently seek solace in the traditional outlet supplied by vodka.[17]

Among men vodka plays an important part in certain types of friendship groups. In the early days of the Bolshevik regime, it was apparently a common practice for a small group of men, who were meeting for the first time and were faced with sharing common responsibilities, deliberately to get drunk together as the first stage in "getting organized." Possibly this custom has withered to some extent under the pressure of mistrust fostered by the Stalinist regime, since it does not turn up spontaneously in the interview materials. Getting drunk with a relative stranger, as a means of forming intimate or diffuse ties, seems to be a rare occurrence today. When it does take place, it is likely to represent the formation of a specific and temporary tie, in response to a specific favor. The favor often consists of refraining from the application of a rule.[18] Several refugees generalized that one could "get anything with vodka" in the Soviet Union. It would be naïve to accept such statements at face value. But it does appear to be a common practice to give someone a bottle of vodka in anticipation of a specific favor. In this way, vodka helps to extend the circle of acquaintances and to tie them into a network of mutual, yet specific, obligations. The actual consumption of vodka may be more likely to generate a diffuse set of friendship obligations. One gets the impression that nowadays the consumption of alcohol in large quantities tends to take place in a group that has already been established for a fair length of time on some other basis, and is regarded as safe.

On the one hand, vodka is an important value in Soviet society. People will use much ingenuity to obtain it, talk about it, and use it as a medium of social manipulation, in a manner not unlike the way alcohol was treated in the United States during prohibition. On the other hand, it is also feared because it encourages the release of tension, often a dangerous act under Soviet conditions. For the sake of his family, one skilled worker remarked, he tried not to visit friends, because he knew he would get drunk and incur the severe penalty for lateness the next day. He regarded himself as a much more prudent and rational man, because of his family obligations, than most of his friends.[19] Many people are aware that the MVD encourages drinking parties in order to loosen the tongues of persons about whom they have suspicions.[20] A young soldier remarked, "If you get drunk, you would tell everything," and asserted this was the reason why Soviet soldiers were not allowed to mix with the German population.[21] How widespread such fears are is a matter of guesswork, although they are probably far from unusual.

An important part of the MVD's duties consists of ferreting out and punishing rumor-mongers, whether their tongues are loosened by alcohol or for some less material reason. Not only in the Soviet situation but in any society rumor and gossip chains seem to flourish when two conditions are present. They thrive when decisions affecting a group of individuals are made without their knowledge and by persons beyond their control. In such a situation fleeting or even imaginary clues become the substitute for facts and circulate in increasingly distorted forms. Gossip chains also grow when the nature of social life generates a large amount of personal and intergroup hostility. Gossip, which we may regard as fact or rumor pointed and barbed with malice, is the concrete expression of this aggression. No doubt these two conditions are present to some extent in all societies and most subgroupings in them. In modern times perhaps the classic place to find them would be an army encampment on the eve of shipment to an unknown combat area. That they flourish in Soviet society can hardly be doubted. Despite the rationalist theme of Soviet propaganda, that people will behave like good Bolsheviks if everything is explained to them, the Soviet social system requires many arbitrary decisions and a high degree of restriction of information.

In Soviet society, as elsewhere, access to various kinds of word-of-mouth information depends upon a person's place in the social system.[22] It is at least plausible that individuals in high positions in the USSR have access to a wider variety of information and are better able to evaluate it than those near the bottom. But it is not necessarily true that they have better access to the kinds of information that affect their immediate personal fate, since the restrictions on violating confidences, in both the formal sense of giving out classified information and the informal sense of revealing office secrets, are very great in the Soviet Union. The degree to which information will be sought also varies a great deal according to individual temperament. Thus, some refugee intellectuals of high status put considerable emphasis on their place in gossip chains that reached into the sources of power and evidently expended considerable effort in maintaining this position. Others of a more retiring nature professed a certain contempt and distrust for this kind of information.[23]

At lower levels, rumor and gossip sometimes appear to be little more than confused transmissions of official information or the consequence of minor leaks from Party members.[24] On a mass scale, it is clearly impossible for the controls over the exchange of information to be completely effective. We have already had occasion to mention the opportunities of the peasants to talk freely among themselves out of earshot of snooping listeners. At times among the workers, the level of diffuse aggression rises to the point where precaution is thrown to the winds. Thus, a young worker claims to have discussed food shortages, politics, and the war quite freely and openly with co-workers his own age, since things were so bad they didn't care about the risk.[25] The risk is nevertheless known, and the spreading of rumor and gossip must be heavily checked by suspicion of informers. Dissimulation, in the form of making overtly pro-Soviet statements that knowledgeable individuals can interpret in an anti-Soviet manner, is probably very widespread. Several former soldiers have mentioned being caught or catching someone listening to the Voice of America broadcasts, and avoiding trouble with a remark about what trash and nonsense the broadcasts contained.

It is a fairly safe guess that the content of most rumor and gossip is closely related to the individual interests of the person receiving or transmitting it, for example, impending shortages of consumers' goods and the like. There is also unquestionably a strong element of wishful thinking at times. Thus rumors probably contain as much pleasant as unpleasant news. Large-scale items, such as rumors that the United States has already declared war, are likely to find their way into gossip chains only when they have direct personal significance to the individual.

Whether underground information is believed or not probably also depends a great deal upon its relation to individual personal experience. Official propaganda is likely to be believed until it contradicts individual experience, which it very often does. Particularly among peasants in the army, a letter from relatives in the village describing harsh conditions at home will be believed instead of the glowing description of a political lecturer. A furlough at home is also likely to be a shattering experience.[26]

Nevertheless, it is possible for those who have accepted the regime on an emotional basis to build an effective wall of rationalizations to explain away experiences that contradict official propaganda. Such persons are not necessarily Party members. Thus the higher standard of living among workers and peasants in the West proved a source of disenchantment to many Soviet soldiers, but was explained by others as cheap capitalist trickery, the exploitation of traitor union leaders, kulaks, and the like. Communist propaganda provides numerous ready-made rationalizations of this type.

To sum up the discussion so far, the following features of the impact of mass terror upon the population stand out, at least provisionally, in connection with the broader problem of stability or change within the Soviet system. One of them is that the terror appears to the population as capricious. As the Soviet leadership alters its policies in the effort to adapt to changing circumstances at home and abroad, its definition of the sources of internal danger necessarily varies over time. Perhaps the greatest variations, the "elimination of the kulaks as a class" and the blood-bath of the Great Purge, both of which may be regarded as part of the violent establishment and consolidation of the Stalinist system, are already past. But even if no such upheaval is in store for the future, smaller and less dramatic policy changes carry with them their redefinitions of the sources of internal danger and the categories of potential victims. Most of the population, busy with their own affairs, cannot possibly foresee these changes. Therefore an element of apparent capriciousness and arbitrariness is bound to remain as long as terror is a prominent instrument. It is of course impossible to draw a sharp line by asserting that when a certain number of people, or certain strategic groups in the population, no longer believe that this society operates according to their subjective definitions of fairness and justice, this society is doomed. Furthermore, the Soviet government, as we have seen, apparently has considerable capital on which it can draw, in the willingness of many people to overlook the harshness of their own treatment, or to regard it as an accidental matter. With all these qualifications the propositions may be offered that organized terror necessarily seems capricious to the subjects of a totalitarian society and that this capriciousness in turn undermines the essential bases of social organization.

Finally, we may take brief note of some of the dynamic consequences of the restriction and control of the flow of information in the Soviet Union, the typical totalitarian counterpart of terror. The rationalist utopian hope that the masses would follow the "correct" course of action if they were in possession of full information has always been treated ambivalently by Marxists and particularly by Russian Marxists. The practice of the latter has indeed swung to the opposite extreme of maximum restriction of the flow of certain kinds of information. To some extent, and in varying proportions among different groups, rumor and gossip serve as a substitute for the information that is restricted. In turn, and as part of a vicious circle, terror must be used to stamp out the substitute.

Now it may be useful to examine the other side of the coin, by considering the pressures upon the rulers of a socialist state to employ terror as an instrument of policy. This is a problem that transcends the Soviet experience, but upon which the Soviet case sheds some valuable light. It is frequently argued that socialism inevitably brings about the widespread use of terror and the disappearance of legal and other safeguards on the freedom of the individual. Socialism may be defined as a form of economic organization in which the decisions concerning the kinds of commodities to be produced and their manner of distribution to the population are made by a central authority instead of by private individuals with property rights in the means of production. Such a definition excludes states such as Britain under the Labour government, where a substantial portion of the economy remained in private hands. The discussion will also be confined to the problems specific to an industrial society.

In its most persuasive form the argument that terror is the blood relative of socialism runs somewhat as follows. The freedom of the individual in society and his defense against arbitrary attacks upon his person ultimately depend upon the competition of independent interest groups within the society. The struggle among workers, managers, farmers, as well as among noneconomic groups such as organized religion, the military forces, and others, provides the necessary basis for a constitutional order. This play of interests takes place within the framework of general acceptance of the rules of the game, expressed in law, and particularly constitutional law. The latter provides certain permissible methods, such as free elections and the organization of political parties, for carrying on the struggle in the political arena, and prohibits others, such as the use of organized violence. Whatever destroys the play of interest groups within the society and permits a single group to dominate inevitably destroys the only realistic guarantee that organized violence will not be used against dissenting persons or groups in the society. Power is the only effective check on power. Socialism destroys this check. The concentration of economic authority in the hands of a single body inevitably carries with it the concentration of political authority. The economic institutions of socialism, by definition, imply the destruction of independent foci of power and authority within the state and their subordination to a single will.

The reply of the democratic socialist holds that socialism provides both a procedure for making economic decisions in a way that will distribute more goods and services to a greater proportion of the population, and a method through which the population may share in the making of these decisions. Socialists have tended to concentrate on the economic technicalities of the way in which these results might be achieved and to ignore the political side of the question.[27] Nevertheless, the essential point of their argument may be expressed as a claim that socialism provides the individual with a more realistic opportunity for making his wishes felt than does a system of private property.

I do not think that the socialist argument comes to grips with the liberal point that power is the only effective check on power. But it does draw attention to a major aspect of the problem: the necessity to distinguish between centralized economic control that is forcibly imposed in order to carry out a policy opposed by most of the population and one that is the consequence of an attempt to find a more satisfactory way of meeting the wishes of the population. Organized terror in the Soviet Union belongs quite clearly in the first of these two categories. The Soviet case cannot therefore be made to support the argument that *any* form of socialism will require organized terror to maintain it.

Under what circumstances, then, may socialism, or any similar form of centralized economy, be expected to develop the features of organized and more or less permanent terror? The answer may be hazarded that organized terror, in its beginning stages at any rate, does not stem from any particular type of economic structure, but from the attempt to alter the structure of society at a rapid rate and from above through forceful administrative devices. The essence of the situation appears to lie in the crusading spirit, the fanatical conviction in the justice and universal applicability of some ideal about the way life should be organized, along with a lack of serious concern about the consequences of the methods used to pursue this ideal. The liberal suspicion of fanatical and self-righteous utopianism is well founded in this respect, though there is very great difficulty in specifying in concrete terms what is utopian and what is practicable. The attempt to change institutions rapidly nearly always results in opposition by established interests. The more rapid and more thorough the change, the more extensive and bitter is the opposition likely to be. Hence organized terror becomes necessary. It may be employed either by the opponents or the advocates of change, or by both if the society becomes polarized around two camps strongly upholding and opposing the *status quo.*

Insofar as socialism requires terror, it does so primarily in order to change the situation that it inherits from its predecessors. Economic and social change that is not the spontaneous product of attitudes and social relationships widely prevalent throughout the society require terror and enthusiasm as their motive force. Whether spontaneous or forced, a rapid pace of change is likely to produce widespread human suffering. Hence the situation in which a socialist regime comes to power is crucial in determining the probabilities of terror, as is widely recognized in socialist writings. If the socialists are content to take over the situation left by their predecessors without making fundamental changes, relatively little terror may be needed. This was the situation originally anticipated in Marxist theory, where terror would merely brush away the remnants of the old order. If, on the other hand, socialism is to be dynamic after it has come to power, it is likely to require the constant application of terror, both against the population at large and dissidents within its own ranks. Its commitment to terror is as great as its commitment to change that goes against the habits and desires of various sectors of the population.

Revolutionary leaders on this account are frequently faced with a dilemma. If they display too little "revolutionary courage" in the use of force, their opponents may rally and overthrow them. The weakness of the German socialists in this respect is often cited as one of the major elements in the Nazi counterrevolution. If, on the other hand, the revolutionists display too much "revolutionary courage" in destroying the bases of the old order and creating a new one, they may find that their original objectives of greater human freedom have been sacrificed to the necessities of keeping power.

If terror is the product of enthusiasm and one of the necessary instruments of a dynamic regime, it is likewise one of the elements that can destroy this dynamism. Here we arrive at the more specific question of the services and disservices to the present Soviet regime of organized terror and the potential significance of the new stress on legality, first announced, ironically enough, by Beriya in his funeral oration for Stalin on March 9, 1953. In July 1953, Beriya himself was purged, becoming the most prominent victim to date of the policy he had formally promulgated. Since some observers interpret the announcement of the new legality and ensuing developments as a fundamental turning-point in Communist policy which could lead to the eventual emergence of a genuinely democratic form of socialism in the USSR,[28] it is well to examine this point somewhat more closely.

First, it may be helpful to recall the sequence of the major events as they took place up until the early summer of 1953. Beriya's speech was followed on March 28 by a sweeping amnesty decree that released persons sentenced to imprisonment for up to five years, and others, regardless of the length of the sentence, who had committed certain kinds of economic crimes involving the misuse of managerial authority, as well as those who had committed certain lesser offenses against military discipline, such as draft dodging and being AWOL. The amnesty did not apply, however, to persons sentenced to terms of more than five years for counterrevolutionary crimes, major thefts of socialist property, banditry, and premeditated murder. A few days later, on April 3, *Pravda* and *Izvestiya* carried the startling announcement that the doctors accused of hastening the death of Zhdanov and Shcherbakov had been "arrested by the former USSR Ministry of State Security incorrectly, without any lawful basis," that the persons accused of incorrect conduct of the investigation of these doctors had been arrested and the doctors released. On April 6, a *Pravda* editorial accused a former Minister of State Security, Semyon D. Ignatiev, of "political blindness" in connection with the doctors' case, declaring he had been misled by one Ryumin, a deputy minister and head of the investigation section, who had been arrested. "Nobody will be permitted to violate Soviet law," *Pravda* continued in its editorial. "Every worker, every collective farmer, and every Soviet intellectual can work peacefully and confidently, knowing that his civil rights are reliably guarded by Soviet socialist law."

Shortly afterward, the new legality spread to the provinces. The first announcement came from Georgia, where the secretary of the Party, Mgeladze, was removed for having participated with the Georgian Minister of State Security in setting up a "provocational 'case' falsified from beginning to end," one of several indications that the original accusation against the doctors had found echoes in similar cases in the provinces. Mgeladze's reign was a brief one. Originally appointed, supposedly at the personal intervention of Stalin and Beriya, to clean up the situation for which his predecessor, one Charkviani, had been responsible, he began with a revealing denunciation of the situation under Charkviani, which has been cited in Chapter 1 as an illustration of the difficulties of Soviet rule in the provinces. Now by a twist of fate that has many parallels in Soviet history Mgeladze was accused of engaging in the same crimes as Charkviani.[29] During the rest of April, a number of personnel changes also took place in the Ukrainian, Belorussian, Azerbaidzhan, and Armenian Republics, as they adopted reorganizations of their ministries parallel to the one announced for the USSR as a whole shortly after Stalin's death.[30] Presumably similar changes will follow in the remaining republics.

It is quite true that from even the most cold-blooded standpoint of self-interest there comes a point at which the use of terror defeats its purposes. Some awareness of this fact may conceivably have played some part in the reversal of the case of the Kremlin doctors and the enunciation of the policy of strict Soviet legality. If everybody in a society is marked as an actual or potential scoundrel, all sorts of vital social relationships will break down. The subordinate will not obey his superior if he is made to feel that this obedience will soon be held against him as evidence of collaboration in some deep-lying plot against the state. Terror ultimately destroys the network of stable expectations concerning what other people will do that lie at the core of any set of organized human relationships. One can readily imagine, for example, what would happen if all Soviet factory directors suddenly found themselves in a completely indeterminate situation in which there were no rules to go by and no way of anticipating the behavior of their subordinates in the plant or their superiors in the ministry in any concrete instance. The entire economy would rapidly come to a halt. Over and above the understandable need to give the population some psychological reassurance in the particular circumstances of Stalin's death, there is an objective and continuing need for some degree of regularity and predictability, or in other words, legality, in even the most arbitrary despotism that hopes to survive. The individual is unlikely to display even the minimum of initiative necessary to maintain a totalitarian system if terror becomes too arbitrary and capricious.

Law and justice, as formally defined, provide only a small part of the necessary regularity that has to be anticipated by the people who live in a viable social system. In the stress on legality, however, the new Soviet authorities have been saying something more than that the mere formalities of the law would be maintained. The point that they have been trying to get across to the population, rather desperately it seems, is that the Soviet system is basically a fair system that can be counted on to reward those who serve it faithfully and to punish those who serve it ill. This emphasis has been driven home by various propaganda devices, including homely tales of individuals caught in the web of false denunciations. In these accounts there is a new note of candor about the methods of injustice that must make many Soviet readers sit up and rub their eyes, as they read facts they have known for a long time but have never seen before in the turgid pages of their official press.

There are, on the other hand, a number of services that organized terror performs for the regime. In the first place, it helps to generate in some people a sort of generalized fear, a sensation of guilt, that in many cases results in feats of prodigious effort.[31] These exceptional efforts must be balanced against the loss of initiative and the escape from responsibility that the background of terror produces in others. Yet they are immediate evidence that the consequences are by no means altogether negative from the regime's standpoint. In the second place, since the terror hits heavily at the instruments of the dictatorship, it helps to prevent them from obtaining too much independent power and thereby frustrating the will of the dictator. The Great Purge of the late thirties struck heavily at the Party, for which there is fairly detailed evidence, and also at the secret police itself, for which the evidence is much scantier.[32] Terror is a necessary ingredient in the dictator's ability to "shake up the apparatus" and reach down to interfere with its operations at any level. It therefore contitutes an essential element in the dictator's control. It also constitutes a device, albeit an extreme one, through which the Soviet system can handle the problem of initiating shifts in policy and personnel and making the new policy stick. Likewise, the purges help to clear the road for talent, keeping open channels of upward mobility, a necessary feature in any dynamic industrial society. Without more precise statistical information, it is difficult to estimate the significance of the purge in this connection, but it is probably considerable. Finally, one should not overlook its effect in destroying and preventing the formation of organized opposition. Former Soviet citizens, who as a group have the greatest stake in the possibilities of such opposition, are nearly unanimous in their denial that any such opposition exists.* In this respect, terror is a necessary counterpart to the cult of an infallible leadership in preventing alterna-

---

* The contrast with the situation in the early thirties is quite striking. Then an ordinary American Communist could go to the USSR, and upon his disillusionment find himself almost automatically put in touch with an organized grass roots opposition within the Communist Party. See the account of Andrew Smith, *I Was a Soviet Worker* (London, 1937). The dissident Yugoslav Communist, A. Ciliga, in his *Au Pays du Grand Mensonge* (Paris, 1938) also gives evidence of considerable organized opposition within the Party at that time.

tive appraisals of the situation at home and abroad from splitting the Party. This infallibility, for which the seeds were planted by Lenin, was fully cultivated by Stalin, and upon his death transferred to a collective leadership, which so far has presented itself as a rather anonymous and impersonal body to the Soviet public.

Summing up the advantages and disadvantages of organized terror to the Soviet system, one can offer the conclusion that the new regime still requires terror as an essential aspect of its power and that it is unlikely to give it up of its own accord. The regime has to walk a thin and not always easily discernible line between using too much terror or too little. Too much can destroy the minimal framework of regularity and legality necessary to maintain the total system upon which the regime's power depends. Too little terror diminishes control at the center by permitting the growth of independent centers of authority within the bureaucracy. Whether the new leaders will be able to solve this problem remains to be seen. Thus far the concessions made to the population, in the form of retail price cuts, the amnesty decree, and other items mentioned earlier, form part of an overall pattern of reducing commitments at home and abroad. At the same time, the leaders are trying to give an aura of popularity and legality to the new regime. In this way, they can cast the cloak of legitimacy over the reshuffling of lieutenants that is evidently taking place widely, as the new leaders, or factions within the leadership, endeavor to consolidate their hold. The major significance of the new Soviet legality appears to be that heads will roll, but they will roll legally. Some persons will be let out of jail, but others will go in. So far, then, the new legality bears a striking resemblance to its Stalinist parent.

chapter 7

IMAGES OF THE
FUTURE

After examining some of the major institutions in Soviet society, we are now at a point where it is necessary to weave together the implications, scattered throughout earlier chapters, which seemed to point to stability or to various forms of change. The number of ways in which the situation in the Soviet Union *can* turn out is almost certainly limited. Probably most thoughtful people would agree that the future is not a purely random affair in which anything can happen, and that there are limits to effective human action. The difficulties begin when one tries to be specific about these limits and to present the reasons for their existence.

The argument that there is only a limited range of alternatives open to Soviet society rests partly upon the following general considerations. In any large-scale industrial society there is a definite number of activities that must be carried on if that society is to continue in existence. Or, to put the matter in a slightly different way, there are certain decisions that have to be made and certain problems that have to be solved in order for the society to exist. Among them, for example, are the production of manufactured goods and their exchange against food products from the countryside. In the course of the discussion, I shall try to indicate what these activities and problems are in the specific case of the Soviet Union. Furthermore there is, again very probably, only a limited number of ways in which these activities can be carried out, or a limited number of solutions that are possible to these problems. For example, as has been pointed out before, certain kinds of industrial discipline and some aspects of the organization of factory life appear to be just as necessary in Magnitogorsk as they are in Detroit. In this connection, it is necessary to emphasize that any statement to the effect that certain activities must be performed in one or more of a specified variety of ways, if a society is to survive, carries no implication that the society will survive. For a variety of reasons, people may not be able to carry out the necessary adaptation, and the society may cease to exist. In theory at least, complete extinction is one of the concrete possibilities that has to be kept in mind.

Finally, the kind of solution that is adopted for one problem limits the range of workable alternatives that are open for the solution of other problems. Marx was undoubtedly correct in his argument that the way in which a society took care of the problem of producing and distributing material goods limited the way in which other problems, such as the organization of political authority, could be solved. It is not, however, necessarily just the solution to the economic problem that limits the solutions to the others. Human societies have displayed a wide range of emphases—from war and expansion beyond their boundaries through commerce and religion—in the types of activities they have stressed and the problems to whose solution they have given priority. In turn these varying emphases have set the tone for other institutions in these societies.

As these emphases shift in response to internal and external circumstances, the forms of the institutions in a society undergo change. In this way, one kind of a society may in time become transformed into a different kind. Often it is a matter of arbitrary decision to assert where one form has ceased to exist and another has taken its place. In other cases, as when a revolution occurs, it is easier to make a distinction between the old and the new. Such distinctions, are, however, a matter of terminology, rather than of substance. The important point is that this approach does not carry any commitment to a particular form of the status quo in the Soviet Union or anywhere else, any more than it implies that any society is a perfectly integrated set of institutions.

In practically all societies, the process of adaptive change is going on almost all of the time, sometimes in a rational and planned manner, sometimes by purely trial-and-error methods, though the rate and extent of change may at times be so small as to be imperceptible. There is, of course, the very real danger that we may mistake some contemporary and limited adjustment, that is only one possibility among many, for a necessary and inevitable one. Not long ago, it was thought that any industrial society inevitably required private property in the instruments of production in order to exist. Nearly a quarter century of Soviet experience has made this proposition appear extremely dubious. To mistake a limited adjustment for a universally necessary one is, however, a factual error rather than an error in the basic approach and assumptions.

One further point deserves brief discussion before proceeding with the concrete task at hand. Though it might be possible to list the activities carried on by any society in a formal scheme that displayed impeccable logical consistency and was entirely free from overlaps and blurrings at the boundaries of its categories, I doubt that such terminological precision would have great scientific utility.* Furthermore, there is generally no one-to-one correspondence between any particular type of activity and the institutions that have grown up as the organized way of carrying out this activity. In the USSR, for instance, the production of goods and services is carried out partly by economic and partly by political institutions, and to some extent also by the family. The difficulty is increased by the fact that our categories for describing these matters are to a very great extent the product of our own intellectual tradition and social structure, and can only with some wrenching be applied to new and different situa-

---

* On this point I concur wholly with Keller's observations on what he calls the "category fallacy." See W. G. Sumner and A. G. Keller, *The Science of Society* (New Haven, 1929), III, 2201–2203. To sociologists my debts to the intellectual tradition represented in this work, and to the rather different one exemplified in Max Weber and the contemporary structural-functional school, particularly Talcott Parsons and Robert K. Merton, will all be obvious, as will be the extent to which I depart from positions taken by these groups.

tions. For the problem at hand, nevertheless, less ambiguity is likely to arise from the careful and consistent use of ordinary language than from an attempt to use some of the more technical schemes that have been developed by social scientists, or to devise still another set of categories for this special purpose.

In the analysis of Soviet society as a whole, one can begin by pointing to a cluster of five closely related problems that receive strong emphasis and whose solution has a marked effect upon the others. The first problem concerns the allocation of power and responsibility. Some way has to be found for choosing the people who are to make the decisions that affect the entire society and play a major part in holding the society together as a distinctive unit. Soviet institutions, as is widely recognized, fail to provide any dependable way of reaching this kind of a decision that can be counted on to win acceptance from all the individuals vitally involved. Likewise, a more or less peaceable procedure has to be found for choosing the subordinates and lieutenants of whoever holds the supreme power. The problem of allocating power and responsibility can, of course, be broken down very much further, but these aspects are all that need to be mentioned for the moment.

The second problem is familiar under the general term "economic production." Activities carried out in connection with this problem constitute answers, as economists point out, to two questions: what shall this society produce, and in what ways shall human and natural resources, or labor and capital, be combined for this purpose? The Soviet answer, for nearly two decades, has been to industrialize as rapidly as possible through its own efforts, with strong emphasis on the making of producers' goods, at the cost of heavy sacrifices from the population. The commitment to a totalitarian political regime and to rapid industrial expansion are in the Soviet case closely connected, with the consequence that a reversal of either commitment carries important implications for the other.

The third and fourth activities concern the distribution of

goods and services among the Soviet people, and the distribution of the people among the various aspects of the production
process in accord with the requirements of the latter. These activities are answers to the questions: who gets what, and who
does what? Their solution is heavily influenced by the solutions
that have been adopted for the preceding ones. Various forms of
coercion have increasingly supplemented income differentials in
the Soviet search for answers to these twin problems of economic
distribution and economic motivation. The growth of a recognizable class system is also in part traceable to the ways in which
these two problems have been handled and constitutes one of the
institutional devices through which they receive an answer.

While the preceding activities concern some of the positive
sides of rule in that they involve getting people to do something,
there is also, as pointed out earlier in this study, the negative
side of preventing people from doing other things. This negative
task can here be called the control of crime, since crime ordinarily refers to ways of behaving that are forbidden by rulers
and lawmakers and excludes forms of behavior that are merely
the subject of ridicule, shame, and informal popular devices for
checking deviant behavior. The distinction is important, since in
the Soviet Union some forms of behavior that are legally criminal,
such as the failure of a kolkhoz to deliver its full crop quota, are
not judged as reprehensible by substantial segments and possibly even the overwhelming majority of the population. Although there undoubtedly has to be some degree of overlap between popular notions of right and wrong and those imposed by
any dictatorship, the gap is frequently large.

This cluster of five problems requires a set of solutions in any
large society. It is the ways in which they are answered, the
forms of organization that have been devised as adjustments in
the search for their solution, that give the USSR its distinctive
character. For the most part, these activities are carried out
through what are generally spoken of as Soviet political and economic institutions—in concrete terms, the Communist Party, the

secret police, the courts, the ministries in charge of industry, and the collective farms. The Soviet class system also enters into the performance of these activities, but discussion of this aspect of Soviet society may be deferred for a moment.

In the analysis of Soviet political and economic institutions * given in earlier chapters there was considerable stress on the criteria by which "good" decisions were distinguished from "bad" ones, as well as on the many kinds of pressure that influenced individuals to make their decisions one way or another. An examination of the ways in which these criteria can vary will suggest the range of possible variation for these institutions. To carry out such an examination in any exhaustive fashion would be an enormous and perhaps an impossible task. Just to describe all the possible ways in which a factory worker can vary his behavior might easily require a volume as large as this one, even if no attempt were made to relate the consequences of all these choices to the actions of other people in the society. Fortunately, such exhaustiveness is hardly necessary, since the behavior of most people in Soviet society, as in any other, ordinarily varies within a rather narrow range. Furthermore, we are not interested in all possible criteria for the decisions made by every person in every possible niche in the political and economic system, but only in criteria that characterize the behavior, more or less equally, of large groups, such as the peasants, workers, intellectuals, and economic administrators, or of small and politically powerful groups, such as the Party leaders.

As has been suggested at various points in this study, three elements may be distinguished that in varying degrees enter into the criteria that distinguish a "good" from a "bad" decision.

---

* The word "institution" is a red-flag symbol to many social scientists, who are likely to call a halt and demand a definition because of the loose way in which the term is frequently used. Here it refers to any form of group relationship in which the behavior of the people concerned displays recurring and predictable features, as, for example, in the family, factory, or larger social units. The term excludes random and aimless behavior, as well as that which concerns only a single individual.

One element that has been heavily stressed is the power of the highest Communist leadership. By and large, Soviet political and economic institutions constitute a remarkable instrument through which the decisions of a tiny group of men, perhaps frequently a single individual, become transformed into the intense and coördinated labor of millions. The second element is the necessity to adapt to the technical requirements of the human and natural situation, or to find an effective way of getting results, even at some sacrifice in political control. This rational and technical element is found in such varied decisions as the granting of additional autonomy to factory managers and the restriction of the amalgamation program among the kolkhozes to goals considerably short of Khrushchev's "farm cities." In many of the decisions of engineers and scientists it remains unquestionably the most prominent element of all, even though these persons are under close political supervision.

The third element is tradition and precedent, in the sense of resistance to change. Where tradition furnishes the main criterion, a good decision is one that resembles some previous one, while a bad decision breaks with established routines. In this concept of tradition there is also a whiff of authority that is applicable here. Traditional decisions are not only those that follow established routines, but they are also those that are sanctioned by the wishes of persons or groups regarded as legitimately holding high status in a society. For the peasantry, tradition in the form of deadening routine, of trying to do things the way they have been done in the past, is often the natural mode of life, overcome only by external forces. Although perhaps less prominent in Soviet political institutions, this element exists widely in Soviet economic institutions. One need only recall the device commonly used in industry of sticking to plans and production methods of previous years in order to evade the government's incessant demands for increased output of materials and effort.

These three elements — power, rationality, and tradition—do

not necessarily exhaust the criteria according to which decisions can be made in the Soviet system. It is also quite possible that some other classification might yield more useful results. No one of the three can be emphasized to the complete exclusion of the other, and they are not always necessarily contradictory and mutually exclusive. Nevertheless, by considering the extent to which each plays a role, and more especially the possibilities and probable consequences of an increase in the emphasis of any one of them along with a corresponding decrease in the emphasis upon the other two, it may be possible to gain some insight into the range of alternatives before the Soviet political and economic system. The same procedure may also be followed in connection with some of the more important activities and institutions that fall outside the scope of strictly political and economic affairs, to which we shall come in due course.

Under Stalin, the emphasis on power as the criterion of a good decision in all spheres of Soviet life was pushed to a point that seems close to the possible limit. At present there is no way of knowing whether this power was that of the dictator alone, or that of Stalin and a few associates upon whom he had to rely, though the latter seems somewhat more likely. In terms of the essential dynamics of the Soviet system, the distinction is not important.

The major difficulty with straightforward power as the chief criterion for decision-making is that it provides no separate and independent basis for its own allocation. Power differs from technical rationality in that the latter provides for the selection of leaders according to objective merit and technical qualifications. It also differs from tradition, which provides for their selection on the basis of accepted custom and ritual.

If the emphasis on power were pushed much further in Soviet society, it seems likely that any reliable basis for the peaceful allocation of responsibility would disappear, not only at the level of the dictator himself but throughout the administrative apparatus. The ultimate consequence would be a disintegration of Soviet society into a war of all against all. Some reasoning of this sort lies behind the various predictions of upheaval and catastrophe that were expected to follow Stalin's death. On the other hand, there is a point somewhere short of this extreme where the emphasis on power can produce a political and social system that destroys many of the individuals within it, while maintaining its structural features intact. Indeed, as Merle Fainsod suggests in *How Russia Is Ruled,* the insecurity of the individuals within the system can be a major source of the system's perpetuation. The power of the dictator, especially his power to intervene arbitrarily at any level of the administrative hierarchy down to the most remote hamlet in a distant Asiatic province, depends very heavily on his being able to keep all of the officials at a certain level of insecurity.

The consequences of the emphasis on power and its relationship to the subordinates' insecurity may become clearer if we contrast the dynamics of totalitarian rule with those of another situation in which power is also highly concentrated, a large and well-run cargo steamship. On such a vessel, the captain has very wide authority, but there the resemblance to a dictatorship ceases. The subordinates of the captain, down to the lowliest member of the crew, have clearly defined spheres of competence. Each man has a job to do and a specified way in which he is supposed to do it. The chain of command, symbolized in uniforms and titles of rank, is clear to all concerned. Neither those in positions of authority nor those who carry out orders may violate the chain of command by skipping over one of its links. The man who performs his job well according to clearly specified technical criteria can ordinarily expect some reward for so doing and will not, as a rule, regard technical skill as something that exposes him to arbitrary punishment. A dictatorship, on the other hand, avoids clearly defined spheres of competence. The essence of the dictator's power rests upon the ability to skip links in the chain of command and to intervene at any point in order to prevent the consolidation of subordinates in opposition to the leadership. Particularly in the Soviet system, all officials, even those closest to the top, occupy an exposed position. Mere technical performance is no guarantee of security. To maintain power, the top Soviet leadership cannot afford to "leave things alone" in the rest of the society. For its continuation, the Soviet system of rule requires a continuous stirring of the pot, repeated shakings-up. On a ship, on the other hand, such shakings-up are regarded as something that destroys morale and effective working relationhips. A ship represents in its way the epitome of the rational-technical model of decision-making and problem-solving relationships, while a dictatorship, with its stress on power, develops very different forms.[1]

Probably no ship has ever been the perfect model of rational authority.* Even a dictatorship, however, cannot dispense with some elements of rational authority. Some degree of clarity and regularity in the allocation of rights, duties, and functions is necessary for the continuation of any administrative system. There has to be some area of defined competence for the official, even though the edges of this area are blurred. It is necessary to emphasize once again that the ideas of power, rationality, and tradition represent extremes that probably cannot ever be wholly realized in practice. Since the Soviet dictatorship cannot dispense with this rational element, the interesting question arises of whether or not the dictatorship might be rationalizing itself,

---

* The distinction between a dictatorship and other forms of hierarchical organization is also partly a distinction between power relationships and authority relationships. Some writers draw the line very sharply between these two. Thus Sebastian de Grazia, *Errors of Psychotherapy* (New York, 1952), declares, "Authority is not force or coercion. By definition it is power that wants using, that is granted in order to be used, that has the support of those for whom and over whom it is used. In short, rightful power" (p. 42). This definition puts the emphasis on the subjective feelings of those under power or authority, which makes it difficult to use for some purposes. In terms of such a definition authority is, I think, largely absent in Soviet society, but such a statement could not be proved without ascertaining the feelings of every Soviet citizen. Here the term authority will be used merely to denote a greater element of acceptance than does the term power, without implying that the latter rests on coercion or even the threat of coercion alone.

so to speak, against its will. Perhaps the Soviet system is suffering from the disease of creeping rationality, much as some people think ours is suffering from creeping socialism. Beneath the turmoil of the purges, demotions, and meteoric promotions that constitute such a prominent feature in the Soviet political landscape one may detect throughout the history of the regime a steady lumbering movement in the direction of the clearer allocation of responsibility. It is worth while, therefore, to explore what might happen if this trend should display still greater strength with the passage of time.

The end result can be imagined as a technocracy—the rule of the technically competent. By definition, such a development would imply a heavy reduction of emphasis on the power of the dictator and its replacement by technical and rational criteria of behavior and organization. The share in power and prestige held by the instruments of violence and persuasion, the secret police and the Party, would decline. That of the industrial manager, the engineer, and the technical administrator would rise. The roles of the political and the technical administrators would be reversed, in that the instruments of violence and persuasion would become the servants of the technocratic rulers, persuading "backward" elements of the population that industrialization really benefited them. Legality, in the sense of an impersonal definition of crime, would replace the arbitrary elements in the present system. Freed from continued political interference, administrative officials would be secure to enjoy the perquisites of office so long as they continued to perform their duties skillfully and accurately. Promotion in the bureaucratic hierarchy would be according to demonstrated merit. The rapid pace of industrial development would continue, though there might be a greater emphasis on consumers' goods. The mass of the population would receive a larger flow of goods and services than is now the case, but would not have a significantly larger share in the decisions determining their fate. Such a set of political and economic institutions, it may be noted, would not differ greatly from the image of Soviet society that many advocates of economic planning with an authoritarian tinge believed they saw in the Soviet Union of the thirties. It is also a far from inaccurate sketch of proclaimed Communist goals, though a Communist would try to claim that even now the masses participate in the determination of policy.

What are the actual possibilities of such a development? It would require a hardy prophet to declare that it is either inevitable or impossible. The chief basis for anticipating such a possibility lies in the argument that the nature of modern industry is such as to push any industrial society in this general direction. The machine, so the argument runs, disciplines the worker with the discipline of the assembly line, forcing him to acquire the virtues of precision, punctuality, and a close awareness of the relationship between physical cause and effect, in a word, rationality. At the same time, the delicate and intricate dependence of industrial plants on one another for the exchange of goods and services forces a similar rationality upon those in charge of the system. The reliance of a machine civilization on science further promotes the spirit of rationality in intellectual life. All these forces find their reflection in the structure of social institutions. Since the Soviet Union has been industrialized, so the argument continues, it cannot be immune to this development, which has already taken over much of the Western world. The rationalizing power of modern industry was set forth by Marx himself with particular vigor, and the same general viewpoint has recently been applied by Isaac Deutscher to forecast the future of the Soviet Union.[2]

Such an interpretation contains within it the concealed assumption that the material welfare of the population is somehow or other bound to be the chief consideration of the present and future rulers of the USSR. It is quite true that the Bolsheviks came to power with a strong commitment to this eventual goal, one that could conceivably be reactivated under favorable circumstances. But the experience of the past quarter century of Bolshevik rule, if it proves anything, proves the possibility of treating industry as a political instrument to serve political goals. The Soviet industrial system is an elaborate mechanism to prevent industry from serving any immediate goal of mass welfare. Whether the instrument can eventually become the master is beyond accurate prediction. Nevertheless, the weight of the evidence indicates, to me at least, that industry can be forced to continue in the role of servant. Furthermore, it appears very questionable that Stalin's successors, soaked in the Bolshevik conception of the importance of political factors and political strategy, would peacefully relinquish the levers of command to those who represent this point of view. A revolutionary coup, on the other hand, by such elements seems to have very dim prospects under present conditions.

The gradual evolution of Soviet political and economic institutions in a traditionalist direction appears somewhat more plausible, though there appear to be rather narrow limits to any such development. In contrast to the technocratic line of transformation, traditionalist change would imply a decline in the share of power and prestige held by the technical administrator. The Party and the secret police would remain the dominant elements in the state, although the military forces might gain somewhat in influence as Party and police controls over them declined in effectiveness. For the essence of a traditionalist development, as the term is used here, lies in the inability of the dictator to intervene effectively through periodic shake-ups of the bureaucratic machinery at points where it had become subject to the dry rot of routine. By definition, matters would go on as they had before. Nominally and in many respects actually still the leaders, the Communist rulers would no longer be able to reach down to the bottom levels of Soviet society to make their policies effective. Such a limitation on the arbitrary power of the center likewise implies a rise in local autonomy. In this fashion, the Soviet masses would enjoy some increase in the opportunity to affect policy and determine their own fate. Loyalty and obedience to a person would replace that to an abstract office with rapidly changing incumbents. The ties of personal cliques, whose network now spreads through much of the Soviet bureaucracy, might well be the focal point for the creation of such loyalties. In a very extreme form, the end result might approach the forms of European feudalism, which also emerged in part from the decline of the centralized Roman bureaucracy.*

In economic life, under a traditionalist system, the factory manager who "sits with folded arms in search of the quiet life," now a prominent target of Communist invective, would become the dominant type. The Party secretary would cease to be the spark plug of technical innovation. The evasion of pressures from above for greater output would increase far above the present situation, until the pressures themselves dried up. The collective farms would become closer to genuine coöperatives, as they too evaded the demands for turning over their quotas of produce to the government. In this way, the vital connection between town and country would be broken, the network of relations that make the Soviet Union a single society heavily damaged. The *élan* of industrial expansion would vanish.

Indeed, carried to any extreme, the traditionalist line of development would be incompatible with the existence of an industrial society.† Population decline would set in, and would be rapid if the centralized economic apparatus broke down swiftly in the manner just sketched. The consequence would be misery and social disorganization on a wide scale. The reaction might

* Though there are many more differences than similarities in the situations confronting the Roman and the Soviet bureaucracies, it is appropriate to recall that the former lasted for some centuries without any device for a peaceful solution to the problem of succession.

† However, as many writers have noted, industrialism in its advanced stages destroys much of the original technical-rational relationship between individual effort and objective results, while it simultaneously takes on some traditionalist features. The growth of large corporations, large labor unions, the development of social insurance and other factors give the individual a place in a large group and tie him to a *status quo,* which is then less readily changed. Parallel forces, I think, lie just below the surface in the Soviet system. In both cases, they serve to slow up the rate of technological and social changes.

easily be a new variety of totalitarian integration. The traditional-ist outcome, in other words, appears to be possible only if move-ment in this direction is relatively slow. On the whole, the func-tional imperatives of industrialism would appear to set rather sharp limits on any far-reaching evolution of Soviet society in the traditionalist direction.

So far the discussion has referred to the possibility of demo-cratic institutions only in passing. Democracy can be arbitrarily defined as a political system in which are found the secret ballot, organized political parties representing distinct interest groups and currents of opinion, a legislature where elected representa-tives promote and reconcile these interests, and a judiciary with some independence of both the legislative and the executive branches of the government. Historical experience with democ-racy suggests that such a set of arrangements is compatible with some movement in either the technical-rational or the tradi-tionalist direction. However, an extreme development in either direction would probably rule out democracy. The rational-technical extreme imposes the single standard of technical ef-ficiency on all decisions. Its spirit is opposed to the plurality of goals characteristic of democracy. The traditionalist extreme, on the other hand, leads to the break-up of the state into semi-feudal units.

Paper forms more or less appropriate to democratic institutions have been part of the official constitutional structure of the Bol-shevik regime since 1918. Frequently in the course of its history, and particularly after Stalin's death, sympathetic observers have expressed the hope that these forms would come to represent the reality of Communist political behavior. Such a shift in the major trend of Bolshevik history since the foundation of the Party in 1903 seems to me at least extraordinarily unlikely. In the first place, it would imply a reversal of the major working assump-tions of Bolshevik rule. The notion of permitting a free play of in-terests within the state goes completely contrary to the idea of manipulating people and social forces to bring about a predetermined political objective, the characteristic pattern of Communist behavior. In the second place, the historical experience of contemporary Western democratic institutions [3] is one in which various groups through both violent and peaceful means shake themselves free from the controls of royal absolutism, eventually destroying much of the latter's power. While a parallel development cannot be ruled out in the case of the Soviet system, it is difficult to see what these groups might be or how the process could get started as long as some faction of the Communist Party remains in the saddle. In the past, dissident Bolshevik groups, unsuccessful in the internal struggle for power, have developed programs that show considerable similarity to the concept of democracy used here. The effect was to increase the repressive discipline of the dominant faction. Should a succession struggle produce openly organized and competing factions (in itself rather unlikely in the form Bolshevism had reached by the 1950's), it seems very improbable that any victorious group could afford to relax its dictatorial grip. Thus both tradition and circumstance combine to render highly dubious any peaceful transformation of the Communist regime into a democratic system.

So far, it appears that the range of possible alternatives open to any foreseeable Soviet leadership is a rather narrow one. To keep themselves in power, the rulers must maintain a delicate balance between the requirements of clarity and confusion, security and insecurity, legality and arbitrariness, in the situations that face their subordinate commanders and the rank-and-file population. By the same token, they must somehow prevent the paralysis of traditionalism by maintaining the same kind of balance between custom and innovation, routine and initiative.

Whether they will succeed, is another question. Is it possible, for example, that forces outside of the area conventionally marked off by the terms politics and economics might be at work, slowly or rapidly altering this system in such a fashion that it will soon be unrecognizable? Even if it is agreed that politics and economics are the crucial elements in Soviet life, certainly they do not exhaust the whole of human activity. Clearly there are other places where we must look.

One place is the Soviet class system. In the analysis of any society Marxists are likely to look here first of all. Possibly this is one of the reasons why the Soviet Union is so sparing in the facts,[4] particularly the necessary statistical information, that it releases about its own class system. In the Soviet case at least, the analysis of their class system does not require consideration of any new activity in addition to the cluster of five already discussed. Social classes in the Soviet Union, as elsewhere, constitute a device through which human beings are matched with jobs and responsibilities, rights and duties, prestige and rewards, the whole complex of affairs denoted by the term status. Generally speaking, social stratification in a society represents one of the ways through which power, authority, and material goods are unequally distributed or allocated in that society. It differs from political and economic institutions in that it is ordinarily much more diffuse, lacking any organized officials to put its operations into effect.

Discussions of social class are complicated by the fact that the categories which are used by the observer, frequently based on some rough combination of income and occupation, may not correspond very closely with the categories that are actually used by the members of the society themselves, as shown not only in their language but also in their behavior toward one another. In the USSR, the official categories that are used in all Communist discussions of the subject are workers, peasants, and the "toiling intelligentsia." To these three is occasionally added, in the more technical discussions, a fourth category, the *sluzhashchie*, which roughly approximates our notion of white-collar workers and is usually translated as employees. It is obvious that many important nuances of social behavior would escape through so crude a mesh. Nevertheless, the interview materials give the impression that these categories are fairly widely used among the Soviet population and have some rough correspondence with social reality. Further study of how the Soviets themselves perceive their own class system and behave in it, based on refugee sources, can be expected to illuminate this problem.

Roughly speaking, there are two ways in which people can be matched with jobs and prestige. One of them allocates people according to merit, that is, expected capacity to perform new jobs or demonstrated capacity in past ones. The ideal of equality of opportunity stresses one form of this criterion. The application of this principle does not produce a system of hereditary social classes. If the Soviet Union follows something resembling the technocratic path of development, the criterion of merit is the one that will have to be stressed in the future. If it continues along the present lines of a totalitarian dictatorship, a somewhat different version of the merit criterion will also require emphasis, a point that will be argued shortly. The other way in which people can be matched with jobs and prestige is according to some real or supposed quality in the individual or the group to which the person belongs, such as race, religion, language, age, or sex. Some such principle underlies caste systems and many class systems where there is little movement from one class to another. It is compatible with a traditionalist emphasis in Soviet society, and incompatible with an emphasis on either technical rationality or on the totalitarian power of the ruler. Neither the criterion of merit nor that of some real or alleged group quality, can become the sole basis for allocating people to different economic and political tasks in so large and complex a society as the USSR. The two principles represent opposite extremes, neither of which is likely to be fully recognized in practice. But strong accent on one is possible only in circumstances that are very different from those permitting stress upon the other.

There is a basic conflict between the principles of a hereditary class system, with its emphasis on innate and often quasi-biological distinctions among the members of the society, and the principles of totalitarian politics. The logic of a totalitarian system demands the application of the principle of allocation by merit, though indeed a special kind of merit, throughout the society. The totalitarian ruler attempts to determine the rank order of all the citizens according to one major criterion: their contribution to his power. Those who oppose him are excluded from the ranks of the citizenry. They are no longer in his eye members of the society, though in concentration camps they can be compelled to serve some of the ends of power. An essential element of totalitarian rule, especially in its Soviet version, is that in principle every citizen except the dictator is equally exposed to the risk of being cast out of the society. No rights and privileges can be acquired by hereditary prescription. In this very fundamental respect, a dictatorship such as the Bolshevik one requires a continuing high rate of social mobility. Only one aspect of this relationship is contained in the frequent observation that as a land of opportunity, the Soviet Union supposedly has a considerable hold over the able and ambitious among its youth. There is also the darker aspect of the relationship in the connection between rapid mobility, terror, insecurity, and totalitarian control.

Should the Soviet Union become gradually permeated by a rigid and hereditary class structure, it would represent as fundamental a transformation of Russian society as that which took place following the Bolshevik revolution. On the economic side, the rapid pace of industrialization, a powerhouse of change that upsets existing class relationships, would have to be brought to a halt. On the political side, instead of a totalitarian system that endeavors to reach into every facet of life, and whose hand is perhaps heaviest on its own bureaucratic servants, the ruler would have to depend upon an aristocracy, bound to him by ties of personal loyalty. Such an aristocracy could not be entirely absorbed in the administrative apparatus of the ruler, but would require some independent base for its existence as a class. The base might be in property, or in some social function that it performed, such as the service of a quasi-religious belief system, or some combination of these.

Although such an extreme does not seem very probable in any foreseeable future, the beginnings of certain trends are visible in Soviet society, which, if continued, might push this system in the direction of a more traditional structure of authority. Though these trends are not capable of precise quantitative measurement with the data that are available now or are likely to be available for some time, it is perhaps possible to make a rough estimate of their importance.

One significant factor is the separation of the rulers from the people. The social isolation of the Kremlin officials is proverbial. On informal social occasions as well as on matters of state, they chiefly see only one another. The same is true to a lesser extent of local officials, perhaps down to the level of the oblast. There are some clues that the isolation is especially marked among members of the secret police. Among the rulers, distinctions of rank and protocol are highly developed, further isolating one layer from another.[5] Among the children of officialdom there has grown up some sense of "inside dopesterism," a contempt for Party slogans and the masses to whom they are supposed to apply.[6] The situation as a whole favors intermarriage within a narrow group and the development of a distinctive way of life within this group, both major characteristics of a hereditary class system. So far these features remain below the surface, overshadowed by the insecurity and rapid turnover of the elite. Soviet sources provide materials for a study of this turnover rate, and though the labor of collecting them would be immense, the results would probably be quite revealing.

Another significant element to consider, in relation to the possibility of a more rigid stratification in Soviet society, is Soviet policy toward the non-Russian nationalities that constitute, according to official statements, about 40 per cent of the population. Though much of the basic factual spadework remains to be done in this important aspect of Soviet life, certain tentative generalizations may be offered. In the first place, as is now rather widely recognized, the Bolsheviks have never been genuine cultural pluralists. They have not attempted to let the various nationalities work out their own culture and institutions independently or find their own solutions in their own way. Some degree of autonomy has been promised and even permitted at times, chiefly as a lure and a sop, particularly in the early days of the Soviet regime when it was necessary to entice the non-Russian nationalities to accept the Bolsheviks.[7] Also the Stalinist dictatorship, even in its most repressive phases, allowed some autonomy in respect to language, as well as in several politically trivial matters, such as costumes and folk dances. But the essence of Bolshevik policy was to impose, often by harsh and brutal methods, a uniform social order upon the enormous variety of peoples inhabiting the USSR. While some of these peoples, such as the Ukrainians, were relatively "advanced," if one judges by the provincial standards of Western industrial society, others were in a state of development roughly approximating that of many American Indians, with all sorts of variations in between. The bed of Procrustes pales as a metaphor before the practice of the Soviet nationalities policy. The uniformity of its application without regard to the way of life that existed beforehand is truly astonishing. Thus we learn from a brief notice in *Pravda* (December 7, 1949) that 90 per cent of the Eskimos, together with certain other nomadic peoples who had lived primarily from reindeer herding, have joined collective farms! [8]

It is, of course, impossible to overhaul the economic life of a people without simultaneously making over a very large portion of the rest of their lives. Marxists generally would be the first to recognize and to emphasize this relationship. Yet this is exactly what the Bolsheviks did. As Kalinin put it, the aim of Soviet policy was "to teach the people of the Kirghiz steppe, the small Uzbek cotton-grower, and the Turkmenian gardener to accept the ideals of the Leningrad worker." [9] It is logically impossible to be a consistent Marxist and to take the major slogan of Soviet nationalities policy seriously. The slogan calls their policy the promotion of "cultures nationalist in form and socialist in content." [10]

Even if the slogan is a travesty upon Marxist premises, the main lines of the policy itself have followed the logic of totalitarian power. In general, it was one of breaking up enclaves of differing institutions and compelling the adoption of the Soviet system, in short, the typical process of totalitarian atomization. It was also to a great extent a policy of equalization, in that for all groups traditional barriers to the exercise of the dictator's power were broken down. In this sense, the policy was the application of the merit principle in its specifically totalitarian version, whereby people and groups receive their status in accord with their contribution to the power of the ruler, while those who resist are excluded from the society or destroyed.

This policy of totalitarian equality could not be carried out fully, and there have been very important currents of movement in the opposite direction. The net result has been to make Great Russians something rather close to a dominant class. For one thing, the agents of Communist policy were often of necessity Great Russians. Sometimes this fact led to a situation in which the Russians pulled the strings while the native leaders danced the tune. Thus the Kremlin was forced to rely upon a specific segment of the population to execute its policy, a relationship that contains the seed of a traditional class system. During and after the Second World War, the Kremlin evidently decided to make a virtue of this necessity, and even promoted a rather fantastic Russian nationalism. Such a reliance on a particular group, however, runs counter to the logic of a totalitarian system, for the reasons already suggested. After Stalin's death, some of the more extreme features of this policy were reversed. Where before there had been campaigns in the non-Russian areas against the expression of "bourgeois nationalism," under the new regime important republic leaders, such as Melnikov in the Ukraine, were dismissed because they had allegedly failed to promote native cadres. These changes can be explained as concessions to the imperatives of totalitarian rule. Similar oscillations have taken place in the past and may be expected in the future, as long as the Soviet leaders try to reconcile the conflicting requirements of maintaining both totalitarian uniformity and a reliable corps of subordinates.

Still a third point to consider is the fact that the existing allocation of power and division of labor in any society has a tendency to perpetuate itself in a way that produces a class system, unless counteracting tendencies are at work. In a sense, the isolation of the rulers in the USSR, discussed above, is merely a special aspect of this larger phenomenon. Although no firm statistical base exists for such a generalization, it seems highly likely that for a substantial majority of the Soviet population today the position of the parents, particularly the father, constitutes the most important feature that will determine the life chances of any given individual in the growing generation. The son of a rank-and-file kolkhoznik is likely to be a kolkhoznik, or a rank-and-file worker if he moves to the city.[11] A lad who starts off as a worker has perhaps a slightly better chance to move at least one rung up the ladder. Corresponding statements can be made about other segments of the population. In this respect, it is correct to assert that the Soviet Union already has the beginnings of a hereditary class system.

One can conclude, therefore, that the exercise of totalitarian power in the USSR has set in motion certain forces, derived from the necessities of distributing both power and tangible material rewards, which undermine its own basis. How far the creation of a class system can go without destroying the essential features of the totalitarian dictatorship is a question that is difficult to answer. Clearly the emergence of a pure totalitarian system, in which all the citizens were ranked anew every day according to their political contributions and reliability, is a practical impossibility. Any existing dictatorship is bound to create and tolerate some form of internal stratification. If the dictatorship is to continue, however, this emergent stratification must not go so far as to create institutional barriers between the dictator and any segment of the people, giving the latter effective autonomy. The reliance on the Russians cannot, for example, be allowed to grow to the point where Russian secret police officials refuse to punish fellow nationals because of some sense of class or ethnic solidarity. Nor can the peasants be allowed to develop a set of economic and social practices that limits the dictatorship's control over the production and distribution of food. Likewise, stratification cannot be permitted to develop to the point where the dictator is hampered in promoting and demoting his subordinates by considerations related to their social origins within the Soviet system.

To date, the emergence of any stratification that would seriously hinder the dictator's power has been prevented. Nevertheless, the regime is on the point of having to face certain crucial choices. It can either be transformed in the direction of a more rigid class system, in which case some of its totalitarian features will soften and disappear, or else it must take the steps necessary to maintain a high rate of social mobility. Of such steps there are at least three, all of which would probably have to be used together. The first, and probably the most important, would be to continue the rapid pace of industrial expansion. The second is the continuation of the system of organized terror and periodic purges. Mobility might be maintained without purges, but hardly the same degree of control over the entire social system. The purges are vital insofar as they demonstrate that continuation in any office is not a matter of prescriptive right, but depends upon the performance of a task in accord with criteria that are primarily, though not entirely, political. The third device is the maintenance of abundant opportunity to rise through the educational ladder. Very significant clues to the future may therefore be derived through careful observation of the use that the new regime makes of these three measures.

The mention of education brings us to a new series of problems, activities, and institutions. In any society, some way has to be found to regulate relationships between the sexes and to train the younger generation to take its place in that society. In the Soviet Union, as in other modern industrial societies, these activities are carried on chiefly through the institutions of the family and the formal educational system. In addition, the dictatorship's youth organizations, the Pioneers and the Komsomol, play an important part in forming the attitudes of Soviet youth. Through all of these channels, the children acquire a certain fund of factual knowledge, some of the motivations appropriate to their eventual adult status, and also some of the values and standards of behavior required by this status.

In Soviet family and educational institutions one may again perceive a balance between totalitarian, rational-technical, and traditional elements. Traditional elements, however, appear to be stronger in the educational system than elsewhere in the society. The emphasis on these features in education may have important implications for the future, even though at present it is countered by the stress on totalitarian and technical elements in the situation confronting Soviet citizens after they have become adults.

In certain respects, the totalitarian aspects of the Soviet family situation may be regarded as a development out of the rationalist trends that are apparent in any industrial society. As already noted, industrialization, and particularly rapid industrialization of the Soviet variety, requires a high rate of geographical and social mobility. It also involves a sharp reduction in the family's function as a work unit. The authorities, for reasons already discussed, have tried without complete success to bring about these changes among the peasants as well as the city population. All of these forces produce a decline in the range and strength of kinship ties, including even those between husband and wife. Divorce becomes more common, and the range of kinship ties that carry with them obligations of support and affection shrinks. With the partial break-up of the kinship bond, the society travels a considerable distance along the road to atomization, or the disintegration of all social units in which the individual participates with strong emotional bonds. Under complete atomization, the individual would be left naked and defenseless before the huge and impersonal organizations of a mass society, manipulated by a small and powerful elite. This imaginary picture of the future has in recent years become a literary commonplace. Since even an industrial society of the Soviet type generates its own type of personal relationships and friendship groupings, this imaginary state of complete atomization is unlikely ever to be realized.

Nevertheless, totalitarianism adds a new element to the destructive forces attacking the family. Within such a movement it is necessary to prevent the growth of personal ties and obligations that conflict with those of the organization. Communist Party statutes, for example, forbid personal relationships that are damaging to the Party. There is a parallel here with many other organizations that have aimed to impose a new social order and a new philosophy upon their times, and which have tried to forbid marriage altogether for their members. Such prohibitions do not necessarily exclude casual liaisons as long as such connections do not carry with them any permanent transfer of the individual's energy and interest, or more important, any dispersion of the organization's resources. The Catholic Church in its attempt to impose celibacy on the clergy has had extensive experience with this problem. It also occurs in military organizations and perhaps in any that require the total absorption of the individual's energies over an extended period of time.

When such a movement gains control of an entire society, however, it cannot extend an anti-family ethic from its own ranks onto the whole society. Any such extension runs too great a risk that the supporting society may fail to reproduce itself adequately and that the new generation will be inadequately socialized from the new rulers' own point of view. Perhaps some day an ingenious conquering group may discover a set of institutional arrangements that can serve as a substitute for the family. To date this discovery has not taken place. The next best solution, from the point of view of a revolutionary dictator, is to attempt to utilize the family to strengthen the regime and to offset its disadvantages, particularly as the transmission agent of undesirable pre-Revolutionary attitudes, through a system of formal education and by means of propaganda. As is generally known, this has been the path taken by the USSR. Any such solution remains, however, a partial one that limits the effectiveness of totalitarian control and is fraught with internal contradictions.

Only a few aspects of these limitations and contradictions can be discussed here. Soviet legislation and propaganda have in recent years strongly discouraged extramarital sexual relationships. In addition, through difficulties placed in the way of divorce, the authorities have tried to make the marriage relationship a durable one. Such at least is the model set before the Soviet public through the major channels of communication, though it is sometimes reported that the highest Communist leaders do not live up to it in their personal lives. At the same time, the Stalinist dictatorship, particularly in the years following the Second World War, did everything in its power through fiction and propaganda to discourage preoccupation with personal problems and personal life. Romance was tied to the political chariot. Personal attractiveness in the socialist state was not supposed to lie in the physical charms, suggestive clothing, and appropriate body odors stressed by American advertising copy, but in heroic contributions to the victory of socialism.[12] Nor was the de-emphasis on private life limited to sex. It extended to any form of reflection, introspection, or personal sentiment that could compete with politics. In the autumn of 1946 A. A. Zhdanov, by that time somewhat of a Communist Colonel Blimp, constrasted the decadent bourgeois pattern of life, especially its concern with private affairs and the foibles of daily life, with the constructive, forward-looking, progressive, and outgoing personality that supposedly characterized the Soviet citizen. "What would have happened," he asked portentously, "if we had raised our youth in a spirit of melancholy and lack of faith in our task? We would not have won the Great Patriotic War." The immediate source of Zhdanov's indignation was a poem by the lyric poet, Anna Akhmatova, expressing the loneliness she felt and shared with her cat at the time of the evacuation of Leningrad.[13]

The more usual cut-and-dried Communist discussions of the question ordinarily claim that under socialism, personal interests, including those of family members, necessarily coincide with the larger interests of society. Therefore any manifestation of personal interests that do not coincide with social ones are defined as a lapse into petty bourgeois attitudes that supposedly have not yet been altogether rooted out of Soviet society.[14]

The casuistic argument cannot be taken seriously. The comments of former Soviet citizens indicate clearly that a prominent reaction to the incessant demands of the totalitarian state takes the form of flight into a variety of efforts to keep one's personal identity by discovering some tolerable niche within the system. If anything, ordinary Soviet citizens may display in their actual behavior more concern with private and family affairs than is the case in societies with a looser form of political organization. Such a conclusion, however, would be very difficult to prove or disprove with hard factual evidence.

Probably as a concession to popular practices, and perhaps by way of trying a new way to control them more effectively, Stalin's successors have allowed some clues to drop, suggesting that the stricter and more puritan aspects of the official policy might be relaxed. A student was permitted to poke fun at Communist puritanism through a magazine article that reviewed the treatment of romantic themes in Soviet movies. In real life, observed the student, "One does not say to one's beloved: 'Fulfill the quota 100 percent and I shall love you,' or, 'If you become a Stakhanovite coal miner I shall marry you; if you don't—look for another.'"[15] Concessions, even in this relatively trivial aspect of policy, are, however, a hazardous affair. The Communists cannot permit any relaxation to proceed very far toward an indulgent tolerance of personal interests without endangering the foundations of their totalitarian rule.

The key then to Soviet family institutions appears to lie in the fact that the encouragement of a stable, monogamous union partially defeats the objective of total political control over the life of the individual. This risk, however, is one that the Soviet rulers can afford, since the isolated family groupings into which Soviet society is widely fragmented cannot readily engage in concerted action. As many observers have noticed, on the basis of refugee autobiographies, the Soviet citizen often lives a highly compartmentalized existence within a small family and friendship group. The process of totalitarian atomization has, in other words, gone about as far as necessary to control the masses. To push it further might readily invite trouble from other sources.

Potentially a more important source of change lies in the degree to which the Bolsheviks rely upon traditional elements in their formal educational system. These features of the school system in turn support traditional authority in both the family and the state. The Bolsheviks now depend upon the family and the educational system to instill the standards of personal honesty and decorum required for the operation of their society. Though the problem of gangs of wild children, the famous *besprizornye* produced by the chaos of earlier years, was "liquidated" a long time ago, the Soviet press still gives a good deal of attention to the question of "hooliganism." Attitudes of respect toward such figures of authority as the parents, the teacher, famous Russian leaders of the past, and of course a selected and frequently changing gallery of current Soviet leaders, are continually inculcated through the educational system. Veneration for the achievements of the Russian past reached heights after World War II that seemed ludicrous to many foreigners. The ideal that the teacher should teach the student to think for himself, a goal that in our individualist society permeates much educational theory if by no means all of its practice, is now alien to both practice and theory in Soviet education. The introduction of fees for higher education in 1940 and the abolition of coeducation, begun in 1943, represent further aspects of a traditionalist trend. It is worth noticing, however, that occasional criticism of the abolition of coeducation was allowed to appear in the Soviet press after the war.

At the same time, there are strong elements of technical rationalism in the Soviet educational system. A very high proportion of the energies of this system are devoted to the transmission of technical and scientific skills. In the past this stress has been particularly true of education above the elementary level. Now in addition, an effort is to be made to increase the teaching of these subjects to younger students. The Fifth Five Year Plan, adopted in 1952, provides for the transition from seven-year public school education to universal secondary or ten-year education in the major cities of the USSR by the end of the planning period. Moreover, polytechnical instruction is to be introduced into the secondary school curriculum, and general polytechnical education is regarded as the ultimate goal.[16] Furthermore, the stress on the acquisition of technical mastery over a specific subject is now very great in the Soviet educational system. Soviet students at all levels have to prove that they "know something about something." It is not enough to demonstrate that they have the correct ideological attitude toward a subject matter, as was often the case earlier. Though the Party and the Komsomol constitute ubiquitous influences to make certain that the correct ideological viewpoint is presented, by itself political orthodoxy is not sufficient.

To sum up, the conclusion may be hazarded that the totalitarian-political element in both Soviet family and educational institutions already receives as much stress as is compatible with the operation of an industrial society. The same two roads therefore are, broadly speaking, open before this pair of institutions.

The traditional road leads to an increase in the significance of kinship ties over demonstrated or demonstrable competence in matching tasks or jobs with people. Unquestionably such an increase could not proceed at an equal rate through all parts of Soviet society. It would be likely to manifest itself most strongly among the peasantry and, perhaps last of all, in the most advanced work on the frontiers of the natural sciences. Likewise, in education, the traditional road implies an increase in the differences that characterize the formal training given to boys and girls, and to the various strata in the population. For the "lower orders" there could still be considerable emphasis on the acquisition of limited technical skills and a certain fund of concrete factual knowledge. This technical training would not have to exceed the transmission of enough skills to pull the levers and switches of a static industrial technique. Curiosity about theory and basic principles would be discouraged. Political indoctrination might take the form of loyalty to certain institutions and figures of authority. As is perhaps the case in any large and complex society, it would be managed in such a way as to prevent insight into the actual dynamics of the system. For the ruling stratum, on the other hand, education would increasingly come to mean the acquisition of a certain stereotyped lore of statecraft, quite conceivably still in the Marxist tradition. Ritual, etiquette, and the development of attitudes of veneration for the past would absorb attention to the exclusion of critical study of basic principles in both the natural sciences and the study of human affairs. Anyone familiar with the Soviet scene will recognize that this description of a possible future already contains many resemblances to the present.

The rational-technical road leads in the opposite direction. The significance of family ties would decline even further as an element determining the status of the adult individual. Rewards and punishments would no longer be distributed by the political authorities in accord with social categories. Both in the home and in the school, education would stress the acquisition of a knowledge of the predictable rules under which the society operated, and the acquisition of both technical skills and basic principles in the natural and social sciences. There would no longer be such a thing as a "good" or a "bad" social origin to affect the individual's career and even his personal safety. Formally, at least, such is already supposed to be the case. Along this road, the

Bolsheviks have taken a few steps. One was the abolition of social origin as grounds for disfranchisement and the adoption of equal electoral rights for town and country in the Stalin Constitution of 1936. In the absence of any choice among candidates and policies, the meaning of the latter step, however, is confined to providing a clue to a version of Bolshevik intentions they have been unable to realize in practice. More important has been the steadily rising stress on concrete knowledge because of its usefulness as an instrument in pursuing aims that are largely taken for granted. This emphasis constitutes one of the major rational-technical features in this aspect of Soviet society. As long as Russian society continues to demand an ever-rising curve of industrial production, the rational-technical features in education will necessarily predominate over the traditional ones.

So far the discussion has only touched incidentally one major institutional complex, the Communist belief system and the organized methods for its perpetuation. All known societies possess some form of organized belief system or religion, if the latter term is not defined too narrowly. Among the many activities in which this belief system plays a part, three may be selected that are necessary foundations for social life. The first one may be called reality testing. The metaphysical assumption is made here that outside of the human mind there exists an external reality to which minimal adaptation is necessary for the sake of survival. Such adaptation requires concrete and rational knowledge that in the course of group life becomes patterned and organized. The second activity is the establishment of values and goals for the society. A belief system tells people why life is worth living. Some meaning and purpose in life is a necessary foundation for group existence.* In addition to containing a more or less ex-

---

* To assert that social life is impossible without some meaning and purpose transcending the satisfaction of biological needs is not to repeat a piece of unverified or unverifiable philosophical or folk wisdom. By now it can be regarded as an empirically based scientific proposition. The disappearance of nonliterate societies, whose system of values ceased to make sense and for whom life lost its savor and meaning after contact with

plicit formulation of the goals and purposes of individual and group life, any belief system includes ideas about what means should and should not be used to attain these ends. In our own society for example, where the acquisition of wealth is to a great extent an end in itself, certain ways of getting rich are approved of and others are defined as fraudulent. This third aspect of the role of a belief system may be called the establishment of norms.

Taken together, these three activities, the establishment of empirical knowledge, of values and purposes, and of norms governing the attainment of these purposes, may at times be organized into both a coherent intellectual system and a single social structure. The Catholic Church at the height of its power came close to being an all-embracing structure of this type, performing these specialized functions for the whole of Western Christendom. Marxism too, in its contemporary Soviet version, constitutes a complete, and largely self-contained, intellectual system with a corresponding social structure in the Communist Party of the Soviet Union. It contains what purports to be a comprehensive method of reality testing in the theory of dialectical materialism. The meaning, purpose, and aim of life is summed up overtly in the victory of Communism at home and abroad. Bourgeois norms of behavior are rejected in favor of those that will help to realize this objective, though the specification of what is approved and disapproved varies with changing circumstances. However, even where a belief system finds its expression in a specific doctrine and organization, its significance is not limited to the organization itself, whether it is of a secular or a religious type. Some aspect of reality testing, purpose, and norms, may be found in practically any form of social behavior, from the production of goods and services to the rearing of the

---

European culture, constitutes but one fragment of evidence in a large body supporting this proposition. One of the best recent discussions may be found in Paul Kecskemeti, *Meaning, Communication and Value* (Chicago, 1952).

next generation. This behavior will not, as a rule, correspond exactly to that demanded by the organized expression of the belief system, that is, by the official philosophy.

In a sense, therefore, to focus attention on the belief system implies the examination of the whole society from a new vantage point, as well as the analysis of certain new activities and the institutions through which they are carried out. However, since the number of theoretical standpoints from which we could examine Soviet society may well be infinite, it is scarcely worth while or possible to pursue each of them systematically. Instead, it will be more profitable merely to set down whatever clues to the future of the Soviet system may be noticed from this standpoint. Our procedure recalls, after a fashion, Vavilov's metaphorical comparison of scientific work and a mountain journey. As the climber or scientist toils his way upward, pausing occasionally to look up from the path immediately in front of him to the surrounding countryside, certain features of the landscape retain generally the same appearance and relationship from one pause for breath to another. Nevertheless, at each successive pause the horizon recedes and new features come into view, while the relationship among old ones may shift to some extent. There is no such thing as a logical helicopter that will by some magical means take us to the summit of perfect knoweldge to look down upon social life arranged in neat patterns like the alternating fields and woodlands of the valley.

At a number of points in this work, it has been suggested that the Soviet system has gone as far as is possible toward emphasizing the power of its rulers. The attempt has been made to force this value commitment on all Soviet citizens as the real purpose of life on this earth. If we follow up the implications of this commitment in respect to reality testing and the establishment of norms for the pursuit of such a value, certain grounds emerge for concluding that this commitment contains within it the seeds of its own decay and modification in some other direction. Quite possibly a single and exclusive commitment to any value represents as much of an impossibility in the field of social behavior as perpetual motion represents in the behavior of physical objects. However, this general point cannot be pursued here.

Let us again imagine the kind of institutions for reality testing that would be necessary in a society organized totally around the quest for ever greater power on behalf of the ruler or rulers. We may assume that some form of leader cult would be a prominent part of the value system in such a society, or at least some mythology to the effect that whatever the ruler does is right and desirable. At the same time, such an imaginary society would require a highly developed set of institutions to perform the task of reality testing, since it would run into increasingly sharp opposition from both the political and the physical aspects of its environment, as the rulers attempted to subject this environment to their will. This society would also require a belief system that placed a high value on truth, for the rulers at least, and deprecated any mythology as a form of self-deception. Already the potentialities for contradiction that lead to change become evident.

The intelligence services in such a society would require a high level of development. They would have to be staffed by people with a coldly cynical attitude toward any slogans and myths that the rulers used to manipulate the subject population or to deceive other powers. At the same time, the staff would have to be blindly loyal to these rulers, a very difficult combination to manage. Roughly the same problem would arise in relation to the scientists in such a society. Both problems are already acute in the USSR.

The professional reality-testers must, by definition, in such a society, remain the servants of the political authority. Since many kinds of knowledge, if not necessarily all kinds, carry political implications, the problem of controlling the professional reality-testers becomes severe. Three sources of danger to the rulers may be noted. The necessary political mythology may blind the professional reality-testers to crucial aspects of the social and physical features of their environment. In the Soviet case this blinding effect seems to be most prominent among the testers of the social reality, though signs are not lacking of a similar impact among those charged with the examination of the natural environment. On the other hand, if the myth is cast aside, and a special dispensation given to the reality-testers, either of two things may happen. The reality-testers may get out of control and begin to seek power for themselves. Or they may develop ideas that go counter to the ruling myths. Then the rulers must use other and more material controls over the reality-testers, and at the same time alter the myth periodically in order to take account of new discoveries.

At first glance, it would seem that there was a third possibility: the development of a system of multiple truths, one for the rulers and others for the masses. There are, however, rather severe limitations on the possibility of extended development in this direction in a totalitarian society. Indeed a thorough-going application carries certain dangers for a totalitarian system. A system of multiple truths requires several sets of intellectuals, separated by watertight compartments. Though all would be subordinated to the political authorities, one would engage in discovering actual reality, while the others would promulgate the official myth and make whatever adjustments in it were necessary from time to time. But the necessity for readjustment tends to break down the watertight compartments. Still another implication of a system of multiple truths is a rigid class system. Movement from one set of truths to another produces continuing disillusionment and loss of motivation that detracts from the store of energy vital to a dynamic totalitarian system. Since a rigid class system appears to be incompatible with a dynamic totalitarian regime for grounds that have already been stated, a too vigorous movement toward a belief system with multiple truths would destroy the regime.

All of the problems suggested above have, in some measure, been faced by the Bolsheviks. Though an over-all appraisal is difficult, it is not too much to assert that by and large the methods chosen to cope with these problems have been contradictory and often self-defeating. There has been some development toward a system of multiple truths. Increasing secrecy about the true state of political, social, and economic affairs is designed as much to conceal the truth from the Soviet population as it is from the outside world. This device has run into the difficulty that daily experience for Soviet citizens frequently contradicts the glow of official propaganda and leads to a widespread loss of motivation. In the absence of adequate data, it is difficult to judge the extent to which the top Party leaders' own working picture of the world is free of the grosser distortions contained in Communist propaganda. There is some evidence that they have erred in the direction of fairly typical bureaucratic cynicism. For example, Stalin evidently underestimated the revolutionary potential of both the French and the Chinese Communist Parties immediately after the Second World War.[17] Likewise, instead of pushing the system of multiple truths as far as might be compatible with the maintenance of their power, in the last years of the Stalin era the Soviet rulers exerted increasing efforts toward imposing an official orthodoxy upon its scientists. This policy threatened to present the regime with the worst of two possible worlds. They could not gain what advantages they might from a system of multiple truths, nor could they derive the benefits of a relatively unfettered class of intellectuals. Some experimentation and modification may therefore be expected from Stalin's successors, as they too search by trial-and-error methods for a compromise between the conflicting imperatives generated by their own search for power. Either increasing traditionalization, in the direction of a system of multiple truths differentiated according to social status, or increasing rationalization that breaks down the barriers to the search for truth, appear to be the major alternatives here as elsewhere. But one should not underestimate the extent of contradiction that can be tolerated by the Soviet system as well as any other.

Similar questions may be asked concerning the relationship between the commitment to power and the normative aspect of a belief system. If power is the main value sought by the rulers of modern industrial society, what norms, if any, apply to govern the pursuit of this objective? In other words, will there be any moral rules that exclude some of the technically efficient ways of obtaining and holding power? Or will the belief system merely specify the techniques available for the pursuit of power, appraising them only in terms of their effectiveness? In general terms, the answer to this question is rather obvious. No society can maintain peaceful relations among its members if its political ethic is nothing more than a form of reality testing.* The normative side, the establishment of rules that limit the naked struggle for power, constitutes a minimum requisite for group existence. As pointed out earlier in this chapter, power does not provide a basis for its own peaceful allocation.

In analyzing the relationship between the commitment to power and the normative aspect of a belief system in any specific case, it is helpful to make use of the distinction drawn by the American sociologist, William Graham Sumner, between in-group and out-group relationships. Members of the out-group, those defined as outsiders, are generally "fair game." This is another way of saying that the only rules which apply in the pursuit of power over an out-group tend to be those of technical efficiency. Thus a decision whether or not to use deception in relations with an out-group is ordinarily evaluated chiefly in terms of its effectiveness in obtaining power. A decision whether or not to exterminate an out-group in gas chambers can be based on such a strictly amoral basis, and can even be regarded as a mistaken policy for reasons

---

* In which case there would be, strictly speaking, no political ethic at all, but merely a straightforward political science expressed in naturalistic terms. Those who argue that such a naturalist science would be a totally inadequate guide for human conduct are quite correct. The inadequacy of naturalist political and social science can, by what is only a superficial paradox, be readily demonstrated by strictly naturalist methods. For some stimulating, if occasionally extreme, observations along these lines see de Grazia, *The Errors of Psychotherapy.*

that have nothing to do with morality. On the other hand, within the in-group some conception of morality must prevail. Some means of getting power, such as assassination, and ce kinds of deception, have to be ruled out in order to maint rity and permit the survival of the group. Therefore it becomes crucial to discover in any specific case the prevailing definition of in-group and out-group relations. Particularly among the rulers, who is defined as "we" and what is meant by "they" becomes a vital piece of information. A few comments on the growth of this definition in Soviet society may help to reveal the processes through which it is reached.

Before 1917 the Bolsheviks were an in-group whose attitude toward the rest of the world, and toward capitalist society in particular, was defined practically entirely in terms of amoral and technical considerations of power. Lenin's statements on this point are too familiar to require repetition here. In this respect at least, Bolshevik behavior corresponds rather closely to doctrine. Groups in Russian society and in other societies were regarded as enemies or potential allies to be utilized, and if necessary, cast aside, strictly in accordance with their usefulness in increasing Bolshevik power.

Within the Party certain rudimentary rules developed governing the competition for power. Party leaders were supposed to be chosen by election, and the principle of democratic centralism in the formation and execution of policy received at least lip service. Policy was supposed to be hammered out at Party congresses, and the leaders were in theory only the executors of this policy, responsible eventually to the rank and file. Lenin, however, displayed a consistent lack of interest and indeed contempt for these efforts to regulate the competition for power within the in-group. He did not hesitate to violate their letter and spirit when it suited his power-maximizing purposes. His definition of the in-group was so narrow that it is scarcely an exaggeration to assert that on many crucial occasions it included only himself.

The failure to develop more than rudimentary rules and a rudimentary ethic governing the competition for power within the Party has had important consequences down to the present day. Stalin's own rise to power within the Party involved the destruction of what rudimentary rules had existed in Lenin's day. It was governed by the same strictly technical and dog-eat-dog considerations that apply to the acquisition of power generally over an out-group. Though important questions of substantive policy were involved, Stalin changed sides on these questions in order to advance his own position, as he saw various policies leading into blind alleys. The result is that no orderly way exists now for the transfer of power after Stalin's death. Though the various competitors for Stalin's role are likely to have strong reasons for preventing any struggle for power from breaking out into the open, to our knowledge they do not have any set of accepted beliefs and practices to fall back upon to keep the struggle in check. Whether they can hit upon some satisfactory procedure remains to be seen. Ordinarily it takes a great deal of time and a number of successful solutions to this kind of problem before a procedure can be established that commands acceptance.

The seizure of power in the November Revolution compelled the Bolsheviks to extend their definition of the in-group. In at least a few limited respects, all of Russia became included within the in-group. Russia had to be preserved as a base for the revolution, though here too the means tended to predominate over the ends with the passage of time. For public consumption, the in-group was redefined as consisting of two elements: the Communist Party leading the proletariat *and* the Soviet state, with a series of vague boundaries marking off the various compartments in this conglomeration. During the Second World War, the inclusion of Great Russia was played up, and the inclusion of the proletariat was played down, though by no means entirely omitted, in the frequent public definitions of the in-group. After the war, the Russians were for a time given an increasingly predominant place in such definitions, at the expense both of the proletariat and the other nationalities of the Soviet state.

To what extent the Party Presidium's private definitions of the in-group, one of the key unspoken assumptions in any policy decision, have changed under the impact of experience is a question for which no certain answer yet exists. As in any group, the definition probably shifts considerably in accord with the issue that requires decision. There may be occasional euphoric moments when the Soviet leaders actually believe that their policy is directed toward the welfare of all mankind, and that on this account all mankind in a sense belongs to the in-group. But it is one of the cardinal and more permanent features of Leninist doctrine that the masses cannot be permitted to define welfare for themselves. Nor are they regarded as capable of perceiving the road to "real" happiness and welfare. Hence, the masses have to be led, and compelled by terror, to undergo great sufferings. From this standpoint the definition of the in-group narrows tremendously, until it includes only the cream of the Bolshevik elite, and perhaps on occasion only the dictator himself, if his own position is clearly established. Then the Soviet population is seen as a series of categories, on which various degrees of reliance can be placed because of their "objective" circumstances. These objective circumstances, in turn, can be and must be manipulated, according to the Communist belief system. The "liquidation of the kulaks as a class" provides only one of the more striking instances. Recent discussions of the reorganization of peasant life, and even the granting of amnesty for certain categories of offenses, give evidence of being cut from the same cloth. The inherent tendency of the Bolshevik leaders is to regard the Soviet population as an out-group. This tendency implies a treatment of the population according to technical, amoral, and nonlegal procedures. But the necessities of the situation compel concessions, which are reflected in the growth of law and other institutions permitting stable and predictable social relationships as well as sentiments of solidarity.

Whether or not this legacy is a fatal one for the present regime depends upon the extent to which a naked struggle for power at

the top can spread outward and downward through Soviet society. It has been argued through much of this book that the
Soviet system is held together mainly through decisions taken
at the center, that ruthlessly hold in check a variety of divisive
tendencies. Should this linchpin weaken or disappear, the entire
Communist apparatus might well begin to crumble. Once started,
the process might be astonishingly rapid, as key functional groups
from the army to the industrial administrators shook off the Party
and police shackles that bind them together and coördinate their
efforts to produce a dynamic social system. To assert, however,
that weakness at the center might well be fatal is not the same as
to assert that it will necessarily occur in the immediate future. A
single leader can quite conceivably eliminate his rivals in an internal struggle for power and emerge in a position roughly parallel to Stalin's. The elimination of Beriya so soon after Stalin's
death may be a step in the latter direction. At the same time,
should a single leader arise, this fact alone, as the rest of this
chapter has shown, could hardly be taken by itself as an indication that no changes are to be expected in the nature of the Soviet
system. Whichever way the struggle at the top turns out, there
remains a series of problems that have to be solved one way or
another no matter who sits in the Kremlin. The struggle over
the succession constitutes a vital part of the forces affecting the
future of Russia. Yet it is still only a part of the total field of
pressures at work and must find its appropriate place within this
total field in any appraisal that comes close to the mark.

The speed or slowness with which changes take place in the
Kremlin may well be a crucial factor that more or less determines
the road that Russian society will travel. If disintegration at the
center is very rapid, it could produce the end of the Bolshevik regime as such. But since it is hardly likely that Russian society will entirely disappear, any group that succeeds to the Bolshevik heritage will therefore face many and perhaps most of
the same problems that have been outlined in this chapter with
roughly the same range of solutions. On this account, the disap-

pearance of the Bolsheviks in the course of the next half-dozen years, which I am inclined to regard as a rather unlikely extreme, would in any case be merely the prelude to one of the other types of change sketched here.

A change in the composition of the leadership, through the eventual emergence of a technocratic aristocracy in the struggle of elites, would also lead to consequences that can be estimated in at least a rough fashion. A more gradual weakening of the central power, on the other hand, would permit the traditionalist forces latent throughout Russian society to come to the fore, also with consequences that can be established with some confidence. Finally, there is still the very strong possibility that the leaders may settle their internal scores through violence and continue the tried and tested techniques of the Stalinist dictatorship with relatively minor tactical modifications. Should this happen, there are strong grounds for believing that these techniques would continue to work for a long time to come. In this fashion, the struggle for power at the center may be seen against a larger field of potential change, and as one of the major factors that might precipitate these changes.

Drawing the argument together reveals then an apparent range of three major possibilities for the future of Russian society. Though it is not possible to make a genuine scientific prediction as to which will actually take place, partly on account of an irreducible area of indeterminacy in human affairs, this viewpoint may still provide some rational basis for estimating the probable course of future events. A good scientific theory in either the natural or the social sciences does not necessarily predict that a specific event will happen in the future. It may merely tell us what to expect if the conditions specified by the theory are actually found to exist. If the possibilities are correctly formulated, they present an ordered intellectual structure into which it is possible to place future facts about the USSR as they become available and derive estimates of the probability of other events. In the meantime, the structure itself also undergoes correction, modification, and quite possibly complete rejection, in the light of both new data and theoretical reflection.

It is necessary to make one more general observation by emphasizing that extreme development in any of these three directions is an impossibility. No one of the three criteria—power, technical rationality, or tradition—can ever become the sole basis for the organization of all decisions and behavior in any human society. Some combination of the three, if in very different proportions, will always be found. Where we are in trouble theoretically is in the difficulty we have in making precise and meaningful statements about the extent to which these elements can be successfully combined.* Clearly it is possible to have a strong dose of tradition among the peasantry, a strong dose of technical rationality among a body of professional scientists, and a strong dose of straightforward power seeking among the rulers, and maintain some sort of a going society for quite a period of time, even if there are all sorts of groanings and creakings in the machinery.

About the best that can be said now is that an emphasis on one of the three criteria excludes emphasis on either of the other two. This relationship of mutual exclusion is quite clear in the case of totalitarian power and tradition. Totalitarian power is dynamic and generally acts as a corrosive on tradition, though as in Nazi Germany it may sometimes wear the mask of tradition for its own purposes. The relationship is also clear in the case of power and

---

* A tremendous amount of empirical work and reflection remains ahead of social scientists before they will be able to make both precise and general statements about the ways in which various criteria and types of institutions can be combined, if indeed they do eventually succeed. Perhaps the greatest success has been achieved by anthropologists in the study of kinship systems. An excellent example is G. P. Murdock, *Social Structure* (New York, 1949). Though I am willing to grant that some of the difficulties in the study of politics may stem from the lack of adequate conceptual tools, it seems to me that in the area of kinship the raw data automatically appear with much more clean-cut lines of division that permit a sharper statement of the range of possible combinations. For example, descent can be traced either through the male or the female or through both of them. Political and economic institutions are much more amorphous, and the difficulties increase as one tries to analyze whole societies.

rationality, although there are times when we might be inclined to think otherwise. Before and during the Second World War, the Nazi regime was often cited as an illustration of technical rationality completely subordinated as an instrument in the search for power. The opening of the Nazi archives has led to a sharp revision of this opinion, as the conflict between political imperatives and those of economics and technical military strategy stand revealed in the struggles of the German leaders. Enough has been said in earlier pages to make it unnecessary to continue around the circle with comments on the remaining incompatibilities.

In concrete terms, the first possibility facing the Soviet regime may be regarded as a continuation and possibly even some intensification of the dynamic, totalitarian, and expansionist characteristics of the Stalinist system. Since the greater portion of this book has been concerned with the nature of the Soviet system in the form it had reached by the 1950's, a programmatic listing of its salient features can be dispensed with here. For reasons that have been presented earlier, it is also doubtful that any great intensification of these features is still possible without seriously weakening social institutions that are necessary for the functioning of an industrial society. A successful solution of the succession crisis and the emergence of an undisputed leader, either through peaceful or violent methods or a combination of the two, appears to be an essential prerequisite for the continued operation of this system. To state these two requirements—limiting the further extension of totalitarian devices and the discovery of a leader—does not imply that the requirements will be met, even if the statement could be demonstrated as impeccable truth. Dangerous consequences do not prevent rulers from embarking on disastrous policies.

The second possibility is that the technical-rational and formal legal features that exist in the Soviet system might come to predominate over the totalitarian ones. This appears to be the central idea behind the predictions of a "managerial revolution" in the USSR. Again, for reasons that have been given earlier in this chapter, I do not think that such a turn could take the form of a parliamentary democracy if it were an outgrowth or extension of the Bolshevik regime. But a political system approaching a technocracy has more than mere plausibility. Probably the readily discernible movement in this direction will stop somewhere short of its logical culmination. The absorption of the political Party official into the role of a technical administrator, discussed in an earlier chapter, is perhaps just as unlikely to continue to the end as is the reverse process of making a political animal out of the technician.

Nevertheless, the possibility of a pronounced technical-rational development does not appear out of the question. The system then would display roughly the following features. First of all, technical and rational criteria would largely replace political ones in the appraisal of economic activities, while the rapid pace of economic growth continued, but in a very different direction. Though the power of the central authorities would remain very great, enforced conformity to a code of law would replace the present device of frequent shake-ups in the administrative apparatus as a means through which power and authority were exercised. By the same token, the importance of organized terror would greatly decline, though some aspects would unquestionably remain to enforce acceptance among the population of materialist and technical values held by the rulers. There would also be some increase in the personal security of the officials, inasmuch as conformity with objective rules and objectively appraised performance would become the chief basis for tenure in office. Social mobility would remain at a high level, as the acquisition of technical skills provided the major avenue of upward mobility, which may possibly be the case at present. Meanwhile the less competent children of gifted fathers would tend to slide down the social ladder, to the extent that their advantages of education and position failed to compensate for the lack of native ability in equipping them with necessary talents.

The consequence of such a high rate of upward and downward mobility, and of an emphasis on merit as the criterion for retaining any status, might be a rather high level of personal insecurity, particularly in the urban population, though deriving from sources quite different from present ones. Partly as a result of the high rate of mobility, but also because of the emphasis on merit as the basis for status, the family unit would tend to remain small and kinship ties of minor significance in comparison with pre-industrial times. Finally, the belief system might be expected to stress the importance of studying the physical rather than the social environment. The purpose of life would be expressed primarily in secular and materialist terms, emphasizing the society as a whole rather than the individual as the object to which benefits ought to accrue. Norms of behavior would be subject to change and display a largely rationalist justification. What a person ought to do would be explained in terms of why a particular course of action brings certain results rather than in terms of more absolute standards. It might be described as a morality of "No smoking—Fire hazard" signs. For the most part, its rules would be applied impartially. Industrialization exerts very strong pressures toward creating a society such as this. It could only come into full bloom, however, if industrialization and the creation of more material goods became more of an end in itself than has so far been possible for the Bolshevik regime.

For the latent traditionalist elements in Soviet society to assert themselves both the emphasis on industrialization and the power of the dictator, two elements now closely connected, would have to be sharply reduced. In this case too, it might be expected that the process would stop far short of a disintegration into the European type of feudal society, but might remain a form resembling an Oriental despotism. That is to say, there would still be a central ruler and a bureaucratic apparatus that ruled the country, but it would do so with much less of an effective effort to control the details of daily life. Meanwhile, industry, the state of the technical arts, and population would level off and remain more or less static.* In the terms used here, there would occur a de-emphasis of political criteria in the appraisal of economic behavior and an end to the rapid pace of economic growth. There would also be an increase in the authority of local officials and a corresponding loss of power on the part of the Kremlin. An important part of this change would be manifested in the way personal connections took increasing precedence over merit and objective performance as the basis of allegiance and obedience. Terror as a major instrument of control and the enforcement of the writ of the center would diminish as this writ became weaker.

Corresponding to these changes would be an increase in personal security and tenure for officialdom, for reasons that are very different from an improvement in their status under technocratic conditions. A much more rigid class system, with sharp educational and cultural distinctions that marked off one stratum from another would also play a part in the allocation of political authority and material goods. Since the number of economic and other activities flowing through kinship and personal channels would increase, the importance of the family as the basic social cell would rise. The shrinkage of meaningful kinship ties, in other words, would very likely be reversed. Finally, the belief system could be expected to set rather close limitations on the exploration of both physical and social reality. In a fully traditional society, the purpose of life is more or less defined as the maintenance of the *status quo*. Though it may seem difficult to imagine Marxist doctrine in such a form, important features already serve this purpose. In further contrast with the super-rationalist order, a traditionalist Communist morality would display norms of behavior that were not subject to ready adaptive change. Also these norms would be justified in terms that did not refer to their immediate practical usefulness in achieving some material end, but according to some more general standard.

* This possibility has been discussed rather frequently in disillusioned Communist circles and has found its way into scholarly interpretations partly through the writings of an Oriental specialist among them, Karl A. Wittfogel, though he cannot be held responsible for the interpretation suggested here.

A traditionalist Russia approximating the sketch just given could scarcely come into being in a world of highly competitive power politics. For the traditionalist forces to come to the surface and take firm hold, the conflict between Moscow and Washington, which has governed international relationships since the end of World War II, would somehow have to be brought to a close. At first glance, therefore, it would appear that external pressures rule out this possibility. But it cannot be dismissed quite so readily. We are so accustomed to the vicious spiral of an arms race and its parallel manifestations in the domestic affairs of both the United States and the USSR that we find it difficult to imagine any unwinding of this spiral. There are also, it is true, some strong general grounds for doubting the possibility of a reversal of this process. Ordinarily in international affairs, when two powers settle their differences, the settlement takes place on account of increasingly clear signs of threat to both their interests from some third power.

Nevertheless, if strong internal forces are at work in both the major antagonists to diminish expansionist pressures, there is at least a possibility of settling outstanding differences. Such forces are quite visible but do not predominate in the Soviet Union. At the moment, any extended American withdrawal runs too great a risk to be considered seriously by those who hold political responsibility in this country. In time, however, a growth of traditionalist forces in Russia might parallel certain American domestic pressures, such as a resurgence of isolationism and a demand for a smaller allocation of our national resources to foreign aid and the military establishment, to produce a slackening of international tension. Once begun, this reversal of the vicious spiral could have cumulative effects in both the United States and the Soviet Union.

Whether this particular combination of circumstances will occur is of course another matter. The present slightly reduced level of international tension does not point to full-scale war in the very near future. At the moment therefore it does not seem

wise or profitable to speculate on the ways in which such a conflict might push Soviet society in one direction or another. Moreover, to permit even hazardous guesses we would have to foresee
accurately the specific conditions with which the Soviet regime
and population might be faced—such as delayed or initial vic-
tories, mass bombardment, and many others—as well as be able
to appraise correctly the state of Soviet society and its relation
with other countries.

Short of war, the impact of external forces could conceivably
have a significant bearing on the further rise of rational-technical elements in competition with totalitarian ones. The rationalist
model, at least in the form described here as a real possibility,
can adapt itself to a more competitive political environment than
can the traditionalist system. The emphasis on continuing industrialization, even if it laid greater stress on the satisfaction of
consumer needs, would still provide the necessary base of strength
for the Soviet Union's effective participation in international
power politics. At the same time, some lowering of the heat in
the international arena would have to occur before the Bolsheviks
could be expected to honor their commitment to provide a better
material life for the masses and make this the core of their policy.

Persons sympathetic to the Bolsheviks have occasionally taken
this point as the center of their argument and tried to prove that
the totalitarian features of the regime were forced upon it by
the requirements of adapting to a hostile world that tried to
strangle the infant socialist state in the midst of its birth pangs.
I think that this reading of the historical record is false, and that
the totalitarian roots reach far back into Marxist doctrine and
Russian history.[18] It is necessary to emphasize this point to bring
out the further one that a rationalist and legal order in the USSR
would be a genuine transformation—indeed, scarcely short of a
revolutionary one.

Yet another reason for stressing the strength of the totalitarian
tradition and totalitarian institutions lies in a certain instability
of the rationalist and technical order, that is manifest even in

our own society and might legitimately be expected to be much stronger in post-Stalinist Russia. The essence of the matter lies in the fact that the mere existence of a powerful industrial state dominating much of the Eurasian continent would be a potential threat to other nations, and primarily to the United States, no matter how peaceful its behavior and apparent intentions.

It is, of course, impossible to foresee all the possible combinations and permutations that might arise among the diplomatic antagonists and allies of the USSR. But it is a safe assumption that elementary prudence will compel some powers to maintain a posture of defense toward the USSR, and that they will be strong powers if the Soviets continue to develop their industrial potential, no matter what the direction of this development. In turn, this posture can easily produce a reaction in Russia that carries the subordination of materialist welfare to political objectives.

As pointed out in the first chapter, the Party Presidum's estimate of the world situation forms a major component in its choice and formulation of Soviet objectives, which in turn affect the situation confronting every Soviet citizen. If the Communist leaders want to live up to their frequently expressed prediction that they will inherit the earth, they will have to continue and intensify certain totalitarian features of their society. An expansionist foreign policy implies a further stress on heavy industry, sacrifices from the population, a stiff policy toward the peasantry, and consequently a major role for the police and the armed forces. On the other hand, a withdrawal on the international front could permit a greater flow of consumers' goods and other political and economic concessions that could in time alter the essential structure of the regime.

Bolshevik suspicion of the outside world, however, will not die down readily and cannot be allayed merely through a one-sided withdrawal on the part of Russia's opponents. Even though the new Party catechism comes close to dropping Stalin down the memory hole, it refers to the Party as the "shock brigade of the world revolution." [19] Clearly this hostility is not the reflection of any single personality among the Soviet elite. It is instead both the product and the source of their institutions, continually renewed by them as well as by their own behavior in international politics. In this fashion both the competitive structure of world politics and the legacy of the past work against the chances of a new order.

Yet the contours of future alternatives, struggling to make themselves felt, are clearly visible in the turmoil of the present. Though only time will yield a conclusive answer, I think it would be a mistake to dismiss the moves recently made by the new regime as a purely temporary and tactical withdrawal, a feint without significance for the fundamental character and objectives of the USSR. So far these moves constitute a retreat, executed in good order but evidently in the face of strong and real forces.

In its brief history the Soviet Union has made a number of such withdrawals before superior force and followed them with powerful counterattacks. The relative freedom of the NEP was succeeded by the brutal reassertion of the central power in what is sometimes referred to as the second or Stalinist revolution. On a smaller scale the Great Purge of the thirties can also be regarded as a reaffirmation of the dictator's power, not only against remnants of dissension within the Party but also against the bureaucratic instruments of power, including eventually the secret police which was showing signs of taking advantage of its indispensability. In the language used here, the Great Purge and its consequences constituted a victory for totalitarian elements over rationalist trends. The Bolshevik leaders, despite their talk about inevitable forces in history, have never been content merely to drift with the historical tide. Instead, their tradition teaches them to harness and manipulate the currents of social change and not to hesitate before mass bloodshed in controlling the expression of so-called automatic social forces. There can hardly be any doubt that the present leaders continue the essential elements of this tradition.

NOTES

CHAPTER 1: THE INSTRUMENTS OF CONTROL

1. The action of the Supreme Soviet is mentioned in *Pravda*, August 9, 1953. The record of the other domestic and foreign events I have taken from issues of the *Current Digest of the Soviet Press* and *The New York Times*.

2. See *Sovetskoe Gosudarstvennoe Pravo* (Moscow, 1948), pp. 268–269. An *oblast'* is officially defined as "an intricate economic complex, including industrial centers and agricultural *raions,* an important base of the central soviet and Party organs in the locality." There are, however, some minor exceptions to this arrangement. A territorial division on the oblast scale that contains at least one autonomous unit is called a *krai,* and in the Far East of the RSFSR a krai includes subordinate oblasts. The RSFSR also contains ten national-territorial units, each of which is called an *okrug.*

3. Curiously enough, Russia proper, the RSFSR, has no Communist Party, as its affairs are handled by the Communist Party of the Soviet Union, the central organization. There are fifteen Communist Parties, each with its central committee, for the other fifteen Republics, as well as 8 krai, 167 oblast, 36 okrug, 544 city, and 4,886 raion Party organizations. There are, in addition, according to reports at the Party Congresses of 1939 and 1952, 350,305 Party "cells," or primary organizations, as they are actually known, in factories, collective farms, the military forces, and the "soviet apparatus" itself (*The Land of Socialism Today and Tomorrow: Reports and Speeches at the Eighteenth Congress of the Communist Party of the Soviet Union* [*Bol'shevik*] [Moscow, 1939], p. 38, and *Pravda,* October 9 and 14, 1952). On the structure and role of the Party, see also Merle Fainsod, *How Russia Is Ruled* (Harvard University Press, 1953), Part II.

4. This arrangement was also to apply to the *kraikom.* See *Pravda,* October 13, 1952.

5. For the control of mass media see Alex Inkeles, *Public Opinion in Soviet Russia* (Harvard University Press, 1950). No really serviceable monograph on education exists as yet, but some of the more important data may be found in Maurice J. Shore, *Soviet Education* (New York, 1947).

6. (New York, 1953), pp. 29, 245–246.

7. See *Pravda,* October 7, 1952. This tendency to reach outside the

usual channels by creating special ones of their own may be a normal and necessary trait among effective despots. The actions of Louis XIV provide a familiar illustration. See Ernest Lavisse, *Histoire de France* (Paris, 1905), VII¹, 158.

8. Cf. Rostow, *Dynamics*, p. 179.

9. Alexander Barmine, *One Who Survived* (New York, 1945), pp. 180, 187.

10. Juri Jelagin, *Taming of the Arts* (New York, 1951), pp. 81, 151.

11. *Pravda*, October 6, 1952.

12. "Za vysokuyu printsipial'nost' i umenie ispravlyat' sobstvennye oshibki (S plenuma Tsk KP[b] Uzbekistana)," *Partiinaya Zhizn'*, no. 6 (March 1948), p. 33.

13. A. Nazarov, "Kak rozhdaetsya potok bumag," *ibid.*, no. 4 (February 1948), pp. 40–41.

14. "O rabote sekretarya sel'skogo raikoma (obzor pisem)," *ibid.*, no. 6 (March 1948), p. 64.

15. See Henry V. Dicks, "Observations on Contemporary Russian Behaviour," *Human Relations*, vol. V, no. 2 (1952).

16. The Soviet press is full of references to these webs, at least to those that frustrate the will of the center. For additional insight into their operation I am also indebted to conversations with a former Soviet newspaperman with wide opportunities to observe their operation. See Harvard Project on the Soviet Social System, B 2:359.

17. *Zarya Vostoka*, September 16–18, 1952, as translated in *Current Digest of the Soviet Press* (hereafter cited as *CDSP*), vol. IV, no. 41 (November 22, 1952), pp. 8, 20.

18. *Ibid.*, p. 9.

19. *Pravda*, October 13 and 14, 1952.

20. V. A. Vlasov, *Sovetskii Gosudarstvennyi Apparat* (Moscow, 1951), p. 364. Although a Soviet author, writing several years after the event, does not ordinarily constitute a trustworthy source, it is more likely that in the year 1951 he would underemphasize, rather than stress, the wartime role of the military in civilian affairs.

21. James H. Meisel and Edward S. Kozera, *The Soviet System* (2nd ed.; Ann Arbor, 1953), p. 368, n. 2.

22. E.g., Vlasov, *Sovetskii Gosudarstvennyi Apparat*, p. 370.

23. Col. Louis B. Ely, *The Red Army Today* (3rd ed., Harrisburg, 1953), p. 153.

24. On the problem of controls over the armed forces see Fainsod, *How Russia Is Ruled*, chap. xiv; Z. Brzezinski, "Party Controls in the Soviet Army," *Journal of Politics*, vol. XIV, no. 4 (1952), pp. 565–591. A forthcoming monograph by Louis Nemzer will provide the kind of intensive analytical study that is badly needed despite the pioneering historical survey by D. F. White, *The Growth of the Red Army* (Princeton, 1944).

25. *Pravda,* October 10, 1952.

26. This information comes from a copy of the 1941 economic plan, marked "Not for publication," which was captured first by the Germans, later by Americans, and eventually published. It is worth noting that several of the figures officially released by the Soviet government agree with those given in this source. See *Gosudarstvennyi Plan Razvitiya Narodnogo Khozyaistva SSSR na 1941 god* (Baltimore, n.d.), pp. 483–485.

27. Vlasov, *Sovetskii Gosudarstvennyi Apparat,* p. 405.

28. Party statutes, Section VIII, ¶ 58, *Pravda,* October 14, 1952.

29. F. Beck and W. Godin, *Russian Purge and the Extraction of Confession* (New York, 1951), p. 167; Alexander Weissberg, *The Accused* (New York, 1951), chap. xiii.

CHAPTER 2: THE POLITICS OF INDUSTRIALIZATION

1. For the most recent attempt, see Abram Bergson, editor, *Soviet Economic Growth* (Evanston, 1953) and the literature cited therein, particularly the works of his major critic, Naum Jasny. These two writers bracket, so to speak, the range of professional opinion on this point.

2. A. Kursky, *The Planning of the National Economy of the USSR* (Moscow, 1949), pp. 110, 111.

3. *Pravda,* August 9, 1953.

4. "Gosudarstvennyi planovyi komitet," *Bol'shaya Sovetskaya Entsiklopediya* (hereafter cited as BSE), XII (1952), 323.

5. "Biudzhet gosudarstvennyi," *ibid.,* VI (1951), 460.

6. E. Lokshin, "Voprosy planirovaniya material'no-tekhnicheskogo snabzheniya narodnogo khozyaistva SSSR," *Planovoe Khozyaistvo,* 1950, no. 2, p. 47.

7. B. Miroshnichenko, "Planirovanie promyshlennogo proizvodstva," *ibid.,* 1951, no. 3, pp. 90–91.

8. "Dogovor," *BSE,* XIV (1952), 623–624.

9. Lokshin, in *Planovoe Khozyaistvo,* 1950, no. 2, pp. 47–48. For the text of the latest regulations known to me (April 21, 1949), see *Sobranie Postanovlenii i Rasporyazhenii Soveta Ministrov SSSR,* no. 9 (July 30, 1949), section 68. For somewhat different interpretations see Harold J. Berman, *Justice in Russia* (Harvard University Press, 1950), pp. 70–76, and Vladimir Gsovski, *Soviet Civil Law* (Ann Arbor, 1948), I, 436–438.

10. The clearest concrete description known to me is A. Zertsalov, "O metode opredeleniya potrebnosti v material'nykh resursakh dlya kapital'nogo stroitel'stva," *Planovoe Khozyaistvo,* 1951, no. 2, pp. 85–90.

11. Editorial, "Uluchshit' planirovanie kapital'nogo stroitel'stva,"

ibid., 1952, no. 2, pp. 14–15, for recent efforts to cope with this problem.

12. Cf. Lokshin, *ibid.*, 1950, no. 2, p. 54.

13. I. Baranov, "Khozyaistvennyi dogovor—orudie vypolneniya gosudarstvennykh planov," *ibid.*, 1949, no. 5, pp. 67–68.

14. A. D. Gusakov and I. A. Dymshits, *Denezhnoe Obrashchenie i Kredit SSSR* (Moscow, 1951), pp. 219, 227.

15. B. Miroshnichenko, "Assortiment i kachestvo produktsii—vashneishie zadaniya gosudarstvennogo plana," *Planovoe Khozyaistvo*, 1952, no. 3, p. 15.

16. Noted in the decree of April 21, 1949.

17. A. Zverev, "Finansovaya distsiplina i kontrol' rublëm v narodnom khozyaistve SSSR," *Bol'shevik*, no. 12 (June 1952), p. 29; see also Lokshin, in *Planovoe Khozyaistva*, 1950, no. 2, p. 52.

18. "Gosudarstvennyi Bank SSSR," *BSE*, XII (1952), 315–316.

19. "Dogovor," *BSE*, XIV (1952), 624.

20. "Ekonomicheskie problemy sotsializma v SSSR," *Pravda*, October 3, 1952.

21. E.g., V. D'yachenko, "Khozraschët kak sotsialisticheskii metod khozyaistvovaniya," *Voprosy Ekonomiki*, 1951 no. 2, pp. 3–23. The author of this work is presently under a cloud for having praised Voznesensky, but his description of the role of *khozraschët* may be taken as an accurate account of what the Soviets have been trying to achieve for many years with this device.

22. D. Kondrashev, "Price-fixing in the USSR," *Finansy i Kredit SSSR*, no. 4 (October 1952), pp. 29–37, as condensed in CDSP, V, no. 17 (June 6, 1953), p. 11.

23. Naum Jasny, *The Soviet Price System* (Stanford, 1951), p. 10.

24. Kondrashev, in *CDSP*, June 6, 1953, pp. 10, 11.

25. *Ibid.*, p. 11.

26. For a concrete case, see Stalin's essay, "Ekonomicheskie problemy sotsializma v SSSR," *Pravda*, October 3, 1952.

27. "Gosudarstvennyi kontrol'," *BSE*, XII (1952), 321–322.

28. *Ibid.*

29. N. N. Rovinskii, *Organizatsiya Finansirovaniya i Kreditovaniya Kapitalnykh Vlozheniya* (Moscow, 1951), p. 230.

30. See Solomon M. Schwarz, *Labor in the Soviet Union* (New York, 1952), pp. 209–214, 250–257, and sources cited there.

31. Gusakov and Dymshits, *Denezhoe Obrashchenie*, p. 220.

32. *Ibid.*, pp. 192–193, 200.

33. A. E. Pasherstnik, *Pravovye Voprosy Voznagrazhdeniya za Trud Rabochikh i Sluzhashchikh* (Moscow-Leningrad, 1949), pp. 215, 339.

34. *Ibid.*, pp. 214–222.

35. E. Manevich, "Zarabotnaya plata i eë organizatsiya pri sotsializme," *Voprosy Ekonomiki*, 1952, no. 4, p. 92.

36. *Ibid.*, p. 93.

37. Illustrative scales may be found in N. G. Aleksandrov and D. M. Genkin, eds., *Sovetskoe Trudovoe Pravo* (Moscow, 1946), p. 218.

38. E. Manevich, "Novye stimuly k trudu i zarabotnaya plata pri sotsializme," *Voprosy Ekonomiki*, 1948, no. 10, p. 28.

39. *Labor in the Soviet Union*, p. 223.

40. *Pravda*, October 6, 1952.

41. *Labor in the Soviet Union*, chap. iii.

42. Harry Schwartz, *Russia's Soviet Economy* (New York, 1950), p. 449 and sources cited there.

43. B. Markus, "Trud," *BSE*, special volume "*SSSR*" (Moscow, 1948), col. 1129.

44. Schwartz, *Russia's Soviet Economy*, p. 449.

45. E. Mokhova, "Gosudarstvennye trudovye rezervy—osnovnoi istochnik popolneniya rabochevo klassa v SSSR," *Voprosy Ekonomiki*, 1949, no. 4, p. 42.

46. *Pravda*, October 12, 1952.

47. Mokhova, in *Voprosy Ekonomiki*, 1949, no. 4, p. 41. For further data see Schwarz, *Labor in the Soviet Union*, pp. 77–83.

48. See *Pravda*, April 28, 1953, and the statements by Finance Minister A. G. Zverev to the Supreme Soviet in *Pravda*, August 6, 1953.

49. I. I. Evtikhiev and V. A. Vlasov, *Administrativnoe Pravo SSSR* (Moscow, 1946), p. 291.

50. In the analysis of the Soviet factory and its relationship to the larger system of administrative controls I owe much to George C. Homans, *The Human Group* (New York, 1950).

51. D'yachenko, in *Voprosy Ekonomiki*, 1951, no. 2, p. 12. Compare David Granick, *Management of the Industrial Firm in the USSR* (in press). In its form as a Ph.D. thesis Granick's study discusses this problem on pp. 264 ff. Granick goes too far in his assertion that the basic difficulty facing management is the absence of a single and clear criterion of success.

52. Pasherstnik, *Pravovye Voprosy*, pp. 270–271.

53. Joseph S. Berliner, "The Informal Organization of the Soviet Firm," *Quarterly Journal of Economics*, August 1952, p. 348. See also Manevich, in *Voprosy Ekonomiki*, 1948, no. 10, p. 32.

54. Zverev, in *Bol'shevik*, June 1952, pp. 30–31.

55. Vera Panova, *Kruzhilikha* (Moscow-Leningrad, 1948), a very illuminating novel of industrial life, stresses this point.

56. For additional detail see Berliner, in *Quarterly Journal of Economics*, August 1952, pp. 356–358.

57. Zverev, in *Bol'shevik*, June 1952, p. 30.

58. This conflict of interests is heavily stressed by refugees who have been in direct contact with the problem. It is also recognized in the Soviet literature on managerial problems. For a review of this material see A. Birman, "Za dal'neishii rost rentabel'nosti sotsialisticheskikh predpriatii," *Voprosy Ekonomiki*, 1951, no. 3, pp. 117–123.

59. A. Arakelian, *Industrial Management in the USSR*, translated by Ellsworth L. Raymond (Washington, 1950), p. 158. The original edition was published in 1947.

60. See Panova, *Kruzhilikha*.

61. Arakelian, *Industrial Management*, p. 126.

62. Harvard Project on the Soviet Social System, B 2–524:AP.

63. A typical illustration may be found in Harvard Project, B 2–384:AP.

64. *Ibid.*

65. Arakelian, *Industrial Management*, p. 125.

66. Fainsod Report No. 40, Russian Research Center files.

67. Arakelian, *Industrial Management*, pp. 133–134, gives two varying tables of organization. It is not known whether the shop has a separate secret police unit, though this seems unlikely.

68. I. Likachev, "Khozraschët na avtozavode imeni Stalina," *Planovoe Khozyaistvo*, 1948, no. 5, p. 50.

69. A spate of articles describing the experiences of individual plants with decentralized cost accounting procedures may be found in the postwar issues of *Planovoe Khozyaistvo* and *Voprosy Ekonomiki*. Brief surveys are included in D'yachenko, "Khozraschët . . . ," *Voprosy Ekonomiki*, 1951, no. 2, pp. 16–20; "Nauchno-proizvodstvennaya konferentsiya po voprosam vnutrizavodskogo khozraschëta," *ibid.*, 1951, no. 6, pp. 115–116.

70. Harvard Project, A 337.

71. *Ibid.*, A 99.

CHAPTER 3: THE PEASANTS' ROLE
IN THE WORKER'S STATE

1. Stanford, California, 1949.

2. A. Yugow, *Russia's Economic Front for War and Peace* (New York, 1942), p. 46, where the author gives a figure of 99.3 per cent. This does not jibe with his other figures on kolkhoz area (117.2 million hectares) and on total area under cultivation (136.9 million hectares) which yields a ratio of only 86 per cent.

3. I. D. Laptev *et al.*, eds., *Voprosy Kolkhoznogo Stroitel'stva v SSSR* (Moscow, 1951), p. 315.

4. *Ibid.*, p. 266, and Lazar Volin, *A Survey of Soviet Russian Agri-*

culture, U.S. Department of Agriculture Monograph 5 (1951), pp. 58, 68.
5. *Sotsialisticheskoe Zemledelie,* March 3, 1951.
6. Laptev, *Voprosy Kolkhoznogo Stroitel'stva,* p. 321.
7. *BSE,* special vol. "SSSR," col. 874.
8. Jasny, *Socialized Agriculture,* p. 503.
9. Cf. Volin, *Survey of Russian Agriculture,* pp. 68–69.
10. *Pravda,* September 15, 1953.
11. *Ibid.,* September 13, 1953.
12. Manuscript on the NKVD in the files of the Russian Research Center, Harvard University, pp. 32–33.
13. *Pravda,* September 15, 1953.
14. *Ibid.*
15. N. Belyaev, "Podgotovka i vospitanie predsedatelei kolkhozov," *Bol'shevik,* no. 5 (March 1951), p. 64.
16. L. Mel'nikov, "Partiinye organizatsii ukrupnënnykh kolkhozov," *ibid.,* no. 4 (February 1951), p. 54.
17. I. Benediktov, "MTC v bor'be za novyi pod'ëm sotsialisticheskogo sel'skogo khozyaistva," *ibid.,* no. 5 (March 1951), p. 17.
18. Harvard Project on the Soviet Social System, A 133.
19. *Pravda,* September 13, 1953. See also Khrushchev's discussion in *ibid.,* September 15, 1953.
20. *Pravda,* September 15, 1953.
21. I. I. Evtikhiev and V. A. Vlasov, *Administrativnoe Pravo* (Moscow, 1946), pp. 313–314; Ya. F. Mikolenko and A. N. Nikitin, *Kolkhoznoe Pravo* (Moscow, 1946), pp. 37–41.
22. Harvard Project, B 2–48:AP.
23. S. G. Kolesnev, *Organizatsiya Sotsialisticheskikh Sel'skokhozyaistvennikh Predpriyatii* (Moscow, 1947), pp. 62–63.
24. *Pravda,* September 15, 1953.
25. T. L. Basiuk, *Organizatsiya Kolkhoznogo Proizvodstva* (Moscow, 1946), p. 58.
26. "Peredovaya: Vazhneishie zadachi dal'neishevo organizatsionnokhozyaistvennogo ukrepleniya kolkhozov," *Bol'shevik,* no. 22 (November 1951), p. 7.
27. *Pravda,* September 15, 1953.
28. Laptev, *Voprosy Kolkhoznogo Stroitel'stva,* p. 305.
29. *Ibid.,* p. 306.
30. Harvard Project, B 10–124:RF.
31. Volin, *Survey of Russian Agriculture,* p. 188.
32. M. Kraev, "O kolkhoznom trudodne," *Voprosy Ekonomiki,* 1949, no. 3, pp. 37–38.
33. *Pravda,* September 15, 1953.
34. *Pravda Ukrainy,* September 25, 1953, in *CDSP,* vol. IV, no. 41 (November 22, 1952), p. 23.

35. Jasny, *Socialized Agriculture*, pp. 692, 694–695. See also the erratum comment released with Jasny's later monographs, indicating that he would like to revise downward his estimates on the kolkhozniks' cash receipts.

36. *Ibid.*, p. 340.

37. I. Glotov, "Obshchestvennoe i lichnoe v kolkhozakh," *Bol'shevik*, no. 24 (December 1951), p. 47.

38. *Ibid.*

39. *Pravda*, September 15, 1953. See also Malenkov's speech of August 8, 1953.

40. S. V. Serebryakov, *Organizatsiya i Tekhnika Sovetskoi Torgovli* (Moscow, 1949), p. 119.

41. *BSE*, special vol. "SSSR," col. 63.

42. *Pravda*, August 9, 1953.

43. See Jasny's estimate, *Socialized Agriculture*, p. 699.

44. *Pravda*, September 19, 1947.

45. Malenkov reported to the Nineteenth Congress that in 1952 the total amount of land given over to agriculture was 1.4 times the amount in 1913. As estimates on the 1913 area vary by nearly 16 per cent (see Volin, *Survey of Russian Agriculture*, p. 106), there is little value in computing the present area from such information.

46. See table in Jasny, *Socialized Agriculture*, p. 393.

47. Laptev, *Voprosy Kolkhoznogo Stroitel'stva*, p. 289.

48. Letter to the author by Dr. Kulischer of June 23, 1953, referring to L. Karaseva, *Zhenschiny v Kolkhozakh* (Bol'shaya Sila, 1949) for 1943 figure and to *Bakinskii Rabochii*, March 11, 1952, and *Pravda*, August 28, 1950, and November 14, 1950, for local postwar figures.

49. See Khrushchev's comments in *Pravda*, September 15, 1953.

50. Jasny, *Socialized Agriculture*, p. 327.

51. *Ibid.*, p. 336.

52. *The Land of Socialism Today and Tomorrow*, pp. 259, 261.

53. February 19, 1950.

54. *Russia's Soviet Economy*, p. 272.

55. Laptev, *Voprosy Kolkhoznogo Stroitel'stva*, p. 319.

56. A. Savin, "Voprosy ukrupneniya kolkhozov," *Voprosy Ekonomiki*, no. 9 (September 1950), p. 101.

57. Basiuk, *Organizatsiya Kolkhoznogo Proizvodstva*, p. 49.

58. A. Grigor'ev, "Partiinye gruppy v brigadakh i na fermakh kolkhozov," *Bol'shevik*, no. 22 (November 1951), p. 70.

59. Laptev, *Voprosy Kolkhoznogo Stroitel'stra*, pp. 291, 338.

60. *Sotsialisticheskoe Zemledelie*, April 12, 1951.

61. *BSE*, special vol. "SSSR," col. 1809.

62. The number of children under three was somewhat more than 10 per cent of the population in the USSR as a whole, according to

estimates by Frank Lorimer, *The Population of the Soviet Union* (Geneva, 1948), pp. 239 and 113. In rural areas the proportion would probably be higher. War losses in the Ukraine might have reduced the figure, but, on the other hand, the annexation of new territory meant a gain of well over 8,000,000 persons (*ibid.*, p. 187), which means that the estimate of 2,000,000 children is conservative.

63. Only 1,000,000 children attended kindergarten in 1946 in the vast Russian Republic, according to *BSE*, special vol. "SSSR," col. 1220.

64. For an excellent analysis of the contemporary situation see N. S. Timasheff, " Religion in Russia, 1941–1950," in Waldemar Gurian, ed., *The Soviet Union* (Notre Dame, 1951), pp. 153–194. The figure is given on p. 158.

65. Harvard Project, A 191.

66. *Ibid.*, A 133.

CHAPTER 4: COMMUNIST BELIEFS ON SCIENCE AND ART

1. Lenin was aware that his position was an assumption and that the opposite viewpoint could not be refuted by rational argument. See his *Materialism and Empirio-Criticism*, in *Selected Works* (New York, n.d.), XI, 322.

2. Current doctrine on the arts may be found in a publication of the Academy of Sciences, F. V. Konstantinov, ed., *Istoricheskii Materializm* (Moscow, 1951), pp. 591–606. The quotation is on p. 591. More authoritative statements, though less concerned with the arts as a whole, are Zhdanov's postwar speeches on Soviet intellectuals, particularly that which appeared in the Soviet press on September 21, 1946, and the decrees of the Party Central Committee of August 14, 26, and September 4, 1946, concerning various literary journals, the theater, and the cinema.

3. See, for example, Richard von Mises, *Positivism* (Harvard University Press, 1951), chap. xxiv, esp. pp. 304, 306. The author shares with Marxism a somewhat negative attitude toward illusion in art.

4. *Materialism and Empirio-Criticism*, pp. 221–222, 247, 394, 406. In connection with Lenin's almost paranoid rejection of ideas that conflicted with his own, Professor Michael Karpovich has called my attention to the valuable memoirs of N. Valentinov, *Vstrechi s Leninym* (New York, 1953). Valentinov vividly describes the rage into which Lenin flew as he first came into contact with Mach's views in 1904 and his complete refusal to examine these ideas seriously upon their merits (pp. 253–255, 283–305). Much of this anger and unwillingness to understand this current of thought found its way into *Materialism and Empirio-Criticism*.

5. W. T. Stace, *The Theory of Knowledge and Existence* (Oxford, 1932).

6. Morris R. Cohen, *A Preface to Logic* (New York, 1944), pp. 94–97.

7. Konstantinov, *Istoricheskii Materializm*, p. 592.

8. Mach, *Analyse der Empfindungen*, pp. 8, 9, as quoted in *Materialism and Empirio-Criticism*, p. 200.

9. "Marx's Theses on Feuerbach," in Karl Marx, *Selected Works* (New York, n.d.), I, 471, 473.

10. *Materialism and Empirio-Criticism*, p. 201.

11. Professor Geroid T. Robinson in a seminar before the Russian Research Center, Harvard University, December 15, 1951.

12. The intervention of the Central Committee was not revealed to the Soviet public for six years and is mentioned in M. Alekseev and V. Cherkesov, "K voprosu o logike i eë izuchenii," *Bol'shevik*, no. 11 (June 1952), p. 32. This information became available after the publication of Alexander Philipov, *Logic and Dialectic in the Soviet Union* (New York, 1952). See also Gustav A. Wetter, *Der dialektische Materialismus* (Vienna, 1952), Part II, chap. x.

13. Konstantinov, *Istoricheskii Materializm*, p. 603.

14. An illuminating analysis of the relationship between Communism and the secular emphasis of our culture may be found in Waldemar Gurian, *Bolshevism: An Introduction to Soviet Communism* (Notre Dame, 1952).

15. *Pravda*, April 7, 1953.

16. See, e.g., *Pravda*, April 8, 1953.

17. *Izvestiya*, April 30, 1953.

CHAPTER 5: SCIENTIST AND ARTIST IN THE POLICE STATE

1. Jelagin, *Taming of the Arts*, pp. 112–115.

2. *Ibid.*, p. 120.

3. *USSR Information Bulletin*, October 7, 1949, p. 600. Multiple job-holding by Academy members was officially prohibited by a special decree of the presidium of the Academy, October 6, 1949, except in cases where special permission is granted by the presidium. See "Za svobodnuyu, tvorcheskuyu, nauchnuyu kritiku," *Vestnik Akademii Nauk SSSR*, no. 8 (August 1950), p. 19. From complaints in this source and other more recent Soviet press items, however, it seems clear that the practice continues (see note 25 below).

4. *BSE*, special vol. "SSSR," col. 1240.

5. *Izvestiya*, July 14, 1951.

6. *Scientist in Russia* (London, 1947), p. 80.

7. Harvard Project on the Soviet Social System, B 10–372:RAF.

8. The relevant decrees may be conveniently located in M. I. Movshovich, compiler, *Vysshaya Shkola: Osnovnye Postanovleniya Prikazy i Instruktsii* (Moscow, 1945), pp. 170–174.

9. See, e.g., Harvard Project, A 67. For the position of the artist in mass communications see Inkeles, *Public Opinion in Soviet Russia.*

10. On Stalin's personal role, see Jelagin, *Taming of the Arts*, pp. 208, 266, 282, 293.

11. For the details of its history, structure, etc., see Louis Nemzer, "The Kremlin's Professional Staff," *American Political Science Review*, March 1950, pp. 72–78; Inkeles, *Public Opinion*, pp. 30–37.

12. See Nemzer, in *American Political Science Review*, March 1950, pp. 75–76.

13. January 11, 1952.

14. Osip Beskin, *The Place of Art in the Soviet Union*, American-Russian Institute: Special Publication No. 2 (New York, 1936), p. 18, n. 7.

15. I. I. Evtikhiev and V. A. Vlasov, *Administrativnoe Pravo* (Moscow, 1946), pp. 372, 386.

16. *Ibid.*, p. 386.

17. Jelagin, *Taming of the Arts*, p. 308.

18. Decree of the Party Central Committee, August 26, 1946, discussed in *Pravda*, September 8, 1946.

19. *Literaturnaya Gazeta*, July 22, 1952.

20. The creation of the Ministry of Culture was announced in the Soviet press on March 16, 1953.

21. *BSE*, special vol. "SSSR," col. 1478.

22. *Ibid.*, I (1949), 560.

23. See *Akademiya Khudozhestv SSSR, Chetvërtiya Sessiya* (Moscow, 1950).

24. *Literaturnaya Gazeta*, January 19, 1952.

25. See, for example, the decree of the Party Central Committee of August 14, 1946, *Bol'shevik*, no. 15 (August 1946), p. 13; *Literaturnaya Gazeta*, January 19, 1952.

26. Ashby, *Scientist in Russia*, pp. 19–29; S. I. Vavilov, *Sovetskaya Nauka na Novom Etape* (Moscow-Leningrad, 1946), pp. 67–68, 74; Evtikhiev and Vlasov, *Administrativnoe Pravo*, p. 384.

27. G. A. Knyazev, *Kratkii Ocherk Istorii Akademii Nauk SSSR* (Moscow-Leningrad, 1945), pp. 74–77.

28. *BSE*, I (1949), 570.

29. *Gosudarstvennyi Plan Razvitiya Narodnogo Khozyaistva SSSR na 1941 god*, pp. 544–545.

30. See Nesmeyanov's biography in *Pravda*, February 17, 1951.

31. *BSE*, I (1949), 570, gives a brief recent description of the formal organization.

32. *Vestnik Akademii Nauk SSSR*, no. 9 (September 1950), pp. 86–87.

33. *Ibid.*, no. 8 (August 1950), pp. 89–91. For the events in physiology see Ivan D. London, "The Scientific Council on Problems of the Physiological Theory of Academician I. P. Pavlov: A Study in Control," *Science*, July 11, 1952, pp. 23–27.

34. Vavilov, *Sovetskaya Nauka*, pp. 17–18.

35. *BSE*, I (1949), 572.

36. Fainsod Report No. 43, Russian Research Center files.

37. See Topchiev's speech of February 2, 1951, in *Vestnik Akademii Nauk SSSR*, no. 3 (March 1951), pp. 38–65.

38. *Pravda*, August 20, 1949.

39. *Izvestiya*, November 2, 1952.

40. See criticism of this division in *Pravda*, September 17, October 2, 1951; December 15, 1952.

41. *Kultura i Zhizn'*, November 7, 1950.

42. *Pravda*, October 23, 1952.

43. December 15, 1952.

44. *Pravda*, October 8, 1952.

45. Cf. Evtikhiev and Vlasov, *Administrativnoe Pravo*, pp. 372–373.

46. Movshovich, *Vysshaya Shkola*, p. 21, n. 1.

47. Rules governing appointment procedure were issued on February 25, 1940 and may be found in Movshovich, *Vysshaya Shkola*, pp. 283–284.

48. Evtikhiev and Vlasov, *Administrativnoe Pravo*, p. 382.

49. See *Izvestiya*, February 27, 1952.

50. *Sovetskoe Gosudarstvo i Pravo*, 1950, no. 6, p. 89.

51. *Literaturnaya Gazeta*, January 18, 1951. See also *Pravda*, January 6, 1951, for the rules governing graduate work in science.

52. *Izvestiya*, January 11, 1949.

53. *Ibid.*, July 11, 1951.

54. *Ibid.*, January 11, 1949; July 11, 1951.

55. *O Polozhenii v Biologicheskoi Nauke, Stenografcheskii Otchët* (Moscow, 1948), p. 36.

56. *Izvestiya*, July 11, 1951.

57. *Ibid.*, May 11, 1950.

58. *Ibid.*

59. Fainsod Report No. 6; Harvard Project, B 2–441:SH; Ashby, *Scientist in Russia*, pp. 25–26. For understandable reasons Ashby missed the secret police unit. He has nothing to say about the union.

60. *Pravda*, August 3, 1949.

61. *Ibid.*, January 23, 1952.

62. The role of the groups and the duties of the *starosta* were formalized by a decree of March 6, 1944. See Movshovich, *Vysshaya Shkola*, pp. 97–98.

63. Movshovich, pp. 97–98; Jakow Budanow, *Technical Institutes*

in the USSR, East European Fund Publication No. 26 (New York, 1952), pp. 7–8.

64. *Sovetskaya Pedagogika*, Supplement for 1952, Book III, pp. 107–109, 192–194, as translated in *CDSP*, vol. V, no. 11 (April 25, 1953), p. 6.

65. See, e.g., Fainsod Report No. 6.

66. *Pravda*, August 7, 1950, report by Vavilov; *Izvestiya*, November 4, 1951, report by Nesmeyanov.

67. For developments in other sciences consult Raymond A. Bauer, *The New Man in Soviet Psychology* (Harvard University Press, 1952); Ivan D. London, "The Scientific Council on Problems of the Physiological Theory of Academician I. P. Pavlov," *Science*, July 11, 1952, pp. 23–27, and "Contemporary Psychology in the Soviet Union," *ibid.*, August 31, 1951, pp. 227–233; Pamela N. Wrinch, "Science and Politics in the USSR: The Genetics Debate," *World Politics*, July 1951, pp. 486–519; Kurt P. Tauber, "Science and Politics: A Commentary," *ibid.*, April 1952, pp. 432–446.

68. "O prirode fizicheskogo znaniya," *Voprosy Filosofii*, 1947, no. 2, pp. 140–176. For further material on the attitude of Soviet philosophers toward modern physics, particularly quantum theory and relativity, see Wetter, *Der dialektische Materialismus*, pp. 343–366.

69. "O prirode fizicheskogo znaniya," p. 139.

70. *Ibid.*, p. 163.

71. Werner Heisenberg, *The Physical Principles of the Quantum Theory* (Chicago, 1930), p. 20.

72. See his *Essay in Physics* (New York, 1952).

73. *Soviet Science* (London, 1936), pp. 42, 47, 74, 115, 200.

74. *Voprosy Filosofii*, 1948, no. 3, pp. 231–235.

75. See, e.g., M. M. Karpov, "O filosofskikh vzglyadakh A. Einshteina," *Voprosy Filosofii*, 1951, no. 1, pp. 130–141; *Krasny Flot*, June 13, 1952, as translated in *CDSP*, vol. IV, no. 25 (August 2, 1952), pp. 3–4.

76. Among the technical journals examined were the following publications of the USSR Academy of Sciences: *Zhurnal Fizicheskoi Khimii* (1950 issues); *Zhurnal Eksperimental'noi i Teoreticheskoi Fiziki* (1950 issues); *Matematicheskii Sbornik* (1950–51 issues); *Trudy Matematicheskogo Instituta Imeni Steklova* (issues of 1947–48); *Uspekhi Matematicheskikh Nauk* (issues of 1948–49); *Izvestiya Akademii Nauk SSSR, seriya matematicheskaya* (issues of 1948 and 1951).

77. E.g., one writer accused a colleague of undermining the materialist theory of heat, cites Lomonosov (who died in 1765) as an authority, and attacks the "idealist" scientists of the early twentieth century, Mach and Ostwald. See Ya. P. Terletskii, "Diskussiya: O soderzhanii zadachi mnogikh chastits v molekulyarnoi fizike," *Zhurnal*

Eksperimental'noi i Teoreticheskoi Fiziki, vol. XX, no. 9 (1950), pp. 854–855, 859. For many years S. I. Vavilov was the editor of this journal.

78. E. S. Sarkisov, "O periodicheskoi sisteme elementov D. I. Mendeleeva," *Zhurnal Fizicheskoi Khimii,* vol. XXIV, no. 4 (1950), pp. 487–502; V. M. Tatevskii, "O teorii rezonansa," *ibid.,* vol. XXIV, no. 5 (1950), pp. 597–639. The remark about concealed agents is on p. 638 of the latter article.

79. *Pravda,* June 23, 1951.

80. See the preface addressed to Stalin in the Academy publication, *Matematicheskii Sbornik,* vol. XXVI (68), no. 1 (1950), p. 5; and the article by a famous Soviet mathematician, A. D. Aleksandrov, "Ob idealizme v matematike," *Priroda,* July 1951, pp. 3–11. The latter is a semi-popular publication. S. I. Vavilov in 1950 remarked that the time had long been ripe for a discussion in mathematics. See *Pravda,* August 7, 1950.

81. E.g., J. R. Kline, "Soviet Mathematics," *Bulletin of the Atomic Scientists,* February 1952, p. 45.

82. *Voprosy Ekonomiki,* 1948, no. 5, p. 79.

83. *Ibid.,* p. 82.

84. *O Polozhenii v Biologicheskoi Nauke,* p. 472.

85. Nemchinov, "Statistika kak nauka," *Voprosy Ekonomiki,* 1952, no. 10, p. 104.

86. *Ibid.,* p. 102.

87. Stuart A. Rice, "Statistical Conceptions in the Soviet Union Examined from Generally Accepted Scientific Viewpoints," *The Review of Economics and Statistics,* February 1952, pp. 82–86. The quotation from the conference report is on p. 83. For reasons given in the text, I disagree with Rice's interpretation, which sees in this incident merely a conflict between theological dogma and scientific reason.

88. *Voprosy Ekonomiki,* 1948, no. 5, p. 88.

89. *Ibid.,* p. 79.

90. "Bol'shikh chisel zakon," *BSE,* V (1950), 538.

91. T. Kozlov, "K voprosu o predmete i metode statistiki," *Voprosy Ekonomiki,* 1952, no. 4, p. 60.

92. Nemchinov, in *Voprosy Ekonomiki,* 1952, no. 10, p. 112.

93. Cf. Clyde Kluckhohn, "The Study of Culture," in Daniel Lerner and Harold Lasswell, eds., *The Policy Sciences* (Stanford, 1951), p. 90.

94. See Solomon M. Schwarz, "Revising the History of Russian Colonialism," *Foreign Affairs,* April 1952, pp. 488–493.

95. Harvard Project, A 628:1745 (NY).

96. Fainsod Report No. 17.

CHAPTER 6: THE IMPACT AND FUNCTION OF TERROR

1. Naum Jasny, "Labor and Output in Soviet Concentration Camps," *Journal of Political Economy*, vol. LIX, no. 5 (October 1951), p. 416.

2. Raymond A. Bauer, "Arrest in the Soviet Union," unpublished report, prepared under the joint auspices of the Russian Research Center, Harvard University, and the Center for International Studies, Massachusetts Institute of Technology, 1953, p. 5 and Appendix I (by John Rimburg), p. xiii.

3. Harvard Project on the Soviet Social System, A 419.

4. Cf. Beck and Godin, *Russian Purge and the Extraction of Confession*, pp. 74, 85. This is the most enlightening yet sober account of the terror that has so far appeared in print.

5. David J. Dallin and Boris I. Nicolaevsky, *Forced Labor in Soviet Russia* (New Haven, 1947), pp. 265–274. See also Jerzy Gliksman, "Terror as Prophylaxis," paper given at the Conference on Totalitarianism, American Academy of Arts and Sciences, March 6–8, 1953, pp. 9–10 (the proceedings of this conference will be published by the Harvard University Press); Beck and Godin, *Russian Purge*, pp. 228–237.

6. New York, 1941.

7. *Sotsialisticheskoe Zemledelie*, January 12, 1952, as translated in *CDSP*, vol. IV, no. 2 (February 23, 1952), p. 30.

8. *Pravda*, January 11, 1952.

9. *Ibid.*, November 21, 1951; January 15, 1952.

10. H. K. Geiger, "The Solidarity of the Urban Slavic Family under the Soviet System," unpublished report, Russian Research Center, Harvard University, 1953.

11. Cf. David J. Dallin, *The New Soviet Empire* (New Haven, 1951), pp. 180–196; Berliner, "The Informal Organization of the Soviet Firm," *Quarterly Journal of Economics*, August 1952, pp. 356–358.

12. See *New York Times*, January 26, 1953, for the report of a Zionist group that exit visas could be obtained fairly easily by bribing the secret police.

13. Harvard Project, A 530.

14. *Ibid.*, A 133.

15. *Ibid.*, A 628:1745 (NY).

16. See Fainsod Report No. 3.

17. See the vivid account of a former informer in Beck and Godin, *Russian Purge*, pp. 200–209.

18. Harvard Project, A 541, gives a typical illustration, perhaps embroidered but one that can be paralleled by many similar incidents. The informant here claimed that an air force officer escaped a pos-

sible ten-year sentence for anti-Soviet agitation by drinking with a military policeman and presenting the latter with a supply of vodka.

19. *Ibid.*, A 315.

20. See Friedrich Report No. 41 for a typical example.

21. Harvard Project, A 639.

22. See Raymond A. Bauer and David B. Gleicher, "Word-of-Mouth Communication in the Soviet Union," *Public Opinion Quarterly*, Summer 1953.

23. Compare Harvard Project A 179, A 373, and A 628:1745 (NY) with A 454.

24. Harvard Project, A 351, A 419.

25. *Ibid.*, A 530.

26. *Ibid.*, A 514, A 332.

27. Cf. Benjamin E. Lippincott, ed., *On the Economic Theory of Socialism* (Minneapolis, 1938). For a critical survey of the literature see Joseph A. Schumpeter, *Capitalism, Socialism and Democracy* (3rd ed.; New York, 1947), Part III.

28. Among them Isaac Deutscher in his *Russia: What Next?* (New York, 1953).

29. *Zarya Vostoka*, April 16, 1953.

30. Texts from the various provincial papers are in *CDSP*, vol. V, no. 17 (June 6, 1953), pp. 3–8.

31. Cf. Dicks, "Observations on Contemporary Russian Behaviour," *Human Relations*, V, no. 2, esp. pp. 127, 155–156.

32. See Z. Brzezinski, "The Permanent Purge and Soviet Totalitarianism" (Ph.D. thesis, Harvard University, 1953), particularly for evidence concerning the impact of the purge on the Party.

CHAPTER 7: IMAGES OF THE FUTURE

1. The importance of tradition and of personal relationships as bases of group behavior is nevertheless very great. See George C. Homans, "The Small Warship," *American Sociological Review*, June 1946, pp. 294–300.

2. *Russia: What Next?*

3. A valuable and provocative discussion of the historical background of Western democratic institutions is Alexander Rüstow, *Ortsbestimmung der Gegenwart* (Zürich, 1952), vol. II. A brief interpretive survey of the major facts, with a critical bibliographical essay, can be found in Carl J. Friedrich, *The Age of the Baroque* (New York, 1952), chap. ix, and pp. 352–354.

4. The most up-to-date survey and interpretation of the available facts may be found in Alex Inkeles, "Social Stratification and Mobility in the Soviet Union: 1940–1950," *American Sociological Review*, August 1950, pp. 465–479.

5. See the observations of Victor Kravchenko, *I Chose Freedom* (New York, 1946), pp. 393–411, on status distinctions within the Kremlin hierarchy. Hede Massing, *This Deception* (New York, 1951), was for a brief time on intimate terms with secret police officials and comments on their isolation (pp. 258–261).

6. This observation was made to me by George Fischer on the basis of his extensive experience in the Soviet school system during the thirties. Criticisms of this attitude also occur occasionally in the speeches of major Soviet leaders.

7. On this point, see E. H. Carr, *The Bolshevik Revolution, 1917–1923* (New York, 1951), I, Part III, and Richard E. Pipes, *The Formation of the Soviet Union* (in press).

8. See also *Pravda*, May 6, 1952. On occasion the ignorance of Soviet officials is incredible. As any anthropologist knows, all human languages have a definite grammar and structure, no matter how "primitive" the group may be that speaks them. Yet a Soviet official, speaking of certain peoples of the Far North, reports that children attending native schools there can learn practically nothing, owing to the low level of the languages concerned, none of them possessing any system of grammar or any proper literature. See Walter Kolarz, *Russia and Her Colonies* (New York, 1952), p. 63, citing *Uchitelskaya Gazeta*, April 4, 1948. This book by a former Czech journalist is the only up-to-date survey of Soviet nationalities policy and contains much valuable information. But despite the generally anti-Soviet tone of the work, the author swallows statements of this type, and speaks himself of the "impossibility of a national culture" among these groups. There is a serious need for a study of Soviet nationalities policy, or selected aspects, by a qualified anthropologist.

9. M. Kalinin, *Za Ety Gody* (Moscow-Leningrad, 1929), III, 385–386, quoted in Kolarz, *Russia*, p. 7.

10. The phrase occurs, I believe for the first time, in Stalin's report to the Sixteenth Congress of the Communist Party in July 1930.

11. See Robert A. Feldmesser, "The Persistence of Status Advantages in Soviet Russia," *American Journal of Sociology*, July 1953, pp. 19–27.

12. Cf. Vera Sandomirsky, "Sex in the Soviet Union," *The Russian Review*, July 1951, pp. 199–209.

13. "Doklad t. Zhdanova o zhurnalakh 'Zvezda' i 'Leningrad,' " *Bol'shevik*, no. 17–18 (September 1946), p. 9.

14. The official ethic of Soviet society may be found in a conveniently summarized form in P. A. Shariya, *O Nekotorikh Voprosakh Kommunisticheskoi Morali* (Moscow, 1951). The discussion of the family occurs on pp. 128–132.

15. *Sovetskoe Iskusstvo*, May 6, 1953, in *CDSP*, vol. V, no. 18 (June 13, 1953), p. 26.

16. *Pravda*, October 12, 1952.

17. Cf. Isaac Deutscher, *Stalin: A Political Biography* (New York, 1949), pp. 519, 529.

18. See Michael Karpovich, "Historical Background of Soviet Thought Control" in Gurian, ed., *The Soviet Union*, pp. 16–30.

19. *Pravda*, July 26, 1953.

INDEX

Academy of Arts, 121
Academy of Sciences of USSR, 103, 113, 114–115, 123, 124–129, 130–131, 133, 139, 142–143, 144
Actors, 17, 114. *See also* Theater
Aesthetics, 100, 103–104, 105, 110
Aggression, 59, 167, 168
Agitprop, 119, 141
Agriculture, collectivized: manpower problems, 73, 76–77, 88–89, 92; weakness of institutional forms, 74, 90; area collectivized, 75, 76, 238; mechanical resources in, 75–76, 90, 95; administrative apparatus, 81, 96; administrative expenditures, 82; private plot and open market, 85–88; decrease in livestock, 86; and rural sex ratio, 88–89; organization of labor, 89–92; labor and production norms, 91; potential future trends, 95–97; variations in crop yields, 145–146. *See also kolkhoz,* Machine Tractor Stations, Peasantry, Planning, Prices, Resources
Akhmatova, Anna, 205–206
Aleksandrov, N. G., 237
Aleksandrov, A. D., 246
Alekseev, M., 242
All-Union Central Council of Trade Unions (AUCCTU), 52
All-Union Committee on the Affairs of Higher Education, 129
Amnesty, 5, 174
Andreev, A. A., 78, 87, 88, 90
Anti-Semitism, 112. *See also* Nationalities
Arakelian, A., 238
Army, *see* Military forces
Arrest: figures on, 155–156; interpretation by victims, 156–157, 158; and family solidarity, 160; methods of appeal from, 163; of Kremlin doctors, 174. *See also* Purges, Terror
Art: development of patterns in,

98; Soviet, 100, 105–106, 110, 111, 120
Artists, 117–119, 121–123, 149–150, 151
Ashby, Eric, 115, 243, 244
Atomic research, *see* Physics
Atomization, *see* Totalitarianism
Authority: power bases needed to maintain, 16; double system of status in, 17–19; allocation and social stratification, 195–196, 201. *See also* Criteria, Dictatorship, Factory, Ministries

Baranov, I., 236
Barmine, Alexander, 234
Basiuk, T. L., 239
Bauer, Raymond A., 245, 247, 248
Beck, F., 235, 247
Belief systems: general functions, 210–212; role of values, 210–211, 216–217; reality-testing, 210, 211; normative aspects, 211; in power oriented society, 213–214; and multiple truths, 214. *See also* Criteria, Rationalism, Totalitarianism, Traditionalism
Belyaev, N., 239
Benediktov, I., 239
Bergson, Abram, 235
Beriya, Lavrentii P., 1, 6, 22, 23, 28, 30, 174, 175, 220
Berliner, Joseph S., 237, 247
Berman, Harold J., 235
Beskin, Osip, 243
Biology, 138, 153
Birman, A., 238
blat, 162–163. *See also* Bureaucracy
Bolshevism: leaders' power as goal, 12–13, 35; role of personal relationships, 20–21, 204–206; agricultural aims, 74–75, 89, 95–97; intellectual assumptions, 99–108, 111–112, 139, 152–153; provisions for doctrinal change, 108–

112, 153; and welfare of masses, 190, 219, 228, 229; and democratic processes, 193–194; function as belief system, 211; rules on pursuit of power, 217–219; and world revolution, 229–230. *See also* Classes, Communist Party, Criteria, Dictatorship, Totalitarianism

Bonus, *see* Incentives

Brzezinski, Z., 234, 248

Budanow, Jakow, 244

Budget, national, 28, 39, 41–42, 60, 124. *See also* Planning

Bureaucracy: need for rationalism, 12–13, 19–21, 188–189; confusion and overlapping in, 13, 16–19, 55, 79–80, 81, 82, 95–96; personal insecurity of officials, 14, 21, 30, 63, 68, 187–188, 198; and Prussian model, 20; manipulating environment of, 36–37, 43–44, 51, 59, 61–62, 91, 150–151, 159–160, 162–163, 213. *See also* Authority, Dictatorship

Carr, E. H., 249

Central Committee (Party): range of daily problems, 15; and economic policy, 64n, 76–77, 80; as intellectual authority, 106, 108, 110, 119, 127–128; role in scientific planning, 127–128
decrees: on logic, 110, 242; on scientific literature, 112n; on arts, 241; on literary journals, 243
See also Agitprop, Communist Party

Central Aero-Hydrodynamic Institute, 123–124

Central Statistical Administration, 145

Charkviani, 175

Cheka, *see* Secret police

Chekhov, A. P., 81

Chemistry, 125, 133, 138, 139, 142–143. *See also* Science

Cherkesov, V., 242

China, 6

Church, Catholic, 204, 211

Church, Russian Orthodox, 93. *See also* Religion

Ciliga, A., 177n

Classes, social: stratification in Soviet society, 15, 183, 198–202; and belief in rumors, 167–169; function of social mobility, 177, 197, 202, 224–225; general role of stratification, 195; Soviet definition of, 195; in-group and out-group relationships, 216–219. *See also* Merit, Purges, Social change, Traditionalism

Cliques: general function, 21–22; and nationalities problem, 22–23; in work situation, 45, 161; in local Party units, 122; among intellectuals, 122, 149–150; and organized terror, 161, 163; role of vodka in, 165–166. *See also* Evasions

Cohen, Morris R., 103, 242

Collectivization, *see* Agriculture

Commissariats, Peoples', 28, 29. *See also* Ministries, NKVD

Committee on the Arts, 120

Committee *or* Commission on Party Control, 23, 78

Communism, *see* Bolshevism

Communist Party of the Soviet Union (CPSU): administrative structure, 8–9, 233; and personnel appointments, 16, 50, 120, 130, 135, 175, 177; policy on personal relationships, 19–21, 122, 204–206; shaking up the apparatus, 20, 23, 41, 177; and the army, 23–24, 26–27; and the secret police, 27–31; safety from arrest, 156–157; founding of, 193
leadership: appraisal of world situation, 4–5, 6–7, 229–230; post-Stalinist policies, 5–7, 86–87, 96, 97, 112, 174–175, 178, 200, 206, 230, 231; cynicism among, 10, 198, 215; succession problem, 15–16, 36, 55–56, 109, 193, 217–218, 219–221, 223; as intellectual authority, 105, 108, 109–111, 112, 113, 116–117, 118–120, 121–123, 127–128, 132–133, 153; social

isolation of, 198, 201; definition of in-group and out-group, 217–219 local and regional officials: responsibilities of *Partorg*, 9, 17, 63–64, 79–80, 134, 136; absorption in technical jobs, 16–19, 25–26, 27, 79, 224; status relationships among, 17, 78–79, 80, 122, 135

membership: figures on, 233; among army officers, 26; on collective farms, 78; among scientists, 125, 134–135

Congresses: Sixteenth (July 1930), 249; Eighteenth (March 1939), 78, 89–91; Nineteenth (October 1952), 8–9, 15, 18, 23, 53, 64n, 128 *See also* Bolshevism, Central Committee, Controls, Dictatorship, Presidium, Purges, Terror, Youth groups

Communist parties: Chinese, 6, 215; German, 6; Georgian, 22–23, 175; Ukrainian, 84; Turkmenistan, 119; American, 177n; French, 215

Concentration camps, 28, 38, 51, 155, 197. *See also* Arrest, Industry, State Labor Reserves

Consensus, popular, 2, 10

Consumers' goods, 6, 37, 57, 65, 95, 229. *See also* Industry

Contracts: between ministries, 42–45, 56; between factories, 43; between factories and scientific institutes, 128. *See also* Planning

Controls, Soviet system of: general structure, 7–9, 13–14, 183–184; main functions, 8–11; relationship among instruments of, 30–31; in industry, 38–39, 40–42, 46, 49–51, 57, 59, 61, 63–65, 66–67, 70; in agriculture, 75, 77–83, 89–90, 93, 95, 97; in science and art, 108–112, 114, 116, 117, 118–121, 122–123, 124, 127, 128–129, 130–132, 133–134, 137–138, 147–153. *See also* Authority, Bureaucracy, Communist Party, Dictatorship, Evasions, Planning, Terror

Cosmogony, 138

Cosmopolitanism, bourgeois, 112, 142

Cost accounting (*khozraschët*), 47

Council of Ministers, 1, 40, 46, 50, 52, 57, 120, 123

Crèches, 92

Crime, 174, 183. *See also* Amnesty

Criteria of decision-making: in use of terror, 11, 157–158, 175–176, 202; general range, 12–13, 184–185; in economic system, 34–36, 39–40, 41, 55–57, 58, 60, 68, 70–71, 185; in intellectual life, 105, 109, 110–111, 116, 123, 153, 185, 215; relationship of mutual exclusion, 185–186, 196, 212–213, 222–223. *See also* Bolshevism, Power, Rationalism, Totalitarianism, Traditionalism

Crowther, J. G., 141

Currency, devaluation of, 6

Dallin, David J., 247

Darwin, Charles, 126

De Grazia, Sebastian, 188n, 216n

Democracy, 171, 174, 193–194, 224

Democratic centralism, 217

Determinism, 147, 230

Deutscher, Isaac, 190, 248, 250

Dicks, Henry V., 234, 248

Dictatorship, Soviet: and bureaucratization of society, 2–3, 19–21, 162; need for arbitrary intervention, 10, 20, 23, 41, 177–178, 187–188; reliance on terror, 11, 170–173, 177–178, 219; fragmentation of authority, 14, 17, 70; need for dynamic leadership, 14, 36–37, 70–71, 220, 223; insecurity of individuals, 14, 15, 21, 30, 187–189, 200–201; conflict of political and technical requirements, 16–19, 24, 25, 26, 27, 31, 40–41, 70–71, 121–122, 153, 185, 188–189, 194, 223, 224; need for regularity in human relationships, 19, 50, 176, 177, 194, 219. *See also* Bolshevism, Communist

Party, Criteria, Nationalities, Power, Totalitarianism

Discussions, *see* Science

Dissertations, doctoral, 130–131, 132–133

Divorce, 110, 203, 205

Docents, 115, 132

Doctors, Kremlin, 7, 174, 175

D'yachenko, V., 236, 237, 238

Dyatkin, M. E., 142

Dymshits, I. A., 236

Dzerzhinskii, F. E., 163

Econometrics, 144

Economics, *see* Statistics

Education: supervision by Party, 9; training program in agriculture, 77; crèches and kindergartens, 92–93, 241; totalitarian features, 203, 208; traditionalist features, 207–208; technical-rationalist features, 208

higher institutions: personnel, 115; compulsory job assignments, 116; types of, 123–124, 130n; *spetsotdel* in, 129; academic appointments, 129–130; control of dissertations, 130–131; fees, 130, 207; abolition of coeducation, 207

See also Family, Intellectuals, Professors, Scientists, Youth groups

Ely, Louis B., 234

Engels, Friedrich, 100

Equality, totalitarian, 197, 200

Eskimos, 199

Evasions: in industry, 12, 40, 44–45, 49, 51–52, 68–69, 162; and growth of cliques, 21–23, 161–162; in agriculture, 75, 82, 87–88, 89, 91, 162; and escapism, 151–152, 206; to avoid arrest, 159–160; in intellectual life, 162; among police informers, 165. *See also* Cliques

Evtikhiev, I. I., 237, 239, 243, 244

Expansionism, 4, 5, 180, 229, 231. *See also* International situation

Factory: as miniature society, 38, 58, 70; income and profit, 47; pay-rolls, 51–52; control over, 57–58; tensions within, 58; working capital of, 60–61; problems faced by lower supervisory personnel, 67–69

director: relationships with other officials, 16, 63–67; authority of, 39, 63–64, 67, 185; how appointed, 50; functions and problems, 59–60, 61, 62

See also Evasions, Motivation, Secret police, *Tolkach*, Wages, Workers

Fainsod, Merle, xiii, xiv, xv, 187, 233, 234, 238, 244, 246, 247

Family: impact of terror on, 160–161; as economic unit, 181, 203; in industrial society, 202–203; and totalitarianism, 203–207

rural: as basic work unit, 74, 85, 88–89, 90, 92, 95; social functions of, 92; and religion, 93–94

See also Bolshevism, Education, Religion, Sex

Far East, Soviet, 53

Feldmesser, Robert A., xvi, 249

Feuerbach, Ludwig, 105, 242

Fischer, George, 249

Fok, V. A., 141

Foreign policy, *see* International situation

France, 73, 215

Frank, Philipp, xvi

Frenkel, Ya. I., 141, 142

Friedrich, Carl J., 248

Friedrich, Paul, xiii, 248

Geiger, H. K., 247

Genetics, 108, 110, 111, 133, 135, 138, 142, 144, 150

Genkin, D. M., 237

Georgia, Republic of, 22–23, 175

German Social Democratic Party, 20, 173

Germany, 6, 20, 73, 173, 222, 223

Gerschenkron, Alexander, xvi

Ginzburg, V. L., 132

Gleicher, David B., 248

Gliksman, Jerzy, 247

Glotov, I., 240

Godin, W., 235, 247
Gosplan, 8, 40–41, 48, 128
Gossip, see Rumors
Granick, David, 237
Great Britain, 73, 171
Great Russians, 200, 202, 218. See also Nationalities, RSFSR
Grigor'ev, A., 240
Gsovski, Vladimir, 235
Gurian, Waldemar, 241, 242, 250
Gusakov, A. D., 236

Hegel, G. W. F., 100
Heisenberg, Werner, 140, 245
History, 108, 110, 119, 125, 133
Homans, George C., 237, 248

Idealism, bourgeois, 101, 106, 140, 142, 144
Ignatiev, S. D., 174
Incentives: and system of controls, 9, 51; as political rewards, 71; income differentials, 83–85, 114–115, 183
  in industry: wage rates, 36, 51–53; and output norms, 44; price controls, 46–49; and distribution of labor, 53–54, 65; bonus, 60, 62; profit, 60–61, 62
  in agriculture: 81, 83–85, 90, 95
  in intellectual life: 116
  See also Motivation
Industrialism: and social cohesion, 10; functional requirements of, 12–13, 19, 70, 179–180, 190, 193, 203, 223; incompatibility with traditionalism, 74, 192–193, 225; and atomization of society, 158–159, 203–204; and balance of power, 228–229. See also Rationalism, Totalitarianism
Industry: heavy, 6, 53, 55; traditionalist elements in, 12, 185; decision-making in, 33–34, 69–70, 191; labor draft, 38, 54–55, 69; output norms, 44, 62, 68; potential stagnation in, 44, 49, 62, 71; personnel selection, 50–51, 56; wage rates, 51–53; discipline in,

51, 179–180; labor floating, 53–54, 69; absenteeism and tardiness, 54; and scientific planning, 127–128. See also Consumers' goods, Cost accounting, Incentives, Ministries, Planning, Prices, Resources, Wages
Inkeles, Alex, 233, 243, 248
Institute of Oriental Studies, 125
Intellectuals: social integration, 98, 114; use of term, 99; need for patron, 99, 151; autonomy and freedom of action, 99, 101–102, 117–118, 153; and political conformity, 105–106, 110, 116, 117, 118, 132–133, 152, 153, 215; and foreign scholars, 113; differences in status, 114–116, 149; multiple job-holding, 115, 116, 152; goals defined by Party, 117; procedures for academic jobs, 129–130; pre-Revolutionary, 133, 148, 149–150; impact of terror on, 137, 150, 156, 164, 175; professional solidarity, 149–150; nepotism among, 150; and gossip chains, 167; and system of multiple truths, 214. See also Artists, Bolshevism, Central Committee, Cliques, Communist Party, Motivation, Nationalities, Scientists
International situation: effect on domestic policies, 4–7, 34, 38, 96, 227–230, 231; and scientific knowledge, 107. See also Communist Party

Jasny, Naum, 48, 72, 84, 85, 89, 155, 156, 235, 236, 239, 240, 247
Jelagin, Juri, 234, 242, 243

Kalinin, M. I., 163, 199, 249
Karaseva, L., 240
Karpov, M. M., 245
Karpovich, Michael, xvi, 241, 250
Kecskemeti, Paul, 211n
Keller, A. G., 181n
khozraschët, see Cost accounting
Khrushchev, N. S., 8–9, 76, 78, 79–80, 81, 84, 86, 185, 239, 240

Kirghiz, 199
Kline, J. R., 246
Kluckhohn, Clyde, xvi, 246
Knyazev, G. A., 243
Koestler, Arthur, 158
Kolarz, Walter, 249
Kolesnev, S. G., 239
kolkhoz: average acreage in 1950, 76; amalgamation, 77, 78, 82, 185; number of farms in 1953, 78; problems of chairman, 78, 81–82; role of political deputy director, 79; role of administrative board, 82–83; reserve fund, 83; labor-day system, 83–85, 91, 96; variations in income, 84; private plot and open market, 85–88, 95, 96; brigade and squad systems, 89–91; and crèches, 92. See also Agriculture, Evasions, Incentives, Machine Tractor Stations, Motivation, Peasantry
Kolmogorov, A. N., 146
Komsomol, see Youth groups
Kondrashev, D., 236
Konstantinov, F. V., 241, 242
Korea, 6, 38, 231
Kozera, Edward S., 234
Kozlov, T., 246
Kraev, M., 239
krai, definition of, 233
Kravchenko, Victor, 249
Kulaks, 157, 169, 219
Kulischer, Eugene M., 88, 240
Kursky, A., 235

Labor, see Agriculture, Industry, State Labor Reserves, Workers
Laptev, I. D., 238, 239, 240
Lasswell, Harold, 246
Lavisse, Ernest, 234
Legality, Soviet, 174–176, 178
Lenin, V. I.: and domestic policies, 11, 20, 109, 217; attacks on Western doctrines, 101, 103, 104, 105, 106, 108, 241; artistic tastes of, 118–119; as infallible leader, 178
Lerner, Daniel, 246
Likachev, I., 238
Linguistics, 108, 111, 125, 135, 138

Lippincott, Benjamin E., 248
Logic, 110
Lokshin, E., 235, 236
Lomonosov, M. V., 245
London, Ivan D., 244, 245
Lorimer, Frank, 241
Loyalty, 16, 25, 51, 77, 92–94, 95, 105–106, 115, 137
Lysenko, T. D., 110, 127, 133, 144

Mach, Ernst, 104, 106, 142, 242, 245
Machine Tractor Stations (MTS), 75–77, 79–80, 83, 90, 95, 159. See also Agriculture, kolkhoz
Machism, 142
Malenkov, G. M., 1, 6, 18, 37, 40, 53, 86, 87, 112, 240
Manevich, E., 237
Marcuse, Herbert, xvii
Market, wholesale, 48, 59
Markov, M. A., 139–141, 142
Markus, B., 237
Marx, Karl, 100, 105, 180, 190, 242
Marxism, 12, 101n, 109, 110, 111–112, 135, 139, 142, 145, 170, 173, 211, 228. See also Bolshevism, Determinism, Materialism
Masses: welfare of, 12, 53, 190, 219, 228, 229; as out-group, 198, 219
Massing, Hede, 249
Materialism, dialectical, 100–105, 110, 124, 139–141, 143, 145. See also Bolshevism, Determinism, Marxism
Mathematics, 138, 139, 142, 143–148
Meisel, James H., 234
Mel'nikov, L. G., 200, 239
Mendel, G. J., 144, 145
Mendeleev, D. I., 126
Merit, 196, 197, 225, 226. See also Criteria
Merton, Robert K., 181n
Mgeladze, A. I., 175
Military forces: as control instrument, 7, 16; local authority of, 9, 24; and expansionism, 11, 229; as competitor for power, 24–25, 27–28; role of zampolit, 25–27, 169;

and secret police, 26, 27, 28, 164, 166, 168; Party membership in, 26; belief in propaganda, 168–169
Ministries, economic: role in planning, 40–46, 52, 56, 128; supervision over, 49; role in personnel selection, 50; authority and problems of minister, 55–57. *See also* Authority, Contracts, Council of Ministers
Ministry of Agricultural Machinery, 45
Ministry of Agriculture and Procurements, 75, 77, 80, 81
Ministry of Culture, 8, 77, 120, 124, 129, 132
Ministry of Education, 120, 129, 130–131, 132
Ministry of Finance, 6, 8, 41–42, 48, 51, 60, 67
Ministry of Health, 8
Ministry of Heavy Machine Construction, 64n
Ministry of Labor Reserves, 120
Ministry of Light Industry of RSFSR, 45
Ministry of State Control, 8, 19, 23, 49–50, 57, 67
Miroshnichenko, B., 235
Mises, Richard von, 241
Mokhova, E., 237
Molotov, V. M., 6
Motivation: of factory managers, 61, 71; of peasants, 83; of intellectuals, 115–116, 137, 151, 152. *See also* Criteria, Incentives
Movshovich, M. I., 243, 244
Murdock, G. P., 222n
Music, 16, 119, 120, 121, 123, 153
MVD (Ministry of Internal Affairs), 159, 160, 163, 164, 165, 166–167, 174. *See also* Secret police, Terror

Nationalism: Russian, 112–113, 148–149, 200, 207; bourgeois, 148–149, 200
Nationalities, non-Russian: cliques among, 22–23; and Union of So-
viet Writers, 121; and cleavage among intellectuals, 148–149, 150; and new Soviet legality, 175; and social stratification, 198–200, 200–201; shift in policy toward, 149, 200–201; as out-group, 218
Nazarov, A., 234
Nemchinov, V. S., 144–145, 147, 150, 246
Nemzer, Louis, 234, 243
Nepotism, *see* Cliques, Intellectuals
Nesmeyanov, A. N., 113, 125, 142, 245
NEP (New Economic Policy), 230
Newspaper correspondents, 118
Nicolaevsky, Boris I., 247
Nikitin, A. N., 239
Nikolenko, Ya. F., 239
NKVD (People's Commissariat of Internal Affairs), 28, 29, 30. *See also* MVD, Secret police

obkom, 9
oblast', definition of, 233
okrug, definition of, 233
Ostwald, W., 245

Pacific Institute, 125
Panova, Vera, 237, 238
Parsons, Talcott, 181n
partiinost, 105, 152
Pasherstnik, A. E., 236, 237
Pauling, L., 142
Pavlov, I. P., 126, 244, 245
Peasantry: concessions to, 6, 72, 85–87, 94, 231; traditionalism among, 12, 74, 89, 97, 185; under Tsarism, 72–73; and police controls, 77, 78, 164; share of *kolkhoz* income, 83–85, 91; and religion, 93–94; admission to higher schools, 130; belief in propaganda, 168–169. *See also* Agriculture, Evasions, Family, Incentives, *kolkhoz*, Motivation
Peter the Great, 123
Philipov, Alexander, 242
Philosophy, 125, 133, 138, 139–141, 143
Physico-mathematical sciences, 128, 132, 133

Physics, 138, 139–142, 143
Physiology, 125, 138
Pioneers, *see* Youth groups
Pipes, Richard E., 249
Planning: in agriculture, 76–77, 80, 91; in art, 117; in science, 117, 126–129; in education, 208 in industry: role of NKVD, 28, 29; stated purpose of, 34; annual plan and budget, 39–42; contracts, 42–45; estimates and norms, 43–44, 62, 68; financial controls, 46–49, 51; State Labor Reserves, 54–55 *See also* Council of Ministers, *Gosplan*, Resources
Politburo, 3, 11, 27, 28, 64n, 78. *See also* Communist Party, Presidium
Population of USSR: rural sex ratio, 88–89; figures on children, 92, 240–241; proportion arrested, 155–156; proportion of non-Russians, 198
Positivism, 100, 101, 102, 103, 104–105
Power: and use of terror, 11, 171, 173, 177–178, 230; conflict with other values, 12–13, 70–71, 74–75, 185–188, 197, 212–213, 222–223, 225; norms governing pursuit of, 216–219. *See also* Bolshevism, Criteria, Dictatorship
Pragmatism, 105
Prediction, scientific, 3–4, 179, 221–222
Presidium of Communist Party: problems confronting, 3–4, 15; limits on powers, 5; competitive aspects of membership, 15, 27–28; and cliques, 22; and economic policy, 34–36, 39, 40, 49, 52, 56, 70; and world situation, 34, 229–230. *See also* Communist Party, Dictatorship, Politburo
Presidium of Academy of Sciences, 125
Presidium of Supreme Soviet, 6. *See also* Soviets
Prices: retail cuts, 5–6, 37; controls

over, 38, 46, 59; as incentive and measuring stick, 46–49; reorganization of system, 47; bases for determining, 48–49; for obligatory deliveries of produce, 75, 83, 86, 95; in government stores, 87. *See also* Incentives
Priests, 93
Probability, theory of, 143–148
Professors, 110, 115, 129–130, 132. *See also* Education, Intellectuals
Profit, *see* Incentives, Planning
Propaganda: on collective farms, 79; in school system, 93, 135; and gossip chains, 168–169; belief in, 168–169, 215; on personal relationships, 205, 206. *See also* Agitprop
Purges: of Kremlin doctors, 7, 174, 175; Great Purge of thirties, 30, 157, 169, 177, 230; within secret police, 30, 174, 177, 230; among artists, 122–123; categories of victims, 157–158; in various republics, 175; and social mobility, 177, 189, 197, 202; within Party, 177, 230. *See also* Secret police, Terror

Quantum theory, 139–143

raizemotdel, 80
Rationalism, technical: necessity for adaptation to, 12–13, 19, 70, 185, 188–189, 190; in agriculture, 74, 97; and origins of Marxism, 109, 111–112; in use of terror, 157–158; and criterion of merit, 186, 187–188, 189, 196; characteristics of a technocracy, 189–190, 196, 209–210, 224–225, 228–229; as possible trend in USSR, 190–191, 210, 221, 224, 228, 231; and democratic developments, 193; in educational system, 203, 208, 210. *See also* Bureaucracy, Criteria, Dictatorship, Power
Raymond, Ellsworth L., 238
Realism, socialist, 105
Religion, 93–94, 104, 180, 210. *See also* Belief systems

Relativity, theory of, 139, 141–142
Resonance, theory of, 142–143
Resources and supplies: in agriculture, 75–76, 91, 95, 96
in industry: allocation, 33, 35–36, 37, 38, 39, 41, 42–44, 46, 48, 56, 57–58, 59, 60, 61–62, 64, 70; quality and variety, 44–45, 56–57, 60, 66; illegal reserves, 45–46
See also Agriculture, Industry, Planning, Prices
Rice, Stuart A., 246
Rimburg, John, 247
Robinson, Geroid T., 242
Roman bureaucracy, 192
Rostow, W. W., xv, 11, 234
Rovinskii, N. N., 236
RSFSR (Russian Soviet Federated Socialist Republic), 8, 233, 241. *See also* Great Russians, Nationalities
Rüstow, Alexander, 248
Rumors and gossip chains, 6, 159, 166–169, 170
Ryumin, 174

Samuel, Herbert L., 140
Sandomirsky, Vera, 249
Sarkisov, E. S., 246
Schumpeter, Joseph A., 248
Schwartz, Harry, 90, 237
Schwarz, Solomon M., 53, 54, 236, 246
Science
general aspects: goals and standards, 98–99, 126, 148; reality and abstractions, 102–104, 139, 145; search for absolutes, 104, 112; neutrality of, 106–107, 108
Soviet: task of, 100; rejection of formalism, 102, 103; partisanship of, 106, 107–108; nationalism in, 108, 111; role of tradition, 111; and rationalism, 112, 190; and foreign intellectuals, 113; applied research and industry, 123, 127–128; scientific discussions, 127, 138–139, 142–145; role of Party units, 134–136, 138–139, 150; and secret police, 134, 136, 137, 150;
controls over, 137–138; technical journals, 142
See also Academy of Sciences, Chemistry, Intellectuals, Mathematics, Physics, Youth groups
Scientists: characteristics of younger, 16, 148, 152; recantation of views, 106, 141, 143, 144–145; autonomy and freedom of action, 108, 123, 129, 135, 141–142, 215; demand for, 116, 130, 145, 151; appointment to academic jobs, 129–130; dissertation and research topics, 130–131, 132–133, 142; higher degrees to, 132; pre-Revolutionary, 133, 148, 152; and Party members, 134, 138; defiance of authority, 144, 145, 150. *See also* Academy of Sciences, Evasions, Intellectuals, Nationalities
Secret police: as competitor for power, 16, 27, 28–30; controls over army, 26, 27; and personnel selection, 50, 137; safety from arrest, 156; categories of victims, 157–158, 169; corruptibility of, 162–163
informers: in army, 26, 164; in factories, 57, 63; reliance on quantity of, 159; as source of bureaucratic paralysis, 159–160, 165; identification of, 163–164; recruitment of, 165
spetsotdel: in factories, 64–65, 238; on *kolkhozes,* 77–78; in Ministry of Education, 129; in scientific institutions, 134, 136, 137
See also Arrest, Purges, Terror.
Vodka
Serebryakov, S. V., 240
Sex: rural ratio, 88–89; Bolshevik attitudes on, 204, 205–206. *See also* Family
Shariya, P. A., 249
Shcherbakov, A. S., 174
Shore, Maurice J., 233
sluzhashchie, 195
Smith, Andrew, 177n
Social change: and political goals, 14, 180–181, 230; and intellec-

tuals, 99, 153; and growth of terror, 172–173. *See also* Classes, Purges
Socialism and terror, 170–173
Soviet Writers' Publishing House, 121
Soviets, local, 8, 19, 57, 80. *See also* Presidium, Supreme Soviet
sovkhoz, 97
spetsotdel, see Secret police
Stace, W. T., 242
Stalin, I. V.: foreign policies, 4, 5, 7, 215; and domestic problems, 4, 7, 11, 16–17, 28, 35, 40, 41, 46, 50, 218, 236, 249; death of, 10, 15, 36, 55, 81, 112, 120, 174, 193, 200, 218, 229; as intellectual authority, 105, 108, 118–119, 145, 151, 243, 246; as benevolent despot, 163; and Georgian Party, 175; as infallible leader, 178, 220, 231; and power, 186
Stanislavsky, K. S., 151
State Bank, 46, 47, 52
State Labor Reserves, 54–55, 73–74
State Planning Commission, *see* Gosplan
State Staff Commission, 50
Statistics, applied, 100, 143–148
Status, *see* Classes
Sumner, W. G., 2, 181n, 216
Supreme Certifying Commission, 132
Supreme Soviet, 1, 6, 8, 41, 163
Syrkin, Ya. K., 142

Tatevskii, V. M., 246
Tauber, Kurt P., 245
Tax, turnover, 47
Technical institutes, 123–124, 128, 133
Technocracy, *see* Rationalism
Terletskii, P., 245
Terror: within Party, 11, 173; services to regime, 11, 176–178; popular beliefs on impact, 156–157, 159, 163–164; capriciousness of, 157, 158, 169–170; rational features of, 157–158; disservices to regime, 160–161, 174, 175–176, 178; and growth of gossip chains,

166–169, 170; and stress on new legality, 174–175, 178; and expansionism, 229. *See also* Arrest, Cliques, Dictatorship, Purges, Secret police, Socialism
Theater, 17, 114, 120, 149, 151
Timasheff, N. S., 241
Iolkach, 61
Tolstoy, Aleksei, 114
Topchiev, A. V., 125, 127, 244
Totalitarianism: continuation and intensification of, 7, 186–187, 202, 207, 221, 223, 229; atomization process in, 136, 150, 158–159, 160–161, 200, 203–207; conflict with rationalist requirements, 136, 187–189, 215, 222–223, 228, 230; in family and educational system, 148, 203–207, 208; and rapid industrial expansion, 172–173, 182, 202, 203; and traditionalist developments, 192–193, 194, 196–197, 204–207, 214, 222, 225; special criterion of merit, 196, 198, 200; and system of multiple truths, 214–215; as adaptation to hostile world, 228. *See also* Bolshevism, Criteria, Dictatorship, Industrialism, Power, Terror
Trade unions, 52, 65, 130, 134
Traditionalism: and industrialism, 12, 74–75, 185, 192–193; among peasantry, 12, 74, 89, 97, 185; and growth of cliques, 22–23; as possible future trend in USSR, 97, 191, 193, 198, 221, 225, 227, 231; and Bolshevik anti-traditionalism, 111, 152–153; concept of tradition, 185, 186; features of traditionalist system, 191–192, 196, 197–198, 208–209, 225–226; and democratic developments, 193; in family and educational institutions, 203, 207–208. *See also* Criteria, Family, Industry, Peasantry
Turkmenistan, 119, 199

Ukraine, 92, 136, 175, 241
Union of Soviet Artists, 121
Union of Soviet Composers, 121

Union of Soviet Writers, 121
United States, 168, 227, 229
Universities, see Education
Uzbekistan, 18, 199

Valentinov, N., 241
Values, see Belief systems, Bolshevism, Criteria
Varga, E. S., 143, 144
Vavilov, S. I., 125, 126, 139, 212, 243, 244, 245, 246
Vlasov, V. A., 234, 235, 237, 239, 243, 244
Vodka, 165–166
Volin, Lazar, 238, 239, 240
Voroshilov, Marshal K. E., 28
Voznesensky, N. A., 236

Wages: determination of rates, 36, 51–53, 65; controls over, 38, 51; payment of, 51–52; wage differentials, 52–53, 110. See also Incentives
War, 54, 59–60, 71, 90, 180, 227–228. See also World War II
Weissberg, Alexander, 235
Wetter, Gustav A., 101, 242, 245

White, D. F., 234
Women, 88–89, 92, 155
Workers, 51–52, 53–55, 68, 69–70, 71, 130, 162, 166, 168, 175, 195. See also Concentration camps, Evasions, Factory, Incentives, Industry, Wages
World War II, 76, 108
Wrinch, Pamela N., 245
Writers, 121–123, 149. See also Intellectuals

Yagoda, H. G., 30
Yezhov, N. I., 30, 157
Yezhovshchina, 157
Youth groups, 26, 130, 135, 136–137, 203, 208
Yugow, A., 238

zampolit, 25, 27
Zertsalov, A., 235
Zhdanov, A. A., 105, 112, 141, 174, 205, 241, 249
Zhebrak, 144
Zhukov, Marshal G. D., 28
Zverev, A. G., 60–61, 236, 237, 238

All these points must be kept in mind in assessing the meaning of any particular step in either the rationalist or the traditionalist direction. The key question, however, is not what the Communist leaders *want* to do about these forces but what they *can* do. With the Korean truce it appears they have had to cut their losses and to cease, at least temporarily, their external expansion in Asia, in a manner reminiscent of their actions in the West at the time of the Berlin air-lift. At home, by the early fall of 1953, it was evidently their judgment that pressure on the peasants would have to be relaxed, the industrialization drive somewhat slackened, more goods allowed to reach the population, the bureaucracy partly rationalized, and the terror made less obvious. No single one of these steps is irreversible nor, perhaps, is the series as a whole. But it is doubtful that the present "collective" leadership is strong enough to reverse them with the forceful and harsh methods of a Stalin, even if the leaders as a whole, or a dominant faction among them, wanted to. The concessions to the peasantry, particularly the stress on the private plot, favor traditionalist forces. The others favor primarily rationalist and technocratic ones. If peace should continue for a decade or more, the rationalist or the traditionalist forces in Soviet society, or some unstable combination of the two, may do their work of erosion upon the Soviet totalitarian edifice.